Philippa Tomczak presents a detailed and nuanced account of the roles and effect of the charitable sector in prisons in England and Wales. In so doing, she develops a fresh approach to penal power that should reorient the field of study.

Mary Bosworth, *Professor of Criminology and Assistant Director of the Centre for Criminology, University of Oxford, UK*

This book challenges some of the orthodox claims that the voluntary sector has been captured by either states or markets. Using actor-network analysis, it argues that the responses of voluntary sector to decades of neo-liberalism and penal punitiveness are nuanced, fluid and complex. Philippa Tomczak makes a compelling, critical intervention in a rapidly evolving and exciting field of study. It is high on my reading list.

Mary Corcoran, *Senior Lecturer in Criminology, Keele University, UK, and editor of* The Voluntary Sector and Criminal Justice *(Palgrave Macmillan, 2016)*

In the past few decades we have seen the emergence of an increasingly complex, hybrid and privatized landscape of penal service delivery, with more and more elements of the voluntary sector being drawn into the new neoliberal marketised penal economy too. This book is a very valuable addition to the literature on the changing relationship between the voluntary sector and the state, raising important questions about the relationship, which organisations are involved, how it works, what effects there are on consumers, and what complexities and concerns there are in new relationship. The book is both insightful and timely and will be of interest to students and scholars of criminal justice, policy-makers and practitioners across the field.

Loraine Gelsthorpe, *Professor of Criminology and Criminal Justice, Deputy Director, Institute of Criminology, University of Cambridge, UK*

Tomczak's sophisticated, empirical exploration of the voluntary sector's involvement in that most involuntary of sectors, the UK's penal system, simply could not be more timely or more badly needed. It fills an enormous gap in the criminological literature while opening up dozens of new avenues for new research. A real path-breaker.

Shadd Maruna, *Professor of Criminology, University of Manchester, UK*

The Penal Voluntary Sector

The penal voluntary sector and the relationships between punishment and charity are more topical than ever before in countries around the world. In recent years in England and Wales, the sector has featured significantly in both policy rhetoric and academic commentary. Penal voluntary organisations are increasingly delivering prison and probation services under contract, and this role is set to expand. However, the diverse voluntary organisations which comprise the sector, their varied relationships with statutory agencies and the effects of such work remain very poorly understood.

This book provides a wide-ranging and rigorous examination of this policy-relevant but complex and little studied area. It explores what voluntary organisations are doing with prisoners and probationers, how they manage to undertake their work, and the effects of charitable work with prisoners and probationers. The author uses original empirical research and an innovative application of actor-network theory to enable a step change in our understanding of this increasingly significant sector, and develops the policy-centric accounts produced in the last decade to illustrate how voluntary organisations can mediate the experiences of imprisonment and probation at the micro and macro levels.

Demonstrating how the legacy of philanthropic work and neoliberal policy reforms over the past thirty years have created a complex three-tier penal voluntary sector of diverse organisations, this cutting-edge interdisciplinary text will be of interest to criminologists, sociologists of work and industry, and those engaged in the voluntary sector.

Philippa Tomczak is a Leverhulme Trust Early Career Fellow at the University of Sheffield's Centre for Criminological Research. She previously studied Criminology and Geography at the Universities of Oxford and Manchester. She is interested in punishment, particularly the regulation of prison suicide, the penal voluntary sector, and actor-network theory.

Routledge Frontiers of Criminal Justice

The Penal Voluntary Sector

Philippa Tomczak

Routledge
Taylor & Francis Group

LONDON AND NEW YORK

First published in paperback 2018

First published 2017
by Routledge
2 Park Square, Milton Park, Abingdon, Oxon OX14 4RN

and by Routledge
711 Third Avenue, New York, NY 10017

Routledge is an imprint of the Taylor & Francis Group, an informa business

British Library Cataloguing in Publication Data
A catalogue record for this book is available from the British Library

Library of Congress Cataloging in Publication Data
A catalog record for this book has been requested

ISBN: 978-1-138-18982-9 (hbk)
ISBN: 978-1-138-50005-1 (pbk)
ISBN: 978-1-315-64142-3 (ebk)

Typeset in Times New Roman
by Wearset Ltd, Boldon, Tyne and Wear

MIX
Paper from responsible sources
FSC   FSC™ C013985
www.fsc.org

Printed in the United Kingdom
by Henry Ling Limited

This is perhaps unconventional, but I'd like to dedicate this book to everyone who is struggling with a project.

All too often publications, brilliant ideas and wide-ranging successes tumble out of people with apparent ease. This has rarely been the case for me.

I'm sure I often don't help myself, but I found writing this book and getting an academic job and doing my PhD really hard. I stuck at it, although sometimes only just. I hope that readers will think the results were worth it.

We only usually see the polished end products of people's efforts and this doesn't depict or even acknowledge the convoluted processes that sit behind every shiny end product. In a small way, this dedication represents the tangled and sometimes painful processes which lie behind achievement. Success is not linear – maybe giving up is.

Contents

Acknowledgements

I would like to acknowledge generous financial support from the Leverhulme Trust *Early Career Fellowship* (2015–2018), the University of Sheffield School of Law (2014–2018) and the University of Manchester *School of Law Scholarship* (2010–2014), which have enabled me to produce this book and the research upon which it is based.

I have greatly benefited from the input of Joanna Shapland while at Sheffield, which has improved my work immensely. I would never have pursued a PhD without the guidance of Mary Bosworth at Oxford, to whom I credit my career. My PhD research was supported by the supervision of Jon Spencer and Jo Deakin at Manchester, and Jon encouraged me use actor-network theory.

At a personal level, I am grateful for the support of Denise and Richard Tomczak, Jake Corrigan and Matt Richards.

Earlier versions of this work have been published as journal articles:

Tomczak, P. (forthcoming) 'The Voluntary Sector and the Mandatory Statutory Supervision Requirement: Expanding the Carceral Net'. *British Journal of Criminology*.

Tomczak, P. and Albertson, K. (2016) 'Prisoner Relationships with Voluntary Sector Practitioners', *The Howard Journal of Criminal Justice*, *55*(1–2): 57–72.

Tomczak, P. (2014) 'The Penal Voluntary Sector in England and Wales: Beyond Neoliberalism?' *Criminology and Criminal Justice*, *14*(4): 470–486. *DOI: 10.1177/1748895813505235.*

Abbreviations

ANT   Actor-network theory
MoJ   Ministry of Justice
NOMS   National Offender Management Service
Pact   Prison Advice and Care Trust
PbR   Payment by Results
POPS   Partners of Prisoners and Families Support Group

1 The penal voluntary sector

1.1 Introduction

The penal voluntary sector and the relationships between punishment and charity are perhaps more topical than ever before. An assortment of countries around the world have seen significant restructuring of public social welfare services in recent decades, involving a general movement away from unified public services and towards the development of quasi-markets (Salamon, 2015; Considine, 2003; Wolch, 1990). Intermediate bodies that sit between the state and the market and have a social benefit mandate are heavily implicated in this restructuring, alongside private companies. I refer to these intermediate bodies as 'voluntary organisations'.[1] Given this context of radical changes to public services, it is problematic and peculiar that partnerships between government and the voluntary sector have 'largely escaped close scrutiny and serious public and policy attention' (Salamon, 2015: 2149).

More specifically, in England and Wales the recent penal policy developments in *Transforming Rehabilitation: A Strategy for Reform* (Ministry of Justice/MoJ, 2013c) and *Breaking the Cycle* Green Paper (MoJ, 2010) suggest a further increasing role for voluntary organisations, or charities, in competitive penal service markets. Despite a flurry of academic commentary responding to these policies and the government's 'dramatically increased engagement' with the voluntary sector as a contractual provider of penal services (Neilson, 2009: 408),[2] little is known about the penal voluntary sector. This is perhaps surprising, as charities have a 'long and rich history' of involvement in criminal justice (Mills *et al.*, 2012: 392; see also Neilson, 2009: 408) and are heavily implicated in the current operation of penal institutions in England and Wales (Martin, 2013; Neuberger, 2009). Indeed, the penal voluntary sector is considered so significant that 'there can *hardly be a prison in the country* that could continue to work as it does if there was a large scale collapse of voluntary, community and social enterprise services for people in custody' (Martin, 2013: no pagination, emphasis added). Although the voluntary sector is broadly underresearched by scholars from various disciplines (Considine, 2003), there is a particular dearth of voluntary sector research in punishment, in relation to studies in areas such as housing and social care (Corcoran, 2011: 33).

Due to this 'limited attention devoted to charitable organisations' by scholars (Armstrong, 2002: 345), understandings of the penal voluntary sector are 'lacking' (Mills *et al.*, 2011: 195). The sector thus remains 'a descriptive rather than theoretically rigorous concept or empirically defined entity' (Corcoran, 2011: 33; see also Mills *et al.*, 2011; Armstrong, 2002). This text addresses this significant gap in knowledge by *conceptualising the penal voluntary sector in England and Wales*. It demonstrates that charitable involvement in criminal justice is more complicated, troubling and full of potential than scholars have opined thus far. It explores the heterogeneity of penal voluntary organisations, considering the what, how and so what questions. Namely, it explores *what* voluntary organisations are doing with prisoners and probationers and *how* voluntary organisations manage to undertake this work, and questions the *effects* of charitable work on prisoners and probationers. The resultant conceptualisation of charitable involvement in criminal justice looks both within and beyond the penal service market and contains multi-level analyses of charities that are fully state funded, partly state funded and not state funded.

This text also offers a detailed and innovative application of actor-network theory (ANT) to a criminological subject. Although this account of the penal voluntary sector was underpinned by ANT, it can still be appreciated by readers who do not wish to engage with ANT, who should feel free to skim or skip ANT sections. However, this text does set out an innovative theoretical and methodological approach to structured research that was inspired by ANT and has many further applications for criminology, penology and beyond. Although I do not claim to provide a programmatic or comprehensive 'ANT approach', I anticipate that the approach I have assembled and applied here will be useful for future research involving multiple partner organisations in the increasingly complex, hybrid and privatised landscape of penal service delivery (such as in restorative justice programmes), and for studying other parts of the voluntary sector at policy and practice level.

This text is situated in the specific jurisdiction of England and Wales, but is highly relevant to studies of the penal voluntary sector in other jurisdictions. Indeed, I hope to stimulate a rich tradition of penal voluntary sector research. Section 1.4 below explores the importance of the voluntary sector in a number of other jurisdictions, and points out important *variations* which affect the applicability of this research to other jurisdictions. I now define and locate the penal voluntary sector.

1.2 Locating the penal voluntary sector

The voluntary sector is comprised of diverse voluntary organisations. In their simplest form, voluntary organisations are located between the market and the state (Considine, 2003; Salamon and Anheier, 1992). Voluntary organisations are formally constituted organisations outside the public sector, whose main distinctive feature is that they do not make profits for shareholders (Maguire, 2012: 493; Corcoran, 2009: 32). The voluntary sector in general contains a 'bewildering variety of organisational forms, activities, motivations and ideologies' (Kendall and Knapp, 1995: 66) and is therefore notoriously difficult to define (Paxton and Pearce, 2005; Martens, 2002). It has even been characterised as 'a loose and baggy monster' for which 'no single "correct" definition ... can or should be uniquely applied in all circumstances' (Kendall and Knapp, 1995: 66).

Part of the 'bagginess' of the voluntary sector results from its position in between and overlapping with the other three sectors of welfare provision, i.e. the public, private and informal sectors. The essential characteristics of the voluntary sector are therefore not always easy to discern (Alcock and Scott, 2007: 85). For example, the penal voluntary sector in England and Wales overlaps with the private/commercial sector of service provision because some voluntary organisations deliver penal services under contract. As such, there are similarities between the activities of companies such as Serco and G4S, and charities such as Nacro, which deliver penal services under contract (see also Neilson, 2009).

In England and Wales, the *penal* voluntary sector is a specialist set of voluntary organisations within the general voluntary sector and is comprised of 'charitable and self-defined voluntary agencies working with prisoners and offenders in prison- and community-based programmes' (Corcoran, 2011: 33). For example, Fine Cell Work trains and pays prisoners to do high quality, creative needlework in their cells and workshops, to foster hope, discipline and employability (Fine Cell Work, 2014: 2) and the Apex Trust helps people with a criminal record to obtain employment, training, education or voluntary work by providing them with the skills they need to access the labour market, working to break down the barriers to their employment and guiding them on the positive disclosure of their conviction(s) (Apex Trust, 2015: 6).

I will add that penal voluntary organisations *also* work with prisoners' families, with victims of crime and in policy advocacy programmes. For example, Partners of Prisoners and Families Support Group (POPS) provide a variety of support and assistance services for anyone who has a link with someone in prison, enabling families to cope with the stress of arrest, sentencing, imprisonment and release (POPS, 2015: 5). Remedi provide restorative justice services directed towards mediation and reconciliation between victims of crime and (ex-)offenders, and work with groups such as youth offending teams and Police and Crime Commissioners (Remedi, 2015: 4–5). The Prison Reform Trust aims to create a 'just, humane and effective penal system' by 'influencing Parliament, Government and officials towards reform' (Prison Reform Trust, 2015: 4). Their key campaigns centre around reducing unnecessary imprisonment and promoting community solutions to crime, and improving treatment and conditions for prisoners and their families (Prison Reform Trust, 2015: 4). I therefore suggest that Corcoran's definition (2011: 33) should be widened to describe penal voluntary organisations as *charitable and self-defined voluntary agencies working with prisoners, (ex-) offenders, their families and their victims in prison, community and policy advocacy programmes.*

The scale of charitable involvement in criminal justice is difficult to establish, as little formal data exist in this area (Meek *et al.*, 2013: 340; see also Corcoran and Hucklesby, 2013; Gojkovic *et al.*, 2011; Meek *et al.*, 2010). Some comment-ators suggest that the sector plays a numerically significant role. In 2005 it was estimated that 1,500 voluntary organisations were working with prisons and pro-bation (Meek *et al.*, 2010: 3), and faith-based organisations alone provided 7,000 volunteers in this area (Neuberger, 2009: 4).

The boundaries of the penal voluntary sector are blurred, but for this research I limited the sector to formally constituted voluntary organisations which are registered as charitable organisations with the Charity Commission[3] and have a principal focus on (ex-)offenders or their families in England and Wales. This excluded grassroots and informal organisations, those with a different geograph-ical focus and those who work with offenders and/or their families amongst mul-tiple groups of clients.[4] I have conceptualised the penal voluntary sector as a distinct entity which can be differentiated from the formal criminal justice system and volunteers within statutory criminal justice agencies, such as Special Constables and magistrates. However, this standpoint does not negate the long history of interactions and the enduring blurred boundaries between voluntary/philanthropic[5] bodies and the formal criminal justice system (see Mills *et al.*, 2011; Silvestri, 2009; Smith *et al.*, 1993; McWilliams, 1983; Ignatieff, 1978; Foucault, 1977). Furthermore, the penal voluntary sector is acknowledged to form part of a broader definition of the criminal justice system, as part of the 'wider cast' of non-statutory actors that play a part in the operation of punish-ment. Examples of this 'wider cast' include private security agents who work as bouncers and guards, private companies that provide prisoner escorts, and the aforementioned 'statutory volunteers' such as Special Constables (Zedner, 2004: 125–126; see also Jones and Newburn, 2002).

The formal criminal justice system is comprised of a number of agencies or institutions such as the police and the Crown Prosecution Service. These agen-cies operate at different scales. The Ministry of Justice (MoJ) is the government department with overall responsibility for criminal justice in England and Wales (Davies *et al.*, 2005: 4). Within the MoJ, the National Offender Management Service (NOMS) is responsible for managing offenders from their sentencing to their resettlement in the community (Davies *et al.*, 2005: 4). When my empirical research was undertaken in 2012, NOMS consisted of the Prison and Probation Services, but following the *Transforming Rehabilitation* reforms to probation (MoJ, 2013c), NOMS now oversees probation delivery through the National Probation Service and privatised Community Rehabilitation Companies. Impris-onment and probation, as delivered by the Prison Service and what was the Pro-bation Service, were the focus of this research, but voluntary organisations do interact with other criminal justice agencies. For example, Citizens Advice is a charitable organisation that mobilises thousands of volunteers to staff the Witness Service operating in every Crown and Magistrates' Court (see Zedner, 2004). The next section explores recent policy developments involving the penal voluntary sector and the academic analysis of these.

1.3 Criminal justice and neoliberalism

Recent policy developments suggest an increasing role for charities in the delivery of penal services under contract in England and Wales (e.g. MoJ, 2013b, 2013c, 2011b, 2010). Neoliberal processes of marketising penal service delivery are related to the privatisation of public services that began in the 1980s, and continued under successive governments (Maguire, 2012; Morgan, 2012; Panchamia, 2012; Ryan, 2011; Corcoran, 2009). Voluntary organisations have a long history of involvement with criminal justice as part of the philanthropic tradition,[6] but have directly featured in neoliberal penal policy rhetoric since 1991 (Corcoran, 2011). Neoliberalism involves privatisation policies aiming to 'desacralise' institutions which previously enjoyed protection from private market competition, e.g. criminal justice and health care (Mudge, 2008: 703–704). The key tenet of neoliberalism is that privatising public services through competitive commissioning markets should stimulate cost-efficiency and save public money (Corcoran, 2009: 33; Garland, 1996: 453).

Public services were privatised by creating competitive service delivery markets under the policies of the Conservative Thatcher government in the 1980s and 1990s (Corcoran, 2011: 36; Ryan, 2011: 517). Thatcher's appetite for privatisation was based on the contested assumption that private sector service provision would be more efficient and cost-effective and catalyse system-wide improvements (Panchamia, 2012). Under the provisions of the Criminal Justice Act 1991, public prisons could be transferred to private sector management, and Probation Boards (which were then in charge of probation areas) were required to commission voluntary and private sector organisations to provide drug programmes (Corcoran, 2011: 36–37; Corcoran, 2009: 33). This Act saw the separation of the purchaser and provider role, the growth of contractual and semi-contractual arrangements and the creation of a quasi-market in punishment (Lacey, 1994), thus unsettling the state monopoly on the allocation and delivery of punishment which had been established about 1877 (Maguire, 2012: 484; Ryan, 2011: 517).

New Labour then 'substantially endorsed' the Conservatives' changes and continued the marketisation of public services (Ryan, 2011: 518; see also Maguire, 2012; Morgan, 2012; Corcoran, 2011). The Offender Management Act 2007 stressed the role of market discipline in improving performance, and enabled some additional responsibilities traditionally associated with probation to be taken on by private and voluntary organisations (Whitehead, 2015: 61; Corcoran, 2011: 37; Mills et al., 2011: 195; Meek et al., 2010: 4). The MoJ also allocated £12 million of short term contract funding to voluntary organisations for the provision of diversionary community-based support to women in response to the 2007 Corston Report[7] (NEF, 2012: 7; see also Annison and Brayford, 2015; Mills et al., 2012, 2011; Home Office, 2007). This MoJ funding was short-term and in 2010 heavy MoJ budget cuts led to the establishment of the £2 million Women's Diversionary Fund, which sustained some services (NEF, 2012; Prison Reform Trust, 2011a).

The *Breaking the Cycle* Green Paper (MoJ, 2010) indicated that the then coalition government was set to further roll back the state and 'continue along Thatcher's radical path' (Ryan, 2011: 518; see also Garside and Mills, 2012). This Green Paper stated the government's 'clear commitment to decentralisation', justifying this stance by emphasising the failures of the 'top-down approach' to penal service delivery (MoJ, 2010: 6, 8). This strategy stressed the role for voluntary and private organisations in criminal justice alongside the public sector, thus combining the political ideal of a smaller regulatory state with the material imperative for fiscal austerity in light of the record UK public deficit (Ryan, 2011: 518). Subsequently, *Transforming Rehabilitation: A Strategy for Reform* emphasised that the market in penal services was to be further opened up to a range of providers from the public, private and voluntary sectors (MoJ, 2013c). This report also stressed the role of payment by results (PbR) financial incentives for service providers in improving competition, performance and effectiveness, and privatised probation supervision for medium and low risk (ex-)offenders by founding Community Rehabilitation Companies (MoJ, 2013c).

These neoliberal reforms of the last three decades have created a mixed economy of penal service provision, in which private and voluntary sector providers operate alongside the public sector to deliver penal services under contract (Cavadino *et al.*, 2013: 177; Panchamia, 2012: 1; Corcoran, 2011: 37; Ryan, 2011: 517; Corcoran, 2009: 33; Garland, 2001: 98). Various aspects of the penal system in England and Wales are now privatised, spanning a spectrum of activities from outsourcing specific regime elements (e.g. contracting-out prison catering services to private companies), to the wholesale transfer of responsibility for the provision and daily running of penal institutions to private contractors (Cavadino *et al.*, 2013: 176; Panchamia, 2012: 6; Zedner, 2004: 276). HMP Wolds opened in 1992 and was the first privately run prison in the UK (Panchamia, 2012; Ryan, 2011). At the time of writing in 2016, there were fourteen private prisons managed under contract by private companies such as Serco, Sodexo Justice Services and G4S Justice Services.[8] The first private probation contract was won by Serco in 2012 and involved supervising probationers on community payback sentences in London (Panchamia, 2012; Travis, 2012; Serco, 2012).

No penal voluntary organisation had taken wholesale responsibility for the construction or management of a penal institution at the time of writing, but charities were directly involved in contracted-out service delivery in a variety of ways. Serco, in 'alliance' with the charities Catch 22 and Turning Point, won a £415 million contract in 2010 to construct the new prison at Belmarsh West and operate it for 26.5 years (Panchamia, 2012; Serco, 2010). This was the first UK prison contract awarded to an alliance of the private and voluntary sectors, with the charities providing rehabilitation and resettlement services for prisoners (Serco, 2010). Whether charities in such consortia are equal partners to their private sector counterparts, or junior partners who are essentially 'bid candy' is, however, debatable (NPC, 2015; Maguire, 2012).

Multiple charities are, however, directly involved in low-level prison privatisation, i.e. the contracting out of specific regime elements (Zedner, 2004: 276). For example, the Prison Advice and Care Trust (Pact) holds a variety of contracts with prison and probation, which include running prison visitor centres e.g. at HMP Bristol (Pact, 2015: 19). Some charities also participated in the establishment of PbR as a mechanism to pay penal service contractors, e.g. in the pilot Social Impact Bond at the private HMP Peterborough. Under PbR, the contractor's payment is linked to results achieved, in order to encourage greater efficiency and effectiveness in service delivery (Maguire, 2012; Fox and Albertson, 2011). The Peterborough pilot was co-ordinated by Social Finance, which raised funding of £5 million to work with short-sentence prisoners in an attempt to reduce reconviction rates. Voluntary organisations involved in the pilot included St Giles Trust and Ormiston Children and Families Trust[9] (Social Finance, 2011).

In combination with the legacy of philanthropic work, neoliberal reforms over the last thirty years have created a three-tier penal voluntary sector of organisations, consisting of those which are largely state funded, those which are partly state funded and those not in receipt of state funding. The research upon which this book is based was conducted amid the neoliberal policy environment described above, and its effects upon diverse charities are considered. However, this text problematises arguments that the entire voluntary sector has been *harnessed* to the 'wider agenda of "post-welfare" state modernization' (Corcoran, 2011: 34, see also Maguire, 2012: 484) and that neoliberal projects have been '*shaping* voluntary sector agents to the demands of the penal marketplace' (Corcoran, 2011: 45, emphasis added).[10] Actual evidence about the effects of marketisation on the independence of penal voluntary organisations across the sector is scarce, and 'much of it is based on speculation' (Helminen, 2016: 2). Nevertheless, commentators have emphasised the likely impact and importance of market reforms for penal voluntary organisations in England and Wales. Marketisation has apparently 'transformed' the voluntary sector's role in punishment, with it 'becoming enmeshed in the day to day operation of the criminal justice system' rather than supplementing statutory services as previously (Hucklesby and Corcoran, 2016: 1). Marketisation has ostensibly raised 'troubling issues for the voluntary sector' (Neilson, 2009: 401), is impacting upon its 'independence and ethos' (Mills *et al.*, 2011: 193) and is threatening its 'distinctiveness and critical voice' (Mills *et al.*, 2011: 193; see also Maguire, 2012; Corcoran 2011).

The impact of neoliberal policy reforms has been a key theme in recent academic commentary, with commentators discussing the sector *in terms of* its links to the marketisation of criminal justice. Although timely and important, these arguments are problematic. Whilst marketised penal reforms certainly affect parts of the penal voluntary sector, I argue that the omnipotence of these reforms has been overstated by commentators. The centrality of marketisation in this literature has resulted in a *partial* analysis of the penal voluntary sector that tends towards economic determinism and neglects the agency and heterogeneity of penal voluntary organisations (Tomczak, 2014). Although the sector's heterogeneity has been briefly acknowledged in existing literature (e.g. Corcoran and Hucklesby, 2013; Corcoran, 2011; Mills *et al.*, 2011), it has not been fully explored by scholars. This is problematic because penal voluntary organisations are not homogeneous: they do different work, have different funding sources, operate at various scales, have different principles and are not uniformly affected by policy changes and market reforms (see also Helminen, 2016; Tomczak, 2014). I address this by examining what penal voluntary organisations are doing and how they manage to undertake their work through varied contractual and non-contractual relationships with statutory criminal justice agencies.

Whilst it is clear that market policy reforms are likely to have a significant impact upon parts of the penal voluntary sector, it is significantly less clear *why*, or indeed *if*, this matters. Although the value and contribution that the sector can make to criminal justice has been cited (e.g. Corcoran and Hucklesby, 2013, no pagination; Maguire, 2012: 484; Mills *et al.*, 2012: 392; Benson and Hedge, 2009: 35; Neuberger, 2009: 2), the evidence base for these claims is not clear. The *distinctive qualities and social benefits* of charitable work, in contrast to public or private sector engagement, have not been substantiated by robust research (Tomczak and Albertson, 2016; Armstrong, 2002). Exactly what the penal voluntary sector does and the contributions it makes to prisoners and probationers are far from clear, both within and beyond the market in penal services, due to gaps in scholarly understandings of the sector. According to Mills *et al.* (2011: 205), 'discussion of how voluntary sector organisations themselves will be affected by recent policy developments remains sparse and underdeveloped'. While this is true, there is a preceding need to understand the *effects* of charitable work upon prisoners and probationers.

When seeking to understand the penal voluntary sector, marketisation is necessary but insufficient: it forms a valid point of entry for analyses, but in practice it directly affects only a small proportion of voluntary organisations (Tomczak, 2014: 479; Maguire, 2012: 488, 491; Corcoran, 2011: 40; Mills *et al.*, 2011: 195; Silvestri, 2009: 4). The centrality afforded to marketisation in recent literature has focussed attention away from non-contractual relationships between voluntary organisations and statutory criminal justice agencies, which has in turn limited our understandings of the penal voluntary sector and the effects of charitable work. This book addresses these gaps in understanding. The next section considers how this book can be understood as a case study of the voluntary sector that is relevant for understanding practices elsewhere.

1.4 A British phenomenon?

While this account and the data within it are situated in the penal and policy contexts and cultures of England and Wales, the voluntary sector and its role in (and beyond) the marketisation of social and penal services are issues of international import. Many countries have restructured public social welfare services in recent decades; I now demonstrate this using four brief examples (the USA, Canada, New Zealand and Australia).

The USA's Reaganite politics from the 1980s saw the creation of a shadow state, or para-state, apparatus of voluntary organisations that grew to carry out traditional welfare state functions (Wolch, 1990). The Clinton administration then undertook a well-documented search for a 'Third Way' of approaching effective welfare delivery (with parallels to the UK Blair government's approach) and the later Bush administration experimented with using not-for-profit groups in the delivery of official welfare programmes (Dollery and Wallis, 2001; see also Kaufman, 2015). As such, the voluntary/nonprofit sector in the USA manages a 'far larger' number of persons under correctional control than for-profit institutions (Armstrong, 2002: 345). Indeed, 'one would be hard pressed to find anywhere in the USA a jurisdiction that does not make use of the Salvation Army ... or some other nonprofit provider in both the assessment and management of criminal offenders' (Armstrong, 2002: 345–346). Furthermore, voluntary and mandatory prisoner re-entry programming for the growing number of released prisoners in the USA 'occurs primarily' in the sector of non-governmental organisations (Kaufman, 2015: 535). But while an ongoing 'lively debate' has discussed the role of the private sector in punishment, the work of voluntary organisations has gone 'largely unnoticed' by scholars (Armstrong, 2002: 345; see also Kort-Butler and Malone, 2015).

The Canadian voluntary sector has become increasingly responsible for providing social services to disadvantaged individuals since the early 1990s. This downloading of services to the voluntary sector has occurred as a consequence of the depletion of federal public services through fiscal restraint, welfare state retrenchment, out-sourcing arrangements, privatisation efforts and new contract governance schemes (Maurutto and Hannah-Moffat, 2016; Ilcan and Basok, 2004; Evans and Shields, 2002). Canadian provincial and federal correctional services work with voluntary organisations operating on a non-profit, fee-for-service basis to provide services such as residential parole supervision and community re-integration of (ex-)offenders (Zubrycki, 2003). For example, according to its website, the John Howard Society of Canada provides various rehabilitative and reintegration services to released prisoners, with most of their front-line programmes delivered under contract with Correctional Services of Canada.

New Zealand saw neoliberal economic reforms in the 1980s and 1990s which included increasing use of purchase-of-service contracts for the voluntary sector and the allocation of funding according to ideas of contestability and efficiency, with contract monitoring undertaken according to rigid specifications (Mills, 2015; Crack et al., 2007; Cribb, 2006). Organisations such as Prisoner Aid, the Prison Fellowship, the Salvation Army and Choices Hawkes Bay provide a range of re-integration services for prisoners and, in recent years, have been supported to 'go much further in working with offenders in the community to reduce re-offending', under results-driven contracts (Department of Corrections, 2012: 1).

In Australia, the Howard government from 1996 experimented with alternative systems of delivering social services, recommending social partnerships among business, government and community organisations (Dollery and Wallis, 2001). These partnerships involved leading charitable and religious bodies such as the Society of St Vincent de Paul, the Salvation Army, the Brotherhood of St Laurence, the Wesley Mission and Anglicare (Dollery and Wallis, 2001). Notably, the private company GEO was awarded the contract to design, build, finance and manage Ravenhall prison in Victoria in September 2014. The prison will open in late 2017 and introduces an Australian-first PbR model. According to its website, GEO will work in partnership with some Victorian voluntary organisations (the YMCA, Melbourne City Mission, Kangan Institute, and the Gathering Place), in an alliance of service providers, to bring about lasting positive change in the lives of prisoners and ex-prisoners.

These parallels between jurisdictions mean that this conceptualisation of the penal voluntary sector is relevant to research in different countries and comparative research. My findings can, and I hope *will*, be utilised as a case study that is relevant for understanding the penal voluntary sector elsewhere. However, it is important to note that the findings presented here are set within the specific penal, policy and economic context and culture of England and Wales, at a particular point in time (see also Dockley and Loader, 2013). *Penal* and *voluntary sector* cultures, operating assumptions and practices differ across territories and time periods. These *contexts matter* when conceptualising and researching penal voluntary sectors. It is therefore important that scholars seeking to apply this work to other jurisdictions scope the legal and policy contexts and cultures applying to both voluntary organisations and punishment, and acknowledge and consider these accordingly. I now outline some significant variations between jurisdictions and encourage others to develop and expand this list of considerations.

Defining the voluntary sector is problematic in one jurisdiction, as explained above, but it is further complicated across jurisdictions because voluntary organisations have different legal statuses and constraints in different countries, which can affect how they operate. For example, the UK and USA have advantageous charity laws providing tax breaks for voluntary organisations, which is not usually the case elsewhere (Martens, 2002). In most countries, only citizens can form voluntary organisations, but this right is extended to all inhabitants in the UK, Ireland, Denmark, France and the Netherlands (Martens, 2002). Only registered organisations can bring legal proceedings to court in France, but official registration is not required for this purpose in the UK, Denmark, Germany and Italy (Martens, 2002). A key variable is the proportion of state funding in the budgets of voluntary organisations, which varies significantly between territories (Salamon and Sokolowski, 2004). I suspect that there are also varying uses of state grant and contract funding, different combinations of marketised and informal work and different proportions of organisations who are mainly, partly and not state funded in the penal voluntary sectors of different countries.

Furthermore, the strength of the welfare state varies between jurisdictions. Some countries have stronger welfare states under which voluntary organisations may offer alternative, substitutive or complementary services to the statutory services provided (Dahlberg, 2005). However, even the Nordic countries, which have traditionally favoured a strong state role in welfare provision, are increasingly utilising private and voluntary bodies in the delivery of public services (Helminen, 2016). By contrast, although France has not seen a politically driven privatisation agenda in probation, the voluntary sector is in virtually sole charge of pre-sentence reports, prisoners' resettlement, prisoners' family support and victims' support, and is increasingly in charge of supporting community re-entry and rehabilitation, half-way houses and treatment programmes (Herzog-Evans, 2014). These varying contexts in which penal voluntary sectors operate should be acknowledged, and may be important when answering the critical questions in relation to penal voluntary sectors in different countries (i.e. *what* voluntary organisations are doing with prisoners and probationers, *how* voluntary organisations manage to undertake their work, and the *effects* of charitable work on prisoners and probationers).

England and Wales have a particular history of statutory and charitable interaction in criminal justice; they have Prison Service Order 4190 which sets out how the Service should relate 'to the voluntary and community organisations upon whom we increasingly rely for the delivery of our work in prisons' (HM Prison Service, 2002); and there is a particular marketised penal policy context including the private and voluntary sectors (as explained above). Penal contexts and cultures also vary, and this may affect what penal voluntary organisations do. For example, the Nordic countries (Finland, Sweden, Norway) have 'exceptional' penal conditions due to comparatively low imprisonment rates and relatively humane prison conditions, and their prisons tend to be small and relatively well staffed (Pratt and Eriksson, 2013). The work of their penal voluntary organisations thus takes place in a very different penal context and might have different effects to the work in England and Wales to which I refer in this book. Future research could usefully examine the relative presence, activities and funding of voluntary organisations in public and private prisons in different jurisdictions, and consider the critical what, how and so what questions in their particular contexts. Such work could certainly draw on this case study of the voluntary sector, which I hope provides a useful framework of results for work to understand and perhaps compare practices elsewhere. However, results should be extrapolated between countries with *caution* and with an awareness of their specific penal and voluntary sector *contexts*. I also hope that the theoretical and methodological approach that I have adopted will be useful, for both future penal voluntary sector and broader criminal justice research. This approach is now explained.

1.5 Theoretical approach

Building analysis of the penal voluntary sector upon neoliberal or market policy reforms may appear reasonable given recent policies which stress the role for charities in the penal service market (e.g. MoJ, 2013c; MoJ, 2010). However, this framework also creates analytical limitations, such as overlooking charitable heterogeneity, agency and autonomy, and neglecting to investigate what charities do without service delivery contracts. Marketised accounts have a tendency to assume critical what, how and so what aspects of penal voluntary organisations' work, thus providing partial and reductionist analyses. This text offers an original conceptualisation of the penal voluntary sector and draws attention to these important factors, which have not been sufficiently investigated. Creating a more complete conceptualisation of the sector that extends beyond marketisation and interrogates the effects of charitable work could be done in more than one way, but I apply ANT theory here. ANT provides an original and structured means of investigating complex penal phenomena at both policy and practice level.

ANT is an approach to sociological analysis based on a theory of agency, knowledge and organisation (Steins, 2001; Law and Hassard, 1999; see also Chapter 3). It is a method to investigate situations, providing a loose intellectual toolkit aiming to sensitise researchers to complex and multiple realities that might otherwise have remained obscure (Nimmo, 2011: 109; Law, 2004: 157). It rejects the basic dualism between micro and macro scale actors (or, in another form, nature and society) which troubles the social sciences, and insists that both can be examined in the same manner (Herbert-Cheshire, 2003: 460). It is therefore useful for bridging problematic analytic divides between the general and the particular, enabling scholars to examine local and national, or macro and micro scale, activities on the same terms and to integrate these accounts (Pollack *et al.*, 2013: 1119). ANT is applied here[11] to conceptualise the penal voluntary sector more fully. It provides a novel way of thinking about the penal voluntary sector, a means of illuminating charitable heterogeneity by considering scale and agency, and a *structured method* of analysing the diverse relationships between charities and statutory criminal justice agencies, and their effects. This diversity and complexity might otherwise have remained obscure amid the macro level debate about the marketisation of penal services.

Two core ANT techniques are applied here: the *principle of generalised symmetry* and the process of *translation*. The principle of generalised symmetry involves approaching apparently disparate bodies of actors from the same analytical perspective, i.e. symmetrically (Nimmo, 2011: 111; Carrabine, 2000: 312). While ANT is consistent with Foucault's emphasis on investigating how power works through disciplinary strategies, it provides conceptual tools which address the absence of a coherent theory of agency within the Foucauldian tradition (Herbert-Cheshire, 2003: 458–459; see also Chapter 3). Here the principle of generalised symmetry is applied to explore questions of agency and scale in relation to voluntary organisations, which entails studying micro and macro scale voluntary organisations, their activities and their agency on the same terms (see Carrabine, 2000: 312). As such, the analyses in Chapters 4 and 5 draw attention to smaller charities and charitable programmes that are not driven by macro scale marketised policy reforms.

The four-phase process of translation supplies an accessible and structured method of studying relationship building and interactions and illustrates how actors can impose themselves and their definitions of a situation on other actors (Sage *et al.*, 2011; Callon, 1986). Studying translations moves away from analysis of organisation as 'a discrete structural entity and towards the study of processes and practices of organising' (Alcadipani and Hassard, 2010: 420). Here translation is applied to examine how relationships are constructed between statutory criminal justice agencies and charities of various sizes. The structured approach is particularly useful because of the heterogeneity of voluntary organisations and their diverse relationships with statutory criminal justice agencies. Two overall translations are analysed in this text. The first translation examines small scale translations, informed by the principle of generalised symmetry. It is currently unclear how relationships between statutory criminal justice agencies and charities are constructed when a commissioning process is not relevant, e.g. where there is no contract funding provided for a charitable service by the MoJ or another statutory agency. As such, we have a limited understanding of exactly how the 'vital array' of charitable work that does not feature in recent criminal justice policy reforms (Martin, 2013: no pagination) is actually facilitated and undertaken. This translation is presented in Chapter 5. The second translation illustrates how some voluntary organisations were translated into a macro scale network of marketised penal service delivery, following recent policy reforms. This translation is presented in Chapter 6.

The effects of charitable work with prisoners and probationers are then explored. Existing literature indicates an important tension in this area. It is unclear whether charities are empowering prisoners and probationers, and enabling them to build social and human capital (Bilby *et al.*, 2013; Henley *et al.*, 2012; Tett *et al.*, 2012; Cohen, 2009; Digard *et al.*, 2007; Lewis *et al.*, 2007; Lippke, 2003), or whether 'benevolent' charitable work extends control, increases the scale of penality, and shores up coercive carceral regimes (Armstrong, 2002; Cohen, 1985; McWilliams, 1983; Ignatieff, 1978; Foucault, 1977; see also Tomczak, forthcoming).

In ANT terms, actors can be either intermediaries or mediators of an actor-network (Latour, 2005,1996; see also Chapter 3). Intermediaries transport meaning or force without transformation and can be black-boxed in analysis, while mediators *transform, distort and modify* the meanings and elements that they are supposed to carry (Afarikumah and Kwankam, 2013). The control and net-widening literature (e.g. Ignatieff, 1978; Foucault, 1977) broadly implies an intermediary role for charities, which are considered to *transport and extend* the force of the formal penal system without *transforming* it (see Afarikumah and Kwankam, 2013; Latour, 2005). Literature which points to the potential enabling functions of charitable work (e.g. Bilby *et al.*, 2013; Lewis *et al.*, 2007) broadly implies that charities are mediators of punishment and are considered to *transform, distort and modify the meanings, elements and experience of punishment* (see Afarikumah and Kwankam, 2013; Latour, 2005). The potential effects of the work of penal voluntary organisations are explored in Chapter 7. Following ANT's aim of learning from actors without imposing an a priori definition of the effects of their actions upon them (Nimmo, 2011: 109; Law, 2004: 157; see also

Chapter 3), I consider how charities can *reproduce, extend and transform pun-ishment* or, in other words, how charities can act as both intermediaries *and* mediators of punishment.

This text is not intended to critique the marketisation of penal services per se. It does not make a normative argument and imply that charitable work with prisoners and probationers is an adequate or appropriate response to the multiple problems and needs of this group (Corcoran, 2012; Brown and Ross, 2010). Nor does it suggest that the responsibility to work with this group lies with civil society rather than statutory organisations. Rather, the aim is to critique the centrality of marketisation in recent commentary, and to provide a more complete theorisation of the penal voluntary sector than is presently available. My analysis draws on data collected from three sources using two methodologies. I undertook document analysis of the publications of over forty penal voluntary organisations and policy documents such as *Breaking the Cycle* Green Paper (MoJ, 2010). I also carried out semi-structured interviews with eleven charity staff and two statutory-sector staff who had involvement with penal voluntary organisations. The following section of this chapter described the content of this book.

1.6 The book

This book conceptualises the contemporary penal voluntary sector in England and Wales. It explores *what* voluntary organisations are doing with prisoners and probationers, *how* they manage to undertake their work, and the *effects* of charitable work on prisoners and probationers. This book consists of eight chapters. This introductory chapter has contextualised the research project upon which the book is based, defined the penal voluntary sector and illustrated recent policy reforms that affect the sector. In Chapter 2, the historical and contemporary relationships between punishment and charity are reviewed. ANT forms the theoretical framework for the research and is fully explored in Chapter 3, along with the methodologies used to collect the data.

The analysis chapters follow. Chapter 4 *scopes* the penal voluntary sector, considering questions of scale and agency in relation to charities and their relationships with statutory criminal justice agencies. Chapter 4 draws on data from the document analysis of charity publications and sets out the foundations for answering the what and how questions: *what* voluntary organisations are doing with prisoners and probationers and *how* they manage to undertake their work. These questions are further addressed in Chapters 5 and 6. Chapter 5 builds on the scoping chapter and moves beyond analysis of contractual relationships to illustrate how *small scale relationships* between voluntary organisations and statutory criminal justice agencies are built. This chapter draws on data from the document analysis and interviews to demonstrate that relationships are sponsored by local statutory criminal justice agencies *and* individual charities. Such relationships affect prisoners and probationers, yet feature in neither current policy discussions nor existing criminological literature. Chapter 6 maps the macro level *policy translation* that began with the publication of *Breaking the*

Cycle Green Paper (MoJ, 2010) and draws on policy and charity publications. Mapping this translation illustrates how multiple statutory and voluntary sector actors were integrated into a specific marketised service delivery actor-network. This chapter demonstrates how the Green Paper affected charities, and was also affected by them.

Chapter 7 draws the analyses together. It answers the so what question and explores the *effects* of charitable work with prisoners and probationers. It finds evidence for potential benefits of charitable work, along with control and net-widening effects. While the empirical evidence base surrounding the penal voluntary sector remains lacking, this analysis also demonstrates that both the control and the emancipatory literatures appear to be inadequate, suggests that more nuanced hybrid or integrated theorisation is required and accordingly offers the conceptual innovation of 'inclusionary control'. The work of voluntary organisations can apparently result in both control and emancipation, or negative *and* positive effects which appear not to be mutually exclusive. Chapter 8 sets out the conclusions drawn from the study. It brings together all the data and their interpretation, and assesses the implications of this research.

Notes

1 An array of terminologies (and associated acronyms) are used to refer to these intermediate organisations. I have adopted the 'voluntary' label in line with recent policy rhetoric in England and Wales (e.g. MoJ, 2010), but the intermediate bodies to which I refer can also be labelled non-profit, third sector, nongovernmental, civil society, community, philanthropic and charitable organisations (Meek *et al.*, 2013; Maguire, 2012; Goddard and Myers, 2011; Alcock and Scott, 2007; Armstrong, 2002 inter alia). I use the labels 'voluntary' and 'charity' interchangeably in this publication for ease of expression, but not all voluntary organisations are registered charities.
2 See also Helminen, 2016; Hucklesby and Corcoran, 2016; Mills, 2015; Meek *et al.*, 2013; Mythen *et al.*, 2013; Maguire, 2012; Mills *et al.*, 2012; Morgan, 2012; Corcoran, 2011; Gojkovic *et al.*, 2011; Meek *et al.*, 2010; Benson and Hedge, 2009; Silvestri, 2009 inter alia.
3 The Charity Commission registers and regulates charities in England and Wales.
4 Chapter 3 provides a longer description of how the research site was bounded.
5 Philanthropy means 'providing help for others' and is a core purpose of the contemporary voluntary sector (Alcock and Scott, 2007: 84).
6 Chapter 2 provides a fuller exploration of this history.
7 The Corston Report (Home Office, 2007) was a review of women with particular vulnerabilities in the criminal justice system.
8 Full details of private prisons and their operators can be found on the website www. justice.gov.uk.
9 This pilot is discussed in detail in Chapter 6.
10 See also Hucklesby and Corcoran, 2016; Mills, 2015; Meek *et al.*, 2013; Mythen *et al.*, 2013; Maguire, 2012; Mills *et al.*, 2012; Morgan, 2012; Corcoran, 2011; Gojkovic *et al.*, 2011; Meek *et al.*, 2010; Benson and Hedge, 2009; Silvestri, 2009 inter alia.
11 This research is, however, not simply an application of ANT and has been informed by intersecting bodies of scholarship. These include Foucauldian ideas of governmentality (Foucault, 1977), net-widening theory (Cohen, 1985) and political economy (Reiner, 2012; Hart, 2002; Garland, 1990; see also Tomczak, 2014). However, the analytical approach has been inspired by the distinct ideas of ANT (Nimmo, 2011).

References

Alcadipani, R. and Hassard, J. (2010) 'Actor-Network Theory, Organizations and Critique: Towards a politics of organizing', *Organization*, *17*(4): 419–435.

Afarikumah, E. and Kwankam, S. Y. (2013) 'Deploying Actor-Network Theory to Analyse Telemedicine Implementation in Ghana', *Science*, *1*(2): 77–84.

Alcock, P. and Scott, D. (2007) 'Voluntary and Community Sector Welfare', in Powell, M. (ed.) *Understanding the Mixed Economy of Welfare*. Bristol: Policy Press.

Annison, J. and Brayford, J. (2015) 'Corston and Beyond', in Annison, J., Brayford, J. and Deering, J. (eds) *Women and Criminal Justice: From the Corston Report to Transforming Rehabilitation*. Bristol: Policy Press.

Apex Trust (2015) *Trustees' Report and Unaudited Accounts for the Year Ended 31 March 2015*.

Armstrong, S. (2002) 'Punishing Not-For-Profit: Implications of nonprofit privatization in juvenile punishment', *Punishment and Society*, *4(*3): 345–368.

Benson, A. and Hedge, J. (2009) 'Criminal Justice and the Voluntary Sector: A policy that does not compute', *Criminal Justice Matters*, *77*(1): 34–36.

Bilby, C., Caulfield, L. S. and Ridley, L. (2013) *Re-Imagining Futures: Exploring arts interventions and the process of desistance*. London: Arts Alliance. Available at: www.artsalliance.org.uk/sites/default/files/Reimagining_Futures_Research_Report_Final.pdf. Accessed: 3 November 2013.

Brown, M. and Ross, S. (2010) 'Mentoring, Social Capital and Desistance: A study of women released from prison', *Australian and New Zealand Journal of Criminology*, *43*(1): 31–50.

Callon, M. (1986) 'Some Elements of a Sociology of Translation: Domestication of the scallops and the fishermen of St Brieuc Bay', in Law, J. (ed.) *Power, Action and Belief: A new sociology of knowledge?* London: Routledge.

Carrabine, E. (2000) 'Discourse, Governmentality and Translation: Toward a social theory of imprisonment', *Theoretical Criminology*, *4*(3): 309–331.

Cavadino, M., Dignan, J. and Mair, G. (2013) *The Penal System: An introduction*. London: Sage.

Cohen, M. L. (2009) 'Choral Singing and Prison Inmates: Influences of performing in a prison choir', *Journal of Correctional Education*, *60*(1): 52–65.

Cohen, S. (1985) *Visions of Social Control: Crime, punishment and classification*. Cambridge: Polity Press.

Corcoran, M. (2009) 'Bringing the Penal Voluntary Sector to Market', *Criminal Justice Matters*, *77*(1): 32–33.

Corcoran, M. (2011) 'Dilemmas of Institutionalization in the Penal Voluntary Sector', *Critical Social Policy*, *31*(1): 30–52.

Corcoran, M. (2012) 'Be Careful What You Ask For: Findings from the seminar series on the Third Sector in criminal justice', *Prison Service Journal*, *204*: 17–22.

Corcoran, M. and Hucklesby, A. (2013) 'Briefing paper: The Third Sector in Criminal Justice'. Available at: www.law.leeds.ac.uk/assets/files/research/ccjs/130703-thirdsec-crimjust-briefing-2013.pdf. Accessed: 12 August 2013.

Considine, M. (2003) 'Governance and Competition: The role of non-profit organisations in the delivery of public services', *Australian Journal of Political Science*, *38*(1): 63–77.

Crack, S., Turner, S. and Heenan, B. (2007) 'The Changing Face of Voluntary Welfare Provision in New Zealand', *Health and Place*, *13*(1): 188–204.

Cribb, J. (2006) *Being Accountable: Voluntary organisations, government agencies and contracted social services in New Zealand.* Wellington: Institute of Policy Studies.

Dahlberg, L. (2005) 'Interaction between Voluntary and Statutory Social Service Provision in Sweden: A matter of welfare pluralism, substitution or complementarity?' *Social Policy and Administration, 39*(7): 740–763.

Davies, M., Croall, H. and Tyrer, J. (2005) *Criminal Justice: An introduction to the criminal justice system in England and Wales.* Essex: Pearson Education.

Department of Corrections (2012) *Partnering with Iwi and Community Groups Factsheet.* Available at: www.corrections.govt.nz/__data/assets/pdf_file/0011/694550/6_RR_partnering_with_iwi_and_community_groups_update_aug_2013.pdf. Accessed: 26 January 2016.

Digard, L., Grafin von Sponeck, A. and Liebling, A. (2007) 'All Together Now: The therapeutic potential of a prison-based music programme', *Prison Service Journal, 170*: 3–14.

Dockley, A. and Loader, I. (2013) *The Penal Landscape: The Howard League guide to criminal justice in England and Wales.* London: Routledge.

Dollery, B. and Wallis, J. (2001) 'Social Service Delivery and the Voluntary Sector in Contemporary Australia', *Australian Journal of Political Science, 36*(3): 567–575.

Evans, B. M. and Shields, J. (2002) 'The Third Sector: Neo-liberal restructuring, governance, and the remaking of state–civil society relationships', in Dunn, C. (ed.) *The Handbook of Canadian Public Administration.* Toronto: Oxford University Press.

Fine Cell Work (2014) *Trustees' Report and Unaudited Accounts for the Year Ended 31 December 2014.*

Foucault, M. (1977) *Discipline and Punish: The birth of the prison.* London: Allen Lane.

Fox, C. and Albertson, K. (2011) 'Payment by Results and Social Impact Bonds in the Criminal Justice Sector: New challenges for the concept of evidence-based policy?' *Criminology and Criminal Justice, 11*(5): 395–413.

Garland, D. (1990) *Punishment and Modern Society: A study in social theory.* Oxford: Clarendon Press.

Garland, D. (1996) 'The Limits of the Sovereign State: Strategies of crime control in contemporary society', *British Journal of Criminology, 36*(4): 445–471.

Garland, D. (2001) *The Culture of Control: Crime and social order in a contemporary society.* Chicago: University of Chicago Press.

Garside, R. and Mills, H. (2012) *UK Justice Policy Review: Volume 1.* London: Centre for Crime and Justice Studies.

Goddard, T. and Myers, R. (2011) 'Democracy and Demonstration in the Grey Area of Neo-Liberalism: A case study of Free Los Angeles High School', *British Journal of Criminology, 51*(4): 652–670.

Gojkovic, D., Mills, A. and Meek, R. (2011) 'Scoping the Involvement of Third Sector Organisations in the Seven Resettlement Pathways for Offenders', *TSRC Working Paper 57.* Southampton: Third Sector Research Centre.

Hart, G. (2002) 'Geography and Development: Development/s beyond neoliberalism? Power, culture, political economy', *Progress in Human Geography, 26*(2): 812–822.

Helminen, M. (2016) 'Nordic and Scottish Civil Society Organisations Working with Offenders and the Effects of Service Delivery: Is pursuing mission impossible whilst bidding for contracts?' *The Howard Journal of Criminal Justice, 55* (1–2): 73–93.

Henley, J., Caulfield, L. S., Wilson, D. and Wilkinson, D. J. (2012) 'Good Vibrations: Positive change through social music-making', *Music Education Research, 14*(4): 499–520.

Herbert-Cheshire, L. (2003) 'Translating Policy: Power and action in Australia's country towns', *Sociologia Ruralis, 43*(4): 454–473.

Herzog-Evans, M. (2014) 'French Third Sector Participation in Probation and Reentry: Complementary or competitive?' *European Journal of Probation, 6*(1): 42–56.

Home Office (2007) *The Corston Report: A report by Baroness Jean Corston of a review of women with particular vulnerabilities in the criminal justice system.* London: Home Office.

HM Prison Service (2002) *PSO 4190 Strategy For Working With The Voluntary And Community Sector.* London: Prison Service.

Hucklesby, A. and Corcoran, M. (2016) 'Introduction', in Hucklesby, A. and Corcoran, M. (eds) *The Voluntary Sector and Criminal Justice.* Basingstoke: Palgrave.

Ilcan, S. and Basok, T. S. (2004) 'Community Governance: Voluntary agencies, social justice and the responsibilisation of citizens', *Citizenship Studies, (8)*2: 129–144.

Ignatieff, M. (1978) *A Just Measure of Pain.* London: Macmillan Press.

Jones, T. and Newburn, T. (2002) 'The Transformation of Policing? Understanding current trends in policing systems', *British Journal of Criminology, 42*(1): 129–146.

Kaufman, N. (2015) 'Prisoner Incorporation: The work of the state and non-governmental organizations', *Theoretical Criminology, 19*(4): 534–553.

Kendall, J. and Knapp, M. R. J. (1995) 'Boundaries, Definitions and Typologies: A loose and baggy monster', in Davis Smith, J., Rochester, C. and Hedley, D. (eds) *An Introduction to the Voluntary Sector.* London: Routledge.

Kort-Butler, L. A. and Malone, S. E. (2015) 'Citizen Volunteers in Prison: Bringing the outside in, taking the inside out', *Journal of Crime and Justice, 38*(4): 508–521.

Lacey, N. (1994) 'Government as Manager, Citizen as Consumer: The case of the Criminal Justice Act 1991', *The Modern Law Review, 57*(4): 534–554.

Latour, B. (1996) 'On Actor-Network Theory. A few clarifications plus more than a few complications', *Soziale Welt, 47*(4): 369–381.

Latour, B. (2005) *Reassembling the Social: An introduction to Actor-Network Theory.* Oxford: Oxford University Press.

Law, J. (2004) *After Method: Mess in social science research.* Abingdon: Routledge.

Law, J. and Hassard, J. (1999) *Actor Network Theory and After.* Oxford: Blackwell.

Lewis, S., Maguire, M., Raynor, P., Vanstone, M. and Vennard, J. (2007) 'What works in Resettlement? Findings from seven Pathfinders for short-term prisoners in England and Wales', *Criminology and Criminal Justice, 7*(1): 33–53.

Lippke, R. L. (2003) 'Prisoner Access to Recreation, Entertainment and Diversion', *Punishment and Society, 5*(1): 33–52.

Maguire, M. (2012) 'Response 1: Big Society, the voluntary sector and the marketisation of criminal justice', *Criminology and Criminal Justice, 12*(5): 483–505.

Martens, K. (2002) 'Mission Impossible? Defining nongovernmental organizations', *Voluntas: International Journal of Voluntary and Nonprofit Organizations, 13*(3): 271–285.

Martin, C. (2013) *Dazzled by the Fireworks: Realising detail in the overwhelming scale of reform.* Clinks Blog Post. Available at: www.clinks.org/community/blog-posts/dazzled-fireworks-realising-detail-overwhelming-scale-reform. Accessed: 25 May 2013.

Maurutto, P. and Hannah-Moffat. K. (2016) 'Women's Voluntary Organisations and the Canadian Penal "Culture of Control"', in Hucklesby, A. and Corcoran, M. (eds) *The Voluntary Sector and Criminal Justice.* Basingstoke: Palgrave.

McWilliams, W. (1983) 'The Mission to the English Police Courts 1876–1936', *The Howard Journal of Criminal Justice, 22*(3): 129–147.

Meek, R., Gojkovic, D. and Mills, A. (2010) 'The Role of the Third Sector in Work with Offenders: The perceptions of criminal justice and third sector stakeholders', *TSRC Working Paper 34*. Birmingham: Third Sector Research Centre.

Meek, R., Gojkovic, D. and Mills, A. (2013) 'The Involvement of Nonprofit Organizations in Prisoner Reentry in the UK: Prisoner awareness and engagement', *Journal of Offender Rehabilitation, 52*(5): 338–357.

Mills, A. (2015) 'A Gentle Thaw or Continued Deep Freeze? Relationships between voluntary and community organisations and the state in criminal justice in New Zealand', *Third Sector Review, 21*(1): 121–142.

Mills, A., Meek, R. and Gojkovic, D. (2011) 'Exploring the Relationship Between the Voluntary Sector and the State in Criminal Justice', *Voluntary Sector Review, 2*(2): 193–211.

Mills, A., Meek, R. and Gojkovic, D. (2012) 'Partners, Guests or Competitors: Relationships between criminal justice and third sector staff in prisons', *Probation Journal, 59*(4): 391–405.

MoJ (2010) *Breaking the Cycle: Effective punishment, rehabilitation and sentencing of offenders*. London: MoJ.

MoJ (2011b) *Breaking the Cycle: Government response*. Available at: www.gov.uk/government/uploads/system/uploads/attachment_data/file/186345/breaking-the-cycle-government-response.pdf. Accessed: 16 October 2013.

MoJ (2013b) *Transforming Rehabilitation: A revolution in the way we manage offenders*. Available at: https://consult.justice.gov.uk/digital-communications/transforming-rehabilitation. Accessed: 17 October 2013.

MoJ (2013c) *Transforming Rehabilitation: A strategy for reform*. London: MoJ.

Morgan, R. (2012) 'Crime and Justice in the "Big Society"', *Criminology and Criminal Justice, 12*(5): 463–481.

Mudge, S. (2008) 'What is Neo-liberalism?' *Socio-Economic Review, 6*(4): 703–731.

Mythen, G., Walklate, S. and Kemshall, H. (2013) 'Decentralizing Risk: The role of the voluntary and community sector in the management of offenders', *Criminology and Criminal Justice, 13*(4): 363–379.

NEF (2012) *Women's Community Services: A wise commission*. Available at: www.corstoncoalition.org.uk/wp-content/uploads/2012/12/A_Wise_Commission_web Ready.pdf. Accessed: 4 January 2013.

Neilson, A. (2009) 'A Crisis of Identity: NACRO's bid to run a prison and what it means for the voluntary sector', *The Howard Journal of Criminal Justice, 48*(4): 401–410.

Neuberger, J. (2009) *Volunteering Across the Criminal Justice System*. London: The Cabinet Office.

Nimmo, R. (2011) 'Actor-Network Theory and Methodology: Social research in a more-than-human world', *Methodological Innovations Online, 6*(3): 108–119.

NPC (2015) *Transforming Rehabilitation: The voluntary sector perspective*. Available at: www.thinknpc.org/publications/transforming-rehabilitation-the-voluntary-sector-perspective/. Accessed: 23 February 2016.

Pact (2015) *Report and Financial Statements for the Year Ended 31 March 2015*.

Panchamia, N. (2012) *Competition in Prisons*. Institute for Government. Available at: www.instituteforgovernment.org.uk/sites/default/files/publications/Prisons%20briefing%20final.pdf. Accessed: 22 February 2016.

Paxton, W. and Pearce, N. (2005) 'The Voluntary Sector and the State', in Paxton, W., Pearce, N., Unwin, J. and Molyneux, P. (eds) *The Voluntary Sector Delivering Public Services*. York: Joseph Rowntree Foundation.

Pollack, J., Costello, K. and Sankaran, S. (2013) 'Applying Actor-Network Theory as a Sensemaking Framework for Complex Organisational Change Programs', *International Journal of Project Management, 31*(8): 1118–1128.

POPS (2015) Trustees' Report and Financial Statements for the Year Ended 31 March 2015.

Pratt, J. and Eriksson, A. (2013) *Contrasts in Punishment: An explanation of Anglophone excess and Nordic exceptionalism.* London: Routledge.

Prison Reform Trust (2011a) *Reforming Women's Justice: Final report of the Women's Justice Taskforce.* Available at: www.prisonreformtrust.org.uk/Portals/0/Documents/Women's%20Justice%20Taskforce%20Report.pdf. Accessed: 22 February 2016.

Prison Reform Trust (2015) Financial Statements 31 March 2015.

Reiner, R. (2012) 'Casino Capital's Crimes: Political economy, crime, and criminal justice', in Maguire, M., Morgan, R. and Reiner, R., (eds) *The Oxford Handbook of Criminology.* Oxford: Oxford University Press.

Remedi (2015) *Report of the Trustees and Financial Statements for the Year Ended 31 March 2015.*

Ryan, M. (2011) 'Counterblast: Understanding penal change: Towards the Big Society?', *The Howard Journal of Criminal Justice, 50*(5): 516–520.

Sage, D., Dainty, A. and Brookes, N. (2011) 'How Actor-Network Theories Can Help in Understanding Project Complexities', *International Journal of Managing Projects in Business, 4*(2): 274–293.

Salamon, L. M. (2015) 'Introduction: The nonprofitization of the welfare state', *Voluntas: International Journal of Voluntary and Nonprofit Organizations, 26*(6): 2147–2154.

Salamon, L. M. and Anheier, H. K. (1992) 'In Search of the Non-profit Sector. I: The question of definitions', *Voluntas: International Journal of Voluntary and Nonprofit Organizations, 3*(2): 125–151.

Salamon, L. M. and Sokolowski, S. W. (2004) 'Measuring Civil Society: The Johns Hopkins global civil society index', *Global Civil Society: Dimensions of the nonprofit sector, 2:* 61–92.

Serco (2010) 'Serco Signs Contract for Belmarsh West Prison Valued at £415m'. Available at: www.serco.com/media/pressreleases/2010/belmarsh.asp. Accessed: 7 June 2012.

Serco (2012) 'Serco Forms Pioneering Probation Alliance with Voluntary Sector'. Available at: www.serco.com/markets/homeaffairs/Copy_of_lowgrangerep.asp. Accessed: 4 January 2013.

Silvestri, A. (2009) *Partners or Prisoners? Voluntary sector independence in the world of commissioning and contestability.* London: Centre for Crime and Justice Studies.

Smith, D., Paylor, I. and Mitchell, P. (1993) 'Partnerships Between the Independent Sector and the Probation Service', *The Howard Journal of Criminal Justice, 32*(1): 25–39.

Social Finance (2011) *Peterborough Social Impact Bond.* Available at: www.socialfinance.org.uk/sites/default/files/SF_Peterborough_SIB.pdf. Accessed: 3 January 2012.

Steins, N. A. (2001) 'New Directions in Natural Resource Management: The offer of actor-network theory', *IDS Bulletin, 32*(4): 18–25.

Tett, L., Anderson, K., McNeill, F., Overy, K. and Sparks, R. (2012) 'Learning, Rehabilitation and the Arts in Prisons: A Scottish case study', *Studies in the Education of Adults, 44*(2): 171–185.

Tomczak, P. (2014) 'The Penal Voluntary Sector in England and Wales: Beyond neo-liberalism?' *Criminology and Criminal Justice, 14*(4): 470–486.

Tomczak, P. (forthcoming) 'The Voluntary Sector and the Mandatory Statutory Supervision Requirement: Expanding the carceral net', *British Journal of Criminology.*

Tomczak, P. and Albertson, K. (2016) 'Prisoner Relationships with Voluntary Sector Practitioners', *The Howard Journal of Criminal Justice*, 55(1–2): 57–72.

Travis, A. (2012) 'Serco wins First Private Probation Contract'. *Guardian*, 13 July 2012. Available at: www.theguardian.com/society/2012/jul/13/serco-first-private-probation-contract. Accessed: 13 September 2013.

Whitehead, P. (2015) *Reconceptualising the Moral Economy of Criminal Justice: A new perspective*. London: Palgrave.

Wolch, J. R. (1990) *The Shadow State: Government and voluntary sector in transition*. New York: Foundation Center.

Zedner, L. (2004) *Criminal Justice*. Oxford: Oxford University Press.

Zubrycki, R. M. (2003) 'Community-Based Alternatives to Incarceration in Canada', in *United Nations Asia and Far East Institute for the Prevention of Crime and Treatment of Offenders Japan*. Annual Report for 2002 and Resource Material Series No. 61, New York: United Nations Publications. Available at: www.unafei.or.jp/english/pdf/RS_No61/No61_12VE_Zubrycki.pdf. Accessed: 26 January 2016.

2 Punishment and charity
Historical and contemporary context

2.1 Introduction

> In Faith and Hope the world will disagree,
> But all mankind's concern is charity.
>> (Pope, 1969[1]: Epistle IV, line 307)

In contrast to the importance suggested by Pope, surprisingly little scholarship has been concerned with the relationships between punishment and charity (Corcoran, 2011; Mills *et al.*, 2011; Armstrong, 2002). However, charities have a long history of involvement in criminal justice (Cox, 2013; Mills *et al.*, 2012; Smith *et al.*, 1993; McWilliams, 1983; Ignatieff, 1978; Foucault, 1977), are thought to play a significant role in the operation of contemporary criminal justice (Martin, 2013; Mills *et al.*, 2012; Neilson, 2009; Neuberger, 2009; Armstrong, 2002) and have recently been prominent in both penal policy rhetoric and academic literature in England and Wales (as detailed in Chapter 1). Drawing on historical and contemporary literature, this chapter outlines what is known about charitable work in punishment and points out key gaps in understanding. It draws on multiple bodies of scholarship and attempts to integrate the lessons they provide.

The first section harnesses the explanatory value of historical perspective (Zedner, 2006) and considers past relationships between punishment and charity. This literature sheds light on the role of voluntary action/philanthropy in the establishment of the prison and probation services and illustrates subsequent *increases in the scale of punishment and social control* (McWilliams, 1986; Ignatieff, 1978; Foucault, 1977). A key lesson from the historical literature is that the 'benevolent' work of voluntary organisations extends social control, increases the scale of penality, and shores up coercive carceral regimes (e.g. McWilliams, 1983; Ignatieff, 1978; Foucault, 1977). However, these 'control' accounts are also problematised in this section.

Analysis of recent literature follows. This literature has emphasised the significance of neoliberal policy reforms, providing a *marketised understanding* of the sector (e.g. Meek *et al.*, 2013; Maguire, 2012; Mills *et al.*, 2012; Corcoran, 2011; Meek *et al.*, 2010; Benson and Hedge, 2009; Neilson, 2009; Silvestri,

2009). Scholars have used marketised policy reforms as the framework for analysis of the penal voluntary sector. For example, Mills *et al.* (2011: 193) discuss the relationship that is developing between the voluntary sector and the state through commissioning, and Corcoran (2011: 33) stresses that political reforms 'are poised to contribute to the exponential growth of a penal voluntary sector' (see also Maguire, 2012: 484; Mills *et al.*, 2012: 393; Corcoran, 2012: 17; Morgan, 2012: 478; Benson and Hedge, 2009: 34; Neilson, 2009: 401). This centrality of marketisation is problematic because participating in the market for penal services is not possible for the vast majority of charities (Maguire, 2012: 488, 491; Corcoran, 2011: 40; Mills *et al.*, 2011: 195; Silvestri, 2009: 4). We are therefore lacking knowledge about what this vast majority of charities is actually doing amid the expanding market for penal services. Despite significant recent commentary about the impact and import of market reforms for the sector, the *forms of existing relationships* between charities and statutory criminal justice agencies are insufficiently understood (Tomczak, 2014).

Furthermore, because the effects and distinctiveness of charitable work have not been fully established, it is not clear *why*, or indeed *if*, market reforms matter. Although the value and contribution of voluntary organisations has been widely acknowledged (e.g. Corcoran and Hucklesby, 2013; Maguire, 2012; Mills *et al.*, 2012; Benson and Hedge, 2009), the *effects* of charitable work in punishment are not well theorised (Tomczak, forthcoming). Different bodies of literature illustrate a tension. For some, voluntary organisations empower prisoners and probationers, enabling them to build social and human capital and encouraging personal transformation (e.g. Mills, 2015; Bilby *et al.*, 2013; Cohen, 2009; Lewis *et al.*, 2007; Maruna, 2007; Lippke, 2003). The final section explores these positive contributions that charitable work can make to prisoners and probationers and notes that, for others, charitable work has negative, controlling, exclusionary and disabling effects (e.g. Cohen, 1985). Charities' contributions to building social capital and extending social control are not necessarily dichotomous, but it is problematic that we do not better understand the effects of charitable work and whether they are distinctive from the work of statutory and private agencies (Armstrong, 2002).

2.2 Punishment and charity: historical relationships

2.2.1 Introduction

This section explores the longstanding relationships between punishment and charity, and the role of philanthropy in producing the institutions of punishment.[2] Exploring this literature is particularly important because 'changes in contemporary penality cannot be viewed in isolation from past strategies of governing' (Hannah-Moffatt, 2000: 510), but voluntary sector 'debates have tended to lose sight of a long tradition of joint work' between statutory criminal justice agencies and charities (Smith *et al.*, 1993: 25). This section presents some key developments in and ideas about past relationships between punishment and charity, but is not intended to form a complete history thereof. Such an account is beyond the scope of this text.

Charitable action was closely linked to the establishment of both the modern prison and probation services (Mills *et al.*, 2012; Neilson, 2009; McWilliams, 1983; Ignatieff, 1978; Foucault, 1977). Although the reforms which introduced both services were (arguably) driven by benevolent and humanitarian motives, both led to expansions in social control (Moore, 2009; Ignatieff, 1978; Jarvis, 1972). Eighteenth-century philanthropists and penal reformers lobbied for the pentientiary to replace corporal punishment, as a means of incorporating criminals into civil society rather than physically harming or killing them (Garland, 1990; Ignatieff, 1978: 213; Garland, 1985). Community supervision was later undertaken with the intention of saving 'offenders from harsh punishments' in the new penitentiaries (McWilliams, 1987: 114–115). However, both sets of reforms stimulated significant increases in control. Establishing the penitentiary led to dramatic increases in the numbers imprisoned in England (Moore, 2009: 13; Ignatieff, 1978: 108). Petty criminals who would have been privately chastised were instead disciplined through the rules and regulations of the penitentiary, to prevent them proceeding 'unimpeded to the commission of more dangerous offences' (Ignatieff, 1978: 28). Establishing probation also increased the scale of punishment. The early phases of probation were built on the powers of the 1879 Summary Jurisdiction Act, which gave magistrates the power to 'discharge the offender on his own recognizance' (Jarvis, 1972: 10) but initially only for cases 'where the offences were thought *so trifling as to make punishment unnecessary*', thus targeting those that would not previously have been punished (Jarvis, 1972: 10, emphasis added).

Both sets of reforms inserted the power to punish more deeply into the social body (Garland, 1990: 136; Ignatieff, 1978: 214; Foucault, 1977: 82). The rules and regulations of the pentientiary were apparently non-punitive, but they were obligatory and non-compliance was punished. Around sixty years later, probation came to disempower and subjugate (ex-)offenders, as probation officers became diagnosticians with the ability to impose meaning upon their charges (McWilliams, 1986: 241–242). Where (ex-)offenders did not conform with the recommendations of their supervisors, there was the option of enforcement (McWilliams, 1986: 256). These developments are fully explained in this section, which illustrates and attempts to problematise theories demonstrating how the role of charitable action in apparently 'benevolent' and humane penal reforms has increased the scale of punishment and the extent of social control, drawing previously included populations into the orbit of social control and widening the net of carceral power (Cohen, 1985: 268).

This section includes material drawn from histories of *ideas* about punishment (e.g. Ignatieff, 1978; Foucault, 1977) and attempts to problematise these ideas using material drawn from *empirically based* histories of punishment (see De Georgi, 2006; Howe, 1994). As an aside, the histories to which I refer in this section are based in England, France and North America. While this geographical basis is appropriate for my conceptualisation of the penal voluntary sector in

England and Wales, it is problematic that Western institutional forms are generally privileged in accounts of penal history, and that these situated accounts have universalising tendencies (Howe, 1994). The nuances of penal histories in different jurisdictions and for different social groups should therefore be considered by those seeking to use this work as a case study of the voluntary sector that is relevant for understanding practices elsewhere.

2.2.2 The role of philanthropy in establishing the modern prison

Key changes in the economy of punishment took place in the mid- to late-eighteenth century, when the object of punishment shifted from the offender's body to their mind (Garland, 1990: 158; Ignatieff, 1978: 11; Foucault, 1977: 80).[3] Earlier penal measures were generally directed at the offender's body e.g. hanging, whipping, branding and the stocks (Ignatieff, 1978: xiii; Foucault, 1977: 49). Later penitentiary regimes targeted the offender's soul, aiming to reform the criminal individual through disciplinary measures such as prison rules and timetables (Foucault, 1977: 3, 6, 125). Through the spread of these apparently non-punitive measures, the population came to be regulated thoroughly and at all times (Garland, 1990: 136; Foucault, 1977: 80, 89). Prisons were a key mode through which this regulation was spread, but other institutions such as schools and Magdalen Hospitals performed similar functions (Nash, 1984; Foucault, 1977). As part of a heterogeneous group of penal reformers (including politicians, industrialists, scientists and doctors), philanthropists[4] played an 'instrumental' role in the establishment of the penitentiary and the 'humanisation' of the penal system through the transition from corporal to carceral punishment (Ignatieff, 1978: 63). As such, philanthropists in this reform movement were central to the development, growth and legitimacy of the modern prison (Moore, 2009: 13; Foucault, 1977: 23).

The penal reformers largely succeeded in convincing the public that displays of corporal punishment were 'degrading and brutal spectacles' (Ignatieff, 1978: 24) and criticised the lack of discipline in existing self-governing prisons (Ignatieff, 1978: 38, 39, 42). The reformers vigorously promoted the *transformative potential of disciplinary prison regimes* as a humane and orderly alternative (Garland, 1990: 142, 168; Foucault, 1977: 23). For example, the philanthropist John Howard published *The State of the Prisons* in 1777 (Ignatieff, 1978). In place of the gothic mode of correction through terror, Howard proposed the amendment of the criminal mind through a programme of penitentiary discipline. Through this regular and steady discipline, e.g. fixed hours of rising, bible study, praying and meals, the lost souls within could be transformed into 'useful members of society' (Ignatieff, 1978: 56, see also 53, 74).

Before the advent of the penitentiary, the role of imprisonment in the economy of punishment was restrained. Court data from London suggests that prison was generally used to punish minor offenders with short sentences which usually lasted less than a year (Ignatieff, 1978: 15; see also Green, 2014; Tarlow, 2007). Before the advent of the penitentiary, petty offenders were unlikely to have been prosecuted and would at most have been whipped or reprimanded (Ignatieff, 1978: 208). But the establishment of the penitentiary saw the capacity of civil society diminish. Ignatieff suggests that employers increasingly brought 'disobedient servants to the bench instead of chastising them privately' (1978: 108), as the reformers successfully argued that failing to repress minor offences enabled petty criminals to commit more dangerous offences (Ignatieff, 1978: 28). Through this desire to formally discipline petty criminals, the reformers were the 'driving forces' behind *dramatic increases in incarceration* in England (Moore, 2009: 13). Petty offenders who would have rarely been prosecuted in the eighteenth century therefore faced imprisonment in the nineteenth, and under very different conditions.

Treatment in the penitentiaries was dependent to some extent on prisoners' willingness to comply with 'a disciplinary regimen of surveillance, hard labour, and submission to rules' (Ignatieff, 1978: 69, see also 214). Those that refused to comply faced the pain of the straitjacket, the handcrank and the treadwheel as a 'deterring form of hard labour' (Ignatieff, 1978: 177, see also 208). As such, the conditions within the new prisons demonstrate a shift in the locus of social control (Ignatieff, 1978: 108). Through the introduction of carceral discipline, the boundary limiting the power of society's powerful over the poor was redrawn and the power to punish was inserted more deeply into the social body (Garland, 1990: 136; Ignatieff, 1978: xiii; Foucault, 1977: 82).

The shift from corporal punishment to carceral discipline saw an associated fragmentation and expansion of the legal power to punish, with experts such as psychiatrists, psychologists, educationalists and social workers introduced to the judicial process over time. These experts were concerned with the correction and reform of individual offenders (Garland, 1990: 136; Foucault, 1977: 10, 11). As such, a 'whole army of technicians took over from the executioner' (Foucault, 1977: 11) and the power of judgment was dispersed among multiple authorities (Foucault, 1977: 22). The existence of these 'minor civil servants of moral ortho-paedics' is held to mean that the modern criminal justice system is 'constantly growing' (Foucault, 1977: 10). New institutional regimes within the penitentiary, such as expert examinations and assessments, produced knowledge about the criminal individual (Garland, 1990: 455). By subjecting the criminal to intense study and control, the prison enabled the production, identification and attempted normalisation of delinquents. The prison's function as an apparatus of know-ledge therefore allows it to fabricate the delinquents that it purports to transform (Garland, 1990: 148–149; Ignatieff, 1978: 77, 164; Foucault, 1977: 126).

A body of scholarship thus argues that, by creating and sustaining delin-quency, the prison achieves important social effects (Garland, 1990: 150; Foucault, 1977: part 4). It enables the authorities to keep habitual criminals under surveillance and separates crime from politics by providing an apparently 'natural' link between crime and punishment (Foucault, 1977: 232). Rather than controlling criminals, the prison keeps the poor under control by equating the poor with the criminal (Garland, 1990: 150; Ignatieff, 1978: 164–165; Foucault, 1977: 272). This utility means that critiques of the institution tend to be followed by the reassertion of good penitentiary practice rather than the abolition of the prison and diverts attention from the socio-economic causes of 'criminality' (Garland, 1990: 149; Ignatieff, 1978: 165). Although these accounts are important and raise awareness about increasing social control, they have also been subject to a variety of criticisms and revisions (e.g. De Georgi, 2006; Howe, 1994). While a full account of these is beyond the scope of this work, I now problematise the effects of charitable work.

Some significant benefits did result from the establishment of the penitentiary. Brutal displays of state violence abated (Ignatieff, 1978: xiii; Foucault, 1977: 80) and criminals were recognised as human beings with the right to protection from brutality, extortion and disease (Ignatieff, 1978: 214). The reformers were instrumental in improving prison sanitation and health, ensuring the proper feeding and clothing of prisoners by the state (as opposed to charitable benefactors or prisoners' families, as in the earlier jails) and attempting to end their exploitation by warders and other inmates (Garland, 1990: 159). These qualitative changes to the experience of imprisonment should not be overlooked.

Furthermore, the intentions and purposes of philanthropy pose a 'very perplexing historical problem' (Nash, 1984: 624). The apparent benevolence of the penal reformers has been characterised as a *ruse* which obfuscates how reform embedded 'the power to punish more deeply into the social body' and extended control (Foucault, 1977: 23, see also 82). Similarly, Ignatieff argues that Howard disguised his disciplinary and reformative ideals as apolitical philanthropy by positioning his campaign in opposition to an abstract 'evil' rather than particular groups of men, thus obscuring how the reforms legitimised the intensification of carceral power (1978: 58, 212). However, other accounts note that the reformers' motivations included 'authentic benevolence or religious conviction' (Garland, 1990: 159; see also Nash, 1984; Spierenburg, 1984; Rothman, 1980).

Rogers explains how the Foucauldian premise that state and voluntary institutions sought solely to reconstruct their subjects as 'docile bodies' 'has tended to obscure the intimate and affective relationships that sometimes bound reformers and those they hoped to serve' (2014: 2). Rogers provides a case study of the philanthropic exchanges between Sarah Martin, a prison visitor at Great Yarmouth Borough Gaol from 1818 to 1843 and points out that her 'close, personal involvement with inmates' cannot be reduced to normalisation and control (2014: 5). Although some prisoners considered Martin's intervention to be coercive, there is also 'ample evidence that many viewed her as an independent, powerful advocate who might arbitrate between themselves and authority, whether the jailer, magistrates or employers' and she received numerous 'declarations of gratitude' and gifts from grateful former inmates (Rogers, 2014: 6). Considerable numbers went out of their way to inform Martin of their circumstances post-release or to give her a small token gift in return for her care, which can be interpreted as 'a confirmation of the profound impact she made on many individuals, both in terms of their self-respect and the welfare of their families' (Rogers, 2014: 17). Rogers therefore illustrates that interactions between the nineteenth-century prison visitor and former offenders are *not 'entirely reducible to power'* (2014: 9, emphases added). As such, and without denying the dramatic increases in incarceration and social control that followed the introduction of the penitentiary, it is reductionist to overlook the improved conditions therein, to neglect potential valuable contributions of charities, and to infer the tactical motivations of the reformers. This indicates that the control literatures are valuable, but incomplete. The next section illustrates how expansions of control also followed the establishment of probation.

2.2.3 The role of philanthropy in establishing probation

It has been contended that although sentencing alternatives such as probation were intended to reduce the use of imprisonment, in practice they have not had this effect: prison populations have been maintained and increased, while so-called 'alternatives' have proliferated. The conventional wisdom of the critical literature on community corrections is that the development of alternatives has been synonymous with a widening 'net' of penal control.

(McMahon, 1990: 121–122)

The penitentiary quickly became a failed project, principally because the aforementioned dramatic increases in imprisonment resulted in institutional overcrowding (Moore, 2009: 13; Ignatieff, 1978: 108). In the mid-nineteenth century, against the backdrop of the failed penitentiary, alcohol abuse became a new troubling social problem and there was 'a dramatic rise in concern about drunkenness' (Newburn, 2003: 125). The philanthropists developed an alternative mode of discipline to tackle this new problem, thus saving 'offenders from harsh punishments' in the pentientiaries by placing missionaries to supervise them in the community (McWilliams, 1987: 114–115). This work ultimately led to the development of probation, increases in the scale of punishment and further diffusion of control. Non-custodial disposals can certainly be considered 'more humane' than custodial sentences (McWilliams, 1987: 115), but providing this option to the courts increased the numbers being punished, extended control outside the walls of the penitentiary and ultimately subjugated probationers.

Between 1860 and 1876, offences of drunkenness and 'drunk and disorderly' behaviour increased dramatically (McWilliams, 1983: 133). As a response to this social problem, a new system of offender supervision took root in 1876, when the Church of England Total Abstinence Society extended their aim of reforming the intemperate to work with the courts and appointed their first police court missionary (McWilliams, 1983; see also Carey and Walker, 2002: 50). The early missionaries worked to achieve the 'restoration and reclamation of individual drunkards appearing before the summary courts' (McWilliams, 1983: 134) by making requests to the magistrates that defendants should be bound over into the Society's care rather than imprisoned (Newburn, 2003: 126). The number of missionaries quickly expanded and they played a 'central role' in establishing the Probation Service, as the missionaries' court pleas became linked to the idea of supervision (Newburn, 2003: 127; see also McWilliams, 1986: 242; McWilliams, 1983: 258).

The 1879 Summary Jurisdiction Act gave magistrates the power to discharge offenders with reassurance that 'an eye was being kept on those accused allowed their liberty' (McWilliams, 1983: 136). But crucially, these discharges occurred only 'where the offences were thought so trifling as to make punishment unnecessary' (Jarvis, 1972: 10). Formal supervision was facilitated by the provisions of the 1907 Probation of Offenders Act, which demanded regular visits to and reports on the (ex-)offender, thus extending control and giving supervising officers a far stronger hold over their charges (McWilliams, 1985: 258–259). Although the 1907 Act also drew on American experiences of (ex-)offender supervision, the work of the missionaries supplied a model for work with offenders *outside* the English prison and established the means through which a welfare organisation could work with the courts (Newburn, 2003: 127). The proliferation of drunkenness in Victorian England was the product of the socio-economic structure of that time, rather than individual 'psychological aberrations' (Harrison, 1971: 355). But the religious temperance movement as a whole utilised individualist solutions to the problem of drunkenness (McWilliams, 1983: 134), again diverting attention from the socio-economic roots of 'criminality' (Ignatieff, 1978: 165).

It has been argued that probation came to disempower (ex-)offenders from around the 1930s, by imposing meaning upon their circumstances and dictating their route to 'reform'. Probation officers came to define the meaning of facts about their clients (e.g. personal facts and their social circumstances) and then recommend what should be done in light of that meaning (McWilliams, 1986: 242). This approach could involve subjugating client's own requests and preferences (McWilliams, 1986: 241–242). The diagnostic process was justified by its potential to increase the effectiveness of sentencing, yet the use of diagnostic social inquiry reports before sentencing did not lead to any significant reduction in crime (Davies, 1974: 256). Nevertheless, the probationer became 'a co-operative recipient of expert treatment' rather than a prime agent in their own process of rehabilitation (McWilliams, 1986: 256). Where (ex-)offenders did not conform with the recommendations of their supervisors, there was the option of enforcement in prison (McWilliams, 1986: 256). These historical literatures indicate that contemporary charitable work could increase the scale of the penal system, increase levels of social control and further fragment the legal power to punish. Work that considers more recent social policy reforms is examined next and raises similar concerns about expanding social control.

2.2.4 Net-widening in the 1960s

Cohen (1985) writes about social policy reforms in 1960s Britain, North America and Western Europe. Cohen argues that these policy changes emphasised decriminalisation, decarceration, diversion, community alternatives and a minimal state but *supplemented* rather than replaced incarceration and elements of the formal control repertoire (1985: 254). Despite the positive rhetoric of inclusionary policies, the old institutions remained, intervention was intensified, and control was extended because community control expanded (1985: 15). The dispersal of social control that follows decentralisation of power can therefore draw previously 'included' populations into the orbit of social control, thus widening the net of carceral power (Cohen, 1985: 268). For critics of community alternatives to punishment, such programmes do not soften or replace coercive approaches but are rather 'an insidious means of netting more people into the formal criminal justice realm for more reasons, by connecting less formal institutions of control with more formal ones' (Armstrong, 2002: 354).

Although extensive, influential and important, the vagaries of the control and net-widening literatures have been highlighted. McMahon (1990) points out that the concept of net-widening is valid but serves to direct attention away from any moderation of penal control which might have taken place, and from the superseding of some previous forms of penal control by preferable ones. Scholars have pointed out that there was a striking rate of deinstitutionalisation in England and Wales between 1880 and 1940, which the development of probation is held to have influenced (McMahon, 1990; Downes, 1988; Rutherford, 1984). Furthermore, there are cases where community orders have been used in lieu of imprisonment, rather than as a supplement to it, although this diversion tends to be overlooked in lieu of emphasising that around half of such sentences are used where the offender would probably not have been imprisoned anyway (McMahon, 1990). Although the reach of the carceral net was expanded via probation, its intensity has perhaps been diminished in some cases and its quality changed, and the concept of net-widening cannot acknowledge this. It therefore appears that more nuanced hybrid theorisation is required to conceptualise the effects of charitable work more fully. More recent literature which considers market reforms affecting the voluntary sector is now examined.

2.3 Punishment and charity: contemporary commentary

2.3.1 The risks of marketisation for the voluntary sector

Recent scholarship has stressed the significance of marketisation for the voluntary sector (e.g. Hucklesby and Corcoran, 2016; Mills, 2015; Meek *et al.*, 2013, 2010; Mythen *et al.*, 2013; Corcoran, 2012, 2011; Maguire, 2012; Mills *et al.*, 2012; Morgan, 2012; Gojkovic *et al.*, 2011; Senior, 2011; Benson and Hedge, 2009; Silvestri, 2009). A key focus of this literature has been the increasing role for voluntary organisations in the delivery of criminal justice services under contract (Maguire, 2012: 483). This increasing role is linked to the neoliberal policy developments described in Chapter 1. The key features of this scholarship and its limitations are now explored.

Increasing the role of charities in the delivery of penal services 'undoubtedly has its attractive aspects' (Maguire, 2012: 484), which are stressed in the policy rhetoric. For example, the *Breaking the Cycle* Green Paper emphasises that decentralising penal services 'provides a once in a generation opportunity', enabling providers from all sectors to work alongside the criminal justice system in order to make a 'real difference' (MoJ, 2010: 9). Despite this positive rhetoric, commentators have highlighted that participating in the market for penal services poses a series of risks for the voluntary sector (Maguire, 2012: 491; Corcoran, 2011: 33; Mills *et al.*, 2011: 193; Neilson, 2009: 401; Silvestri, 2009: 3; Corcoran 2008: 37), and, presumably, for the (ex-)offenders, families and victims that it serves. Marketisation is causing 'contemporary dilemmas of institutionalization' (Corcoran, 2011: 33; see also Mythen *et al.*, 2013) and raising 'troubling issues' for the voluntary sector (Neilson, 2009: 401; see also Maguire, 2012: 484).

These risks are encapsulated by the apparent clash in ideals between the voluntary and public sectors. The voluntary sector is seen to hold social welfarist ideals, focussing on the socialisation and economic integration of (ex-)offenders (Goddard, 2012: 357). Scholars have highlighted a distinctive 'voluntary sector' ethics of compassion and rehabilitative approach, which prioritises the needs of individual (ex-)offenders (Mills *et al.*, 2012: 394; Silvestri, 2009: 3,4; Corcoran, 2008: 37). By contrast, penal policy has often implied 'greater use of imprisonment, for longer periods, and more intensive supervision in the community' (Faulkner, 2007: 144; see also Maguire, 2012: 486). As such, reformative voluntary sector agendas are considered at risk of appropriation by security and punitive agendas through marketisation (Corcoran, 2012: 18).

The market in penal services puts voluntary organisations at risk of 'goal distortion' or 'mission drift' (Corcoran and Hucklesby, 2013). Goal distortion refers to charities moving away from their original mission and ethos in the pursuit of contract funding, and compromising their social-justice-orientated campaigning and advocacy work in favour of delivering services for statutory organisations (Mills *et al.*, 2011: 207; Neilson, 2009: 407; Kendall, 2003: 78; see also Goddard, 2012). It is feared that increasing numbers of charities will compromise their independence in order to win service delivery contracts, and thus become quasi-governmental organisations that are engaged with and dependent on the government (Neilson, 2009: 408; see also Maguire, 2012: 485; Corcoran, 2011: 46; Mills *et al.*, 2011: 195; Meek *et al.*, 2010: 8). As such, penal voluntary organisations appear under threat of becoming servants of government and, if punitive tendencies endure, agents of penal expansionism (Corcoran, 2012: 18; Maguire, 2012: 486; Meek *et al.*, 2010: 7; Silvestri, 2009: 4; Faulkner, 2007: 144).

The growth of penal service markets poses related risks to the campaigning roles of voluntary organisations.[5] These risks have centred around the landmark 2008 bid made by Nacro, as part of a consortium, to build and run a new prison (Corcoran, 2011; Mills *et al.*, 2011; Neilson, 2009). This bid has a prominent place in the literature, being greeted with 'disbelief, not least because bidding to run a new prison was directly contrary to Nacro's firmly established policy line' against the expanding secure estate (Neilson, 2009: 406, 404; see also Corcoran, 2011: 31; Mills *et al.*, 2011: 195). Although the Nacro bid was ultimately unsuccessful, it exemplified the inconsistency between Nacro's campaigning message and its actions as a provider of contract penal services (Neilson, 2009: 406).

Scholars have indicated that operating in this market could potentially cause the 'loss of the sector's distinctiveness and critical voice' (Mills *et al.*, 2011: 193; see also Neilson, 2009: 406), which has sounded on behalf of offenders, which are one of the most despised groups in society (Silvestri, 2009: 6). Similar marketisation dilemmas apply across the voluntary sector (Carmel and Harlock, 2008; Paxton and Pearce, 2005; Ilcan and Basok, 2004; Kendall, 2003; Evans and Shields, 2002). However, these dangers could be particularly pertinent for the penal voluntary sector, as the 'unpopular nature of work with offenders' arguably means that voluntary organisations working in criminal justice 'are more likely to be dependent on contract' funding, due to constrained fundraising sources (Mills *et al.*, 2011: 207; see also Gojkovic *et al.*, 2011: 18).

In practice, the divergent working cultures and foci of voluntary and statutory sector staff have been observed to cause problems in partnership working (Vennard and Hedderman, 2009: 237; see also Neuberger, 2009; Women in Prison, 2006). For example, the priorities of prison staff are considered likely to clash with voluntary sector workers when working together, as prison staff are 'traditionally more focussed on punishment, controlling offenders and managing risk' (Mills *et al.*, 2012: 394; see also Corcoran, 2011: 42; Mills *et al.*, 2011: 197). In addition, the Prison Service is regimental and hierarchical, but charities tend to have much looser and flatter organisational structures (Hucklesby and Worrall, 2007). In probation, voluntary sector staff may be reluctant to report the non-attendance of probationers at their programmes, as absences may be treated as a breach of parole conditions and result in recall to prison (Women in Prison, 2006: 4). Staff attitudes and working cultures can vary substantially between different statutory criminal justice agencies and between individual prisons (Mills *et al.*, 2012; Liebling, 2008; Liebling *et al.*, 2005). But when voluntary organisations are contracted to deliver penal services, it is unclear how the behaviours and discretion of charitable staff could be affected when dilemmas and working conflicts arise. As such, market policy reforms could see the goals and working practices of voluntary organisations being 'compromised by the need to fit into the goals of the criminal justice system' (Mills *et al.*, 2012: 402).

Marketisation can also be seen as an attempt to 'risk-shift' or responsibilise, representing a wider governmental commitment to displace responsibility and risks from the state to the voluntary and private sectors (Mythen *et al.*, 2013: 2; Phoenix and Kelly, 2013; Ilcan and Basok, 2004; see also Garland, 2001, 1996). Increasing involvement of the penal voluntary sector may represent further privatisation of criminal justice 'by the back door' (Maguire, 2012: 484; Morgan, 2012: 478; Silvestri, 2009: 5), as part of a broader strategy of governance through which an increasing range of non-statutory organisations are made responsible for delivering crime control, instead of the sovereign state monopoly on punishment. Neoliberal reforms could mean that charities:

> have little option but to accept a dominant economic discourse of risk where outcome measures of reconviction and value for money come to supersede

inputs and the principle of 'moral good' that has historically underpinned activities and policy making in the sector.

(Vennard and Hedderman, 2009: 240)

This is particularly concerning in light of the outcome pressures of payment by results, which are likely to see service providers cherry-pick less challenging groups of potentially 'rehabilitative offenders', 'while 'toxic offenders' will be cast aside' by contractors, leaving a difficult rump of 'more risky' offenders for the public sector to manage (Mythen *et al.*, 2013: 7). Groups that are identified and classified as 'less risky' may therefore be targeted for interventions and management by voluntary organisations, particularly during periods of economic austerity and 'scarce funding' (Mythen *et al.*, 2013: 2; see also Fox and Albertson, 2011: 410). This could ultimately see the voluntary sector 'colonized by an economic discourse of risk, where measures of reconviction and value for money come to direct operations' (Mythen *et al.*, 2013: 13–14).

While raising timely and fundamental concerns, and contributing significantly to the literature on the sector, the centrality of marketisation in this recent body of work is problematic. There is little consideration of how pervasive contract funding is likely to be in practice, of voluntary organisations' agency to resist and modify market reforms, and of the longstanding interrelationships between punishment and charity. These neglected elements are now explored.

2.3.2 Funding, heterogeneity and agency

Funding is at the heart of the argument for a marketised understanding of the penal voluntary sector. Commentators suggest that, because many charities are *heavily reliant* on state funding (Maguire, 2012: 485; Corcoran, 2011: 32; Gojkovic *et al.*, 2011: 18; Mills *et al.*, 2011: 193; Ryan, 2011: 519; Meek *et al.*, 2010: 8; Neilson, 2009: 401; Benson and Hedge, 2009: 35; Silvestri, 2009: 3; Garside, 2004: 9), the voluntary sector is vulnerable to 'being drawn into ... marketised penal reform' (Corcoran, 2011: 46). It is therefore feared that voluntary organisations could be compelled to respond to policy developments geared to increase their role in service provision (Mills *et al.*, 2011: 194). If they do not, their survival could be threatened, because 'funding will follow those organisations willing to adapt their priorities to fit those of the criminal justice system' (Mills *et al.*, 2011: 195). As such, charities apparently 'do not have the ... option' to avoid participating in the penal service market (Garside, 2004: 9; see also Mills *et al.*, 2011: 207) and are unable to resist the 'magnetic pull' of state contract funding (Corcoran, 2009: 32). If voluntary organisations like Nacro or SOVA fail to win contracts to deliver criminal justice services, the implications are 'far more serious' as their work with prisoners and probationers is 'what they are all about', whereas private companies such as G4S have diversified operations to fall back on (Garside, 2004: 9).

The growth of competitive service commissioning has occurred alongside reductions in government grant funding, which has apparently amplified the imperative to participate (Maguire, 2012: 485; Meek, *et al.*, 2010: 7). Charities are therefore either 'rolling over' in the face of pressures to compete for service delivery contracts, 'or going under' and failing to survive (Benson and Hedge, 2009: 35). But, just as 'the official conception of the voluntary sector is that of biddable service deliverers' (Corcoran, 2009: 32), scholars have tended to selectively focus on the role of voluntary organisations as *competitors in the market for penal services* (Tomczak, 2014). Following this literature, becoming proactively competitive appears to be a financial necessity for voluntary organisations (Corcoran, 2011: 43), which 'will need to establish themselves as competent and legitimate contributors and partners in the provision of criminal justice' (Corcoran and Hucklesby, 2013: no pagination). However, this apparent financial necessity for charities to compete in the market for penal services (Corcoran and Hucklesby, 2013; Maguire, 2012; Meek *et al.*, 2010; Benson and Hedge, 2009; Corcoran, 2011, 2009; Garside, 2004) has not been well substantiated. Indeed, contradictory evidence can be easily found. Across the general voluntary sector 'three-quarters of charities receive *no government funding*' (Corcoran, 2011: 41, emphasis added). Furthermore, grant-making trusts are 'one of the most significant funders – if not the most significant funder – amongst charities working in the criminal justice system' (Joseph Rank Trust, 2012: 5; see also Gojkovic *et al.*, 2011).[6] The degree to which voluntary organisations rely on state grant and contract funding is therefore questionable.

Using a dataset from the 2008 National Survey of Third Sector Organisations, Gojkovic *et al.* (2011: 17) found that public monies comprised the primary source of funding for 56 to 59 per cent of organisations that work with offenders. This dataset potentially privileges the responses of organisations in receipt of public funding, who probably have a greater interest in returning completed surveys (Gojkovic *et al.*, 2011: 17). Even using this potentially skewed sample, state funding sources are clearly not the only means through which charities sustain their operations. Nevertheless, recent commentary has emphasised the imperative for charities to participate in competitive commissioning. It is therefore unclear where the limits of marketisation lie. Because the necessity for charities to participate in the penal service market has been assumed, there is a limited understanding of which parts of the sector and which types of organisation may be excluded from, less affected by, or able to resist marketisation.

The marketisation literature also neglects diversities in scale. Recent literature dealing with the penal voluntary sector is located within the macro level policy research tradition and assumes that policy reforms drive the activities of the sector. But commentators have pointed out that the contestability process greatly favours the 'Big Players' or corporate-style charities, and excludes smaller organisations (Morgan, 2012: 478; Corcoran, 2012: 21; Benson and Hedge, 2009: 35). These 'Big Players' are: often national; generally more oriented towards corporate business models; employ staff with experience in marketing, financing and contracting; and are better able to raise capital and optimise economies of scale (Benson and Hedge, 2009: 35; Corcoran, 2008: 37). Such charities are considered by some to be private sector 'lookalikes', differing only in their lack of shareholders and legal status (Benson and Hedge, 2009: 35). Although the 'Big Players' are most likely by far to participate in the penal service market, they compose a minority of penal voluntary organisations and are generally 'felt not to be typical of the sector' (Silvestri, 2009: 4; see also Corcoran, 2011: 41; Corcoran, 2008: 37). Those more characteristic smaller voluntary organisations which form the vast majority of the sector (Corcoran, 2011: 40) have been peripheral in recent commentary, although Mills *et al.* (2012: 401) argue that smaller, possibly volunteer-led charities are 'more likely to bring the so-called "added value" to their work with offenders, particularly the building of social cohesion through their connections to the local community'. As such, perhaps scholars have *neglected to analyse the most worthful organisations* in the sector.

Sixty per cent of charities have an annual income that is below £10,000 (Corcoran, 2011: 41), but in recent scholarship these smaller charities are notable only as a result of concerns about their 'future viability', due to their inability to participate in penal service markets (Mills *et al.*, 2011: 195). Small charities have effectively been eliminated from the commissioning process, because few have the capacity or infrastructure to win nationally or regionally commissioned projects involving large numbers of (ex-)offenders (NPC, 2015; Maguire, 2012; Silvestri, 2009; Corcoran, 2008). Although bigger 'lots' are more efficient for government, they exclude local organisations. Smaller charities are thus ostensibly 'being crowded out by a "Tesco-effect" in commissioning cycles, whereby the economies of scale and national programmes provided by large players prove attractive to cautious statutory purchasers' (Corcoran, 2011: 41; see also Tomczak, 2014).

As a result, smaller charities are thought to be joining consortia in order to bid for contracts, forming 'bid candy' that provides evidence of the lead commercial organisation's commitment to certain values (Corcoran, 2012: 21; Morgan, 2012: 485; Benson and Hedge, 2009: 35). This is creating the 'risk that much of the voluntary sector will be swallowed up by the big commercial players, Serco, Capita and so forth' (Morgan, 2012: 478). As such, smaller charities could lose much of their distinctive client-centred ethos, and see their critical and campaigning voices muted through the need to support their public and private sector business partners (Morgan, 2012: 485).

While raising valid concerns, this commentary overstates the reach of market reforms without empirical evidence. Commentators have not yet considered whether those excluded from the penal service market may in fact have options other than 'going under' or joining consortia to bid for contracts (Benson and Hedge, 2009: 35). It is undeniably important to examine the macro level processes and effects of marketisation. These are significant and topical developments. However, it is also important to consider the representativeness of this commentary across the penal voluntary sector, and to recognise that the micro level situation may look different. Existing commentary extrapolates the risks attached to the penal service market across the voluntary sector. But, given that the majority of smaller scale charities receive no government funding (Corcoran,

2011: 41), it is not clear why they will be compelled to participate in marketisation. This suggests that the agency of charities to remain outside the penal service market has not been sufficiently considered. It casts doubts over the 'necessity' for charities to establish themselves as competent and legitimate contributors to and partners in the penal service market (see Corcoran and Hucklesby, 2013). It also raises further questions about what types of non-contractual relationships charities have with statutory criminal justice agencies, and how these relationships are sustained financially.

Market policy reforms appear to have made a significant impact upon some voluntary organisations. However, it is significantly less clear from recent commentary why, or indeed if, market reforms matter. Recent marketisation literature rests on the implication that the penal voluntary sector makes some 'special contribution' to its service users (Maguire, 2012: 490). This contribution is considered at risk from market reforms, which threaten to erode the sector's distinctive character (Maguire, 2012: 491; Corcoran, 2011: 33; Mills *et al.*, 2011: 193; Neilson, 2009: 401; Silvestri, 2009: 3; Corcoran 2008: 37). Although the idea of voluntary action often evokes a powerful and 'richly positive imagery' of inclusion, this impact remains unproven in practice (Armstrong, 2002: 351; see also Crawford, 1999: 151) and there is little empirical evidence to support the notion of a distinctive charitable contribution. Indeed, historical and net-widening literature indicates that charitable work has negative consequences, such as increasing the scale of the penal system and levels of social control. There is clearly a disconnect between these literatures and a limited evidence base, and consequently the effects of charitable work are insufficiently understood (Armstrong, 2002). The next section considers what positive and/or distinctive contributions charities may make to prisoners and probationers, to more thoroughly assess the foundation for concerns about the impact of market policy reforms on the penal voluntary sector and move towards a fuller conceptualisation of the sector.

2.4 Positive effects of charitable work

2.4.1 Introduction

Marketisation is considered to be leading the penal voluntary sector away from traditional models of supplementary penal service provision, and leading charities to provide core penal services (Maguire, 2012: 491; Mills *et al.*, 2011: 193), making involvement with the punitive and coercive aspects of criminal justice work unavoidable (Corcoran and Hucklesby, 2013). While logical, this concern is based on the unsubstantiated notion that charities make a 'special contribution' to service users (Maguire, 2012: 490), perhaps by operating an 'alternative welfare system which has compensated for failures in market and state systems to meet the complex needs of offenders' (Corcoran, 2012: 17; see also Corcoran and Hucklesby, 2013: no pagination; Maguire, 2012: 484; Mills *et al.*, 2012: 392; Meek *et al.*, 2010: 3–4; Neuberger, 2009: 7–17; Silvestri, 2009: 3; see also Lewis *et al.*, 2007).

Although it is generally assumed that voluntary sector programmes are 'inherently less punitive and more rehabilitative' than statutory programmes, this implicit assumption has not been rigorously tested (Armstrong, 2002: 346; see also Meek *et al.*, 2013: 340; Neuberger, 2009: 7). Furthermore, assessing the effects of charitable work with prisoners and probationers is difficult due to the lack of a research tradition in this area, and the context dependency of charitable programmes and their outcomes (Corcoran and Hucklesby, 2013; Meek *et al.*, 2013). The potential positive effects of charitable work are now explored. This section refers to literature which specifically examines the voluntary sector and broader scholarship which demonstrates how charities can make a positive contribution to prisoners and probationers. Four overlapping themes are raised by this scholarship, which are: creating social and human capital (Corcoran, 2012; Brown and Ross, 2010; Lewis *et al.*, 2007), broader provision of services (Bilby *et al.*, 2013; Liebling, 2004; Lippke, 2003), relationships (Phoenix and Kelly, 2013; McNeill, 2006) and enabling desistance from crime (Robinson and McNeill, 2008; Maruna, 2007; Burnett and Maruna, 2006; Burnett and McNeill, 2005).

2.4.2 Positive contributions

The 'traditional justification' for voluntary sector involvement in criminal justice is based on the sector's 'capacity to innovate, to take risks, and to pioneer new ways of working' with (ex-)offenders (Smith *et al.*, 1993: 34; see also Corcoran and Hucklesby, 2013; Benson and Hedge, 2009; Silvestri, 2009). Charitable work can widen the range and quality of social work programmes and resources available to (ex-)offenders (Meek *et al.*, 2010: 3; Smith *et al.* 1993: 26, 29), thus creating further opportunities for this marginalised group. Charities' bases in the community can enable provision of 'through the gate' services and continuity of support for prisoners after release (Mills *et al.*, 2012: 393; Meek *et al.*, 2010: 4).

It has also been argued that charities provide their services distinctively, having a person-centred, non-authoritarian and non-judgemental working style which may mean that prisoners and probationers perceive charitable staff as more approachable and trustworthy than statutory staff (Maguire, 2012: 484; Mills *et al.*, 2012: 393–4; Meek *et al.*, 2010: 3; Light, 1993: 323). Charities may therefore be better able to engage service users (Maguire, 2012: 484; Mills *et al.*, 2012: 393–4; Light, 1993: 323). This trust and engagement between voluntary sector staff and service users has 'traditionally' been seen as 'one of the strongest features of voluntary sector involvement' in criminal justice (Maguire, 2012: 491; Neuberger, 2009: 7; see also Brookman and Holloway, 2008).

Some evidence of this is provided by Lewis *et al.*'s 2007 study, which assessed British voluntary sector resettlement and mentoring Pathfinder projects with short-term prisoners transitioning back into the community. It found that offenders that had post-release contact with voluntary sector mentors 'did significantly better than any other group of prisoners analysed' (Lewis *et al.*, 2007: 47). Prisoners were found to enrol for help with practical problems (e.g. finding accommodation), but in follow-up interviews over half of the participants indicated that the most beneficial aspect of the programme had been 'emotional support' or 'someone to talk to'. This aspect was cited almost four times as frequently as the next most common response, which was 'help with accommodation' (Lewis *et al.*, 2007: 47). Although practical support is an essential aspect of post-release assistance, this study suggested that 'ex-prisoners may benefit particularly from contact with people that have more time to pay attention to *individual needs* and whose distinctive contribution is often the provision of *personal and emotional support*' (Lewis *et al.*, 2007: 47, emphases added). The study therefore provides some explanation of the distinctive voluntary sector quality of person-centredness, although this finding cannot be extrapolated across the sector.

Charities are also considered to hold valuable reserves of social and human capital, which may benefit the (ex-)offenders that they work with (Mills, 2015: 133; Silvestri, 2009: 3). Both social and human capital are productive, and make possible the achievement of certain ends that in their absence would not be possible (Coleman, 1988: 98). Social capital comes about through changes in the *relations* among persons that facilitate action while human capital is created by changes *in persons* that bring about skills and capabilities that make them able to act in new ways (Coleman, 1988: 100). Building social capital involves creating capabilities by establishing *networks* of mutual support and improvement, which operate in what can generally be regarded as the public interest (Faulkner, 2003). For example, increasing the social capital of (ex-)offenders has been linked to desistance from crime (Mills and Codd, 2008: 10; see also Farrall and Maruna, 2004; Wolff and Draine, 2004). Literature on mentoring schemes with women released from prison indicates that such programmes can 'deliver gains in social connectedness and capital' (Brown and Ross, 2010: 31). Reflecting Lewis *et al.* (2007), Brown and Ross (2010: 41) found that relational supports were a key value of mentoring. Relational supports seemed to be particularly valuable because of the high levels of social isolation among released prisoners (Brown and Ross, 2010: 42). Mentors activated their own social capital for the benefit of their mentees in a broad variety of ways; e.g. by providing character references to support employment and housing, and accessing information about education opportunities (Brown and Ross, 2010: 42). Engaging with charitable mentoring and support programmes could therefore activate and enhance the social capital of prisoners and probationers in practical ways.

Furthermore, activating social capital through mentoring provided emotional benefits, congruent with the positive normative orientation models that underpin processes of desistance from crime (Brown and Ross, 2010: 46; see also Burnett and Maruna, 2006). In addition to the practical activation of social capital, the support provided 'evidence of trust and affirmation of their status as a person in a way that was important and meaningful to' mentees (Brown and Ross, 2010: 43). As such, this mentoring scheme also seemed to support the 'complex process of psychological change that must accompany letting go of an old life and personal identity and finding new ways of being in the world' (Brown and Ross, 2010: 48; see also Giordano *et al.*, 2002).

An illustration of constructing social and human capital, and supporting desistance from crime is provided by Corcoran's (2012: 20) brief exploration of the Samaritans' prison listener programme. Under this programme, prisoners are trained by the Samaritans to listen to fellow prisoners in confidence. The scheme aims to reduce prison suicides and self-harm, and alleviate the feelings of prisoners in distress.[7] Prisoners who volunteered as listeners through the programme reported perceived increases in their skills, confidence and self esteem (Corcoran, 2012: 20). Many made the journey from being service users in prison, onto acting as volunteer listeners, then onto being paid staff (Corcoran, 2012: 20). This process indicates that engaging with a voluntary organisation and acting as a listener may enhance prisoner social and human capital, and could support the shifts in personal identity which enable the transition from offender to resettled person, including imagining and believing in a 'replacement self' (Corcoran, 2012: 20; see also Maruna, 2011; Burnett and Maruna, 2006; Giordano *et al.*, 2002). In addition, 'engagement with families, communities, civil society, and the state itself' (McNeill *et al.*, 2012: 2) is necessary to achieve and maintain desistance from crime, so charitable work which builds social capital through supporting or creating social networks and facilitating family contact could enable desistance from crime.

Turning to the breadth of penal service provision, scholars state that charities can widen the range and quality of programmes and resources available to prisoners and probationers (Meek *et al.*, 2010: 3; Smith *et al.*, 1993: 26, 29). Broader literature explains that opportunities to depart from prison routines through charitable enrichment programmes may be valued by prisoners. 'Deadening idleness' has been deemed the hallmark of contemporary imprisonment (Lippke, 2003: 35), so enrichment programmes may provide opportunities to break this idleness and offer associated psychological benefits, such as relief from boredom, anxiety and stress (Digard *et al.*, 2007: 4; Lippke, 2003: 35). Such programmes may also build human capital, by providing avenues of self-development and increasing self-confidence for prisoners and probationers (Bilby *et al.*, 2013; Henley *et al.*, 2012; Tett *et al.*, 2012; Cohen, 2009; Lippke, 2003). Although such 'soft' achievements tend to be regarded as precursors to behavioural change rather than outputs in themselves, they are important in the process of rehabilitation and support desistance from crime (Genders and Player, 1995). After all, desistance is more than just an absence of crime and 'involves the pursuit of a positive life' (Maruna, 2007: 652) for which apparently 'soft' personal qualities are of importance.

Enrichment programmes may promote prisoner and probationer engagement (Bilby *et al.*, 2013: 6), and, in turn, their human capital. This is particularly valuable in criminal justice settings where it is likely that many individuals will have previously struggled to engage with productive activities (Bilby *et al.*, 2013: 6), with prisoners being more likely to have literacy difficulties than the general population and tending to have negative attitudes to learning (Tett *et al.*, 2012: 172). Lewis and Meek (2012) argue that using sport as a rehabilitative tool in prison settings can motivate prisoners that are difficult to engage in other resettlement, educational or psychological programmes. Sport was also found to provide an indirect means of creating capabilities by improving prisoner literacy and numeracy (Lewis and Meek, 2012). Similarly, participating in arts-based activities has been found to create greater openness to engaging with other educational courses and forms of attainment amongst prisoners (Tett *et al.*, 2012). Promoting engagement through enrichment activities may be an important benefit of charitable work.

Turning to relationships, literature regarding desistance from crime and the moral performance of prisons highlights the importance of positive relationships between staff and prisoners/probationers (Phoenix and Kelly, 2013; Robinson and McNeill, 2008; McNeill, 2006; Burnett and McNeill, 2005; Liebling, 2004). However, the same debates are largely absent from the voluntary sector literature. Given that one of the key qualities of charitable work is cited as its person-centred approach and capacity to build trust and engagement with service users (Maguire, 2012; Brookman and Holloway, 2008), this absence is both surprising and problematic.

Scholars have identified that strengths-based, person-centred and collaborative approaches are important factors for desistance-focussed offender management work (McNeill, 2006; Burnett and McNeill, 2005). A strengths-based approach which involves staff placing an 'emphasis on recognition, exploitation and development of competencies, resources, skills and assets' of (ex-)offenders (McNeill, 2006: 50) is helpful. It is also important for staff to display empathy and genuineness towards service users (McNeill, 2006; Burnett and McNeill, 2005). Whether staff members display these qualities in the eyes of service users takes on a 'very important dimension', because it forms the foundation upon which they will co-operate with services and take steps towards desisting from crime (Phoenix and Kelly, 2013: 428; see also Robinson and McNeill, 2008; Burnett and McNeill, 2005).

Liebling's work on the moral performance of prisons also emphasises the importance of relationships between staff and prisoners. Moral performance is 'those aspects of a prisoner's mainly interpersonal and material treatment that render a term of imprisonment more or less dehumanising and/or painful' (2004: 473). Liebling argues that 'prisons should perform well because it is important to treat human beings well' (2004: 473) and notes the potentially transformative impact of interpersonal transactions, providing prisoner accounts detailing how harsh and uncaring treatment in custody can 'turn you into a different person', whereas 'compassionate' treatment can make you feel better and 'completely different' (2004: 143, 145). Compassionate treatment from charitable staff could improve the experience of punishment and prisoner behaviour, and is also more likely to enable prisoners to pursue the 'positive life' required to desist from crime (Maruna, 2007: 652).

It is important to note that prison populations tend to be highly marginal and have severely limited resources of social and human capital (Brown and Ross, 2010: 48). Charitable work is certainly not a panacea or all-inclusive solution to the complex social issues that prisoners and probationers often have (Corcoran,

2012: 22). However, there is some evidence that charitable work may be valuable to prisoners and probationers. Potential valuable contributions include: building social capital; providing emotional support; providing enrichment activities; supporting engagement, education, resettlement and employment; adopting a person-centred approach; contributing to the moral performance of prisons; and contributing to desistance from crime. However, these contributions cannot be assumed to apply to all charitable work carried out across the penal voluntary sector, as they depend on individual programmes and their contexts.

More specific analysis of exactly how charities can positively affect prisoners and probationers is required, along with consideration of whether these contributions are distinct to the penal voluntary sector and/or certain charities within it. Because the distinctive contributions of the voluntary sector are not clear (Armstrong, 2002: 346), the qualities that may be lost through marketisation also remain nebulous. Over a decade ago, Armstrong highlighted that understandings of nonprofit organisations were reliant on 'the imagery of what we think they are and do' (2002: 362), recommending that scholars should stop relying on this imagery and instead 'seek out clear understandings of how they actually behave and interact with government agencies' (2002: 362). Following Armstrong, the analysis chapters will provide clear examples of charitable relationships with statutory criminal justice agencies and consider how these varying relationships might influence the effects of charitable work.

2.5 Discussion

The recent marketisation literature is valuable in many ways. Scholars have raised critical concerns that market reforms may have a detrimental impact on the sector and change its distinctive nature (e.g. Hucklesby and Corcoran, 2016; Mills, 2015; Meek *et al.*, 2013, 2010; Mythen *et al.*, 2013; Corcoran, 2012, 2011; Maguire, 2012; Mills *et al.*, 2012; Morgan, 2012; Gojkovic *et al.*, 2011; Senior, 2011; Benson and Hedge, 2009; Silvestri, 2009). This literature has put the sector on the scholarly 'radar', and made progress towards creating a fuller understanding by beginning to address the relative dearth of penal voluntary sector research (Corcoran, 2011: 33; Mills *et al.*, 2011: 195; Armstrong, 2002: 345). However, the *diversity* of organisations within this heterogeneous sector has not been fully explored and questions of *scale* and charitable *agency* have also received very little attention, perhaps because analysis has been focussed on macro level policy reforms. These oversights limit understandings of the sector.

Furthermore, the net-widening literature has not been accounted for in the marketisation debate. Considering the net-widening literature recasts the terms of this debate, so that it considers whether charitable work has any value or is merely extending the repertoire of control. It could be true that recent market reforms are fundamentally changing the terms of the relationship between some voluntary organisations and criminal justice institutions. However, the historical literature examined here indicates that charities have long been involved with the punitive and coercive aspects of criminal justice work (see Corcoran and

Hucklesby, 2013) and penal expansionism. This literature is essentially over-looked in recent scholarship on the penal voluntary sector but illustrates that the potential control effects of contemporary charitable work, and their interrelation-ships with positive effects, require far more attention.

These gaps in understanding have emerged from recent literature about the voluntary sector in England and Wales, but addressing them would in turn provide a better foundation for this literature. In an eloquent summary of recent scholarship about the voluntary sector, Maguire argues that the 'dystopian vision of a "penal market" dominated by a small number of powerful private companies and corporate-style third sector organisations, from which principled and innovative third sector providers have been largely squeezed out should give serious pause for thought' (2012: 492). This is undeniably true, but a thorough exploration of the role of voluntary organisations in criminal justice is even more urgently required. Impoverished understandings of the voluntary sector's work and its effects are problematic, because some commentators suggest that the sector plays a significant role in the operation of criminal justice (Martin, 2013; Neuberger, 2009; Armstrong, 2002). However, because the sector is insufficiently understood (Martin, 2013; Corcoran, 2011; Mills *et al.*, 2011; Armstrong, 2002) and important questions about the effects of charitable work remain unanswered, it is not clear why, or indeed if, market reforms matter.

We need to build a far more substantive body of evidence about the effects of charitable work and consider whether they are distinctive. We must examine how charitable work can expand control, and consider how it can improve the conditions, experience and outcomes of punishment. It is possible that charitable work has enabling and control effects, which may coexist or overlap, but this has not been explored. We need to assess whether controlling and enabling effects can occur simultaneously, and the conditions under which prisoners and probationers can benefit from charitable programmes. We should also examine whether prisoners and probationers find charitable programmes distinct from or more valuable than opportunities with other service providers, or whether they experience them in terms of surveillance and submission to rules (Armstrong, 2002: 346; Ignatieff, 1978: 69). Although this text begins to answer these questions and commences the process of fully conceptualising the penal voluntary sector, there is far more work to be done in this field. I hope to stimulate further scholarship.

Notes

1 The original text was published in London in 1733–1734.
2 See also Maurutto and Hannah-Moffat, 2016 for an introduction to the history of penal voluntary organisations in Canada; Mills, 2015 for an introduction to the history of penal voluntary organisations in New Zealand; and Freedman, 1984 for a thorough account of the role of women's prison reform in America from 1830 to 1930.
3 Penal change is a process and the 1750s were not an absolute starting point for the penitentiary. Reductions in displays of suffering began in Europe around 1600, when the judicial use of mutilation and maiming declined sharply (Garland, 1990: 158; see also

Spierenburg, 1984). Furthermore, the English penitentiary was preceded by two centuries of experimentation with confinement using debtors' prisons, jails and bridewells/ houses of correction (Ignatieff, 1978: 11, 29). Men had been put to work in bridewells to learn the 'habits of industry' since the Elizabethan period, but on a much smaller scale than in the penitentiaries (Ignatieff, 1978: 11).

4 Philanthropy means 'providing help for others' and is a core purpose of the contemporary voluntary sector (Alcock and Scott, 2007: 84).

5 Some further charitable lobbying will be affected by new rules on the spending of government grant funding which come into effect in May 2016. The new rules mean that grant funds from central government must not be used to lobby government and Parliament, although privately raised funds can still be used for campaigning.

6 The degree to which charities are reliant on state funding is a key variable between jurisdictions. For example, in New Zealand there is not the tradition of large-scale private philanthropy seen in England and Wales, so voluntary organisations across the board are more dependent on state funding (Mills, 2015). However, the USA appears to align with England and Wales as American charities cannot rely only on Department of Correction funding because a small number are granted most of the contracts, so charities also receive funds from 'many other governmental and private funding sources' (Kaufman, 2015: 539).

7 For further information, see www.samaritans.org/your-community/our-work-prisons. Accessed: 19 October 2015.

References

Alcock, P. and Scott, D. (2007) 'Voluntary and Community Sector Welfare', in Powell M. (ed.) *Understanding the Mixed Economy of Welfare*. Bristol: Policy Press.

Armstrong, S. (2002) 'Punishing Not-For-Profit: Implications of nonprofit privatization in juvenile punishment', *Punishment and Society*, *4(*3): 345–368.

Benson, A. and Hedge, J. (2009) 'Criminal Justice and the Voluntary Sector: A policy that does not compute', *Criminal Justice Matters*, *77*(1): 34–36.

Bilby, C., Caulfield, L. S. and Ridley, L. (2013) *Re-Imagining Futures: Exploring arts interventions and the process of desistance*. London: Arts Alliance. Available at: www. artsalliance.org.uk/sites/default/files/Re-imagining_Futures_Research_Report_Final. pdf. Accessed: 3 November 2013.

Brookman, F. and Holloway, K. (2008) *An Evaluation of the Women's Turnaround Project.* Pontypridd: University of Glamorgan.

Brown, M. and Ross, S. (2010) 'Mentoring, Social Capital and Desistance: A study of women released from prison', *Australian and New Zealand Journal of Criminology*, *43*(1): 31–50.

Burnett, R. and Maruna, S. (2006) 'The Kindness of Prisoners: Strengths-based resettlement in theory and action', *Criminology and Criminal Justice*, *6*(1): 83–106.

Burnett, R. and McNeill, F. (2005) 'The Place of the Officer–Offender Relationship in Assisting Offenders to Desist from Crime', *Probation Journal*, *52*(3): 247– 268.

Carey, M. and Walker, R. (2002) 'The Penal Voluntary Sector', in Bryans, S., Martin, C. and Walker, R. (eds) *Prisons and the Voluntary Sector: A bridge into the community.* Winchester: Waterside Press.

Carmel, E. and Harlock, J. (2008) 'Instituting the "Third Sector" as a Governable Terrain: Partnership, procurement and performance in the UK', *Policy and Politics*, *36*(2): 155–171.

Cohen, M. L. (2009) 'Choral Singing and Prison Inmates: Influences of performing in a prison choir', *Journal of Correctional Education*, *60*(1): 52–65.

Cohen, S. (1985) *Visions of Social Control: Crime, punishment and classification*. Cambridge: Polity Press.

Coleman, J. S. (1988) 'Social Capital in the Creation of Human Capital', *American Journal of Sociology, XCIV*: S95-S120.

Corcoran, M. (2008) 'What Does Government Want from the Penal Voluntary Sector?' *Criminal Justice Matters, 71*(1): 36–38.

Corcoran, M. (2009) 'Bringing the Penal Voluntary Sector to Market', *Criminal Justice Matters, 77*(1): 32–33.

Corcoran, M. (2011) 'Dilemmas of Institutionalization in the Penal Voluntary Sector', *Critical Social Policy, 31*(1): 30–52.

Corcoran, M. (2012) 'Be Careful What You Ask For: Findings from the seminar series on the Third Sector in criminal justice', *Prison Service Journal, 204:* 17–22.

Corcoran, M. and Hucklesby, A. (2013) 'Briefing Paper: The Third Sector in criminal justice'. Available at: www.law.leeds.ac.uk/assets/files/research/ccjs/130703-thirdsec-crimjust-briefing-2013.pdf. Accessed: 12 August 2013.

Cox, P. (2013). *Bad Girls in Britain, 1900–1950: Gender, justice, and welfare*. Basingstoke: Palgrave Macmillan.

Crawford, A. (1999) 'Questioning Appeals to Community within Crime Prevention and Control', *European Journal on Criminal Policy and Research, 7*(4): 509–530.

Davies, M. (1974) 'Social Inquiry for the Courts: An examination of the current position in England and Wales', *British Journal of Criminology, 14*(1), 18–33.

De Giorgi, A. (2006). *Re-thinking the Political Economy of Punishment: Perspectives on post-Fordism and penal politics*. Aldershot: Ashgate.

Digard, L., Grafin von Sponeck, A. and Liebling, A. (2007) 'All Together Now: The therapeutic potential of a prison-based music programme', *Prison Service Journal, 170*: 3–14.

Downes, D. (1988) *Contrasts in Tolerance: Post-war penal policy in the Netherlands and England and Wales*. Oxford: Clarendon Press.

Evans, B. M. and Shields, J. (2002) 'The Third Sector: Neo-liberal restructuring, governance, and the remaking of state-civil society relationships', in Dunn, C. (ed.) *The Handbook of Canadian Public Administration*. Toronto: Oxford University Press.

Farrall. S. and Maruna, S. (2004) 'Desistance-Focussed Criminal Justice Policy Research: Introduction to a special issue on desistance from crime and public policy', *The Howard Journal of Criminal Justice, 43*(4): 358—367.

Faulkner, D. (2003) 'Taking Citizenship Seriously: Social capital and criminal justice in a changing world', *Criminal Justice, 3*(3): 287–315.

Faulkner, D. (2007) 'Prospects for Progress in Penal Reform', *Criminology and Criminal Justice, 7*(2): 135–152.

Foucault, M. (1977) *Discipline and Punish: The birth of the prison*. London: Allen Lane.

Fox, C. and Albertson, K. (2011) 'Payment by Results and Social Impact Bonds in the Criminal Justice Sector: New challenges for the concept of evidence-based policy?' *Criminology and Criminal Justice, 11*(5): 395–413.

Freedman, E. B. (1984). *Their Sisters' Keepers: Women's prison reform in America, 1830–1930*. Ann Arbor, MI: University of Michigan Press.

Garland, D. (1985) *Punishment and Welfare: A history of penal strategies*. Aldershot: Gower.

Garland, D. (1990) *Punishment and Modern Society: A study in social theory*. Oxford: Clarendon Press.

Garland, D. (1996) 'The Limits of the Sovereign State: Strategies of crime control in contemporary society', *British Journal of Criminology, 36*(4): 445–471.

Garland, D. (2001) *The Culture of Control: Crime and social order in a contemporary society*. Chicago: University of Chicago Press.

Garside, R. (2004) 'Who Delivers and Why it Matters', *Safer Society*, *21*: 7–9.

Genders, E. and Player, E. (1995) *Grendon: A study of a therapeutic prison*. Oxford: Oxford University Press.

Goddard, T. (2012) 'Post-Welfarist Risk Managers? Risk, crime prevention, and the turn to non-state community-based organizations', *Theoretical Criminology*, *16*(3): 347–363.

Gojkovic, D., Mills, A. and Meek, R. (2011) 'Scoping the Involvement of Third Sector Organisations in the Seven Resettlement Pathways for Offenders'. *TSRC Working Paper 57*. Southampton: Third Sector Research Centre.

Giordano, P. C., Cernkovich, S. A and Rudolph, J. L. (2002) 'Gender, Crime, and Desistance: Toward a theory of cognitive transformation', *American Journal of Sociology*, *107*(4): 990–1064.

Green, S. (2014) *Crime, Community and Morality*. Oxford: Routledge.

Hannah-Moffat, K. (2000) 'Prisons That Empower', *British Journal of Criminology*, *40*(3): 510–531.

Harrison, B. (1971) *Drink and the Victorians: The temperance question in England 1815–72*. London: Faber and Faber.

Henley, J., Caulfield, L. S., Wilson, D. and Wilkinson, D. J. (2012) 'Good Vibrations: Positive change through social music-making', *Music Education Research*, *14*(4): 499–520.

Howe, A. (1994). *Punish and Critique: Towards a feminist analysis of penality*. London: Routledge.

Hucklesby, A. and Corcoran, M. (2016) 'Introduction', in Hucklesby, A. and Corcoran, M. (Eds) *The Voluntary Sector and Criminal Justice*. Basingstoke: Palgrave.

Hucklesby, A. and Worrall, J. (2007) 'The Voluntary Sector and Prisoners' Resettlement', in Hucklesby, A. and Hagley-Dickinson, L. (eds) *Prisoner Resettlement: Policy and practice*. Cullompton: Willan Publishing.

Ilcan, S. and Basok, T. S. (2004) 'Community Governance: Voluntary agencies, social justice and the responsibilisation of citizens', *Citizenship Studies*, *(8)*2: 129–144.

Ignatieff, M. (1978) *A Just Measure of Pain*. London: Macmillan Press.

Jarvis, F. (1972) *Advise, Assist and Befriend: A history of the Probation and After-Care Service*. London: NAPO.

Joseph Rank Trust (2012) *Collaboration or Competition? Cooperation or Contestability?* Available at: http: //theosthinktank.co.uk/research/theos-reports. Accessed: 7 June 2012.

Kaufman, N. (2015) 'Prisoner Incorporation: The work of the state and non-governmental organizations', *Theoretical Criminology*, *19*(4): 534–553.

Kendall, J. (2003) *The Voluntary Sector*. London: Routledge.

Lewis S., Maguire M., Raynor P., Vanstone M. and Vennard J. (2007) 'What works in Resettlement? Findings from seven Pathfinders for short-term prisoners in England and Wales', *Criminology and Criminal Justice*, *7*(1): 33–53.

Lewis, G. and Meek, R. (2012) 'Sport and Physical Education Across the Secure Estate: An exploration of policy and practice', *Criminal Justice Matters*, *90*(1): 32–34.

Liebling, A., with Arnold, H. (2004). *Prisons and Their Moral Performance: A study of values, quality, and prison life*. Oxford: Oxford University Press.

Liebling, A. (2008) 'Why Prison Staff Culture Matters', in Byrne J. M., Hummer, D. and Taxman, F. S. (eds) *The Culture of Prison Violence*. New York: Pearson.

Liebling, A., Tait, S., Stiles, A., Durie, L. and Harvey, J., assisted by Rose, G. (2005) *An Evaluation of the Safer Locals Programme*. Report submitted to the Home Office.

Light, R. (1993) 'Why Support Prisoners' Family-Tie Groups?' *The Howard Journal of Criminal Justice*, *32*(4): 322–329.

Lippke, R. L. (2003) 'Prisoner Access to Recreation, Entertainment and Diversion', *Punishment and Society*, *5*(1): 33–52.

Maguire, M. (2012) 'Response 1: Big Society, the voluntary sector and the marketisation of criminal justice', *Criminology and Criminal Justice*, *12*(5): 483–505.

Martin, C. (2013) *Dazzled by the Fireworks: Realising detail in the overwhelming scale of reform*. Clinks Blog Post. Available at: www.clinks.org/community/blog-posts/dazzled-fireworks-realising-detail-overwhelming-scale-reform. Accessed: 25 May 2013.

Maruna, S. (2007) 'After Prison, What? The ex-prisoners' struggle to desist from crime', in Jewkes, Y. (ed.) *Handbook on Prisons*. Cullompton: Willan Publishing.

Maruna, S. (2011) 'Reentry As a Rite of Passage', *Punishment and Society*, *13*(1): 3–28.

Maurutto, P. and Hannah-Moffat. K. (2016) 'Women's Voluntary Organisations and the Canadian Penal "Culture of Control"', in Hucklesby, A. and Corcoran, M. (eds) *The Voluntary Sector and Criminal Justice*. Basingstoke: Palgrave.

McMahon, M. (1990) '"Net-widening" Vagaries in the Use of a Concept', *British Journal of Criminology*, *30*(2): 121–149.

McNeill, F. (2006) 'A Desistance Paradigm for Offender Management', *Criminology and Criminal Justice*, *6*(1): 39–62.

McNeill, F., Farrall, S., Lightowler, C. and Maruna, S. (2012) 'How and Why People Stop Offending: Discovering desistance' *IRISS Insights 15*. Available at www.iriss.org.uk/resources/how-and-why-people-stop-offending-discovering-desistance. Accessed: 19 February 2014.

McWilliams, W. (1983) 'The Mission to the English Police Courts 1876–1936', *The Howard Journal of Criminal Justice*, *22*(3): 129–147.

McWilliams, W. (1985) 'The Mission Transformed: Professionalisation of probation between the Wars', *The Howard Journal of Criminal Justice*, *24*(4): 257–274.

McWilliams, W. (1986) 'The English Probation System and The Diagnostic Ideal', *The Howard Journal of Criminal Justice*, *25*(4): 241–260.

McWilliams, W. (1987) 'Probation, Pragmatism and Policy', *The Howard Journal of Criminal Justice*, *26*(2): 97–120.

Meek, R., Gojkovic, D. and Mills, A. (2010) 'The Role of the Third Sector in Work with Offenders: The perceptions of criminal justice and third sector stakeholders', *TSRC Working Paper 34*. Birmingham: Third Sector Research Centre.

Meek, R., Gojkovic, D. and Mills, A. (2013) 'The Involvement of Nonprofit Organizations in Prisoner Reentry in the UK: Prisoner awareness and engagement', *Journal of Offender Rehabilitation*, *52*(5): 338–357.

Mills, A. (2015) 'A Gentle Thaw or Continued Deep Freeze? Relationships between voluntary and community organisations and the state in criminal justice in New Zealand', *Third Sector Review*, *21*(1): 121–142.

Mills, A. and Codd, H. (2008) 'Prisoners' Families and Offender Management: Mobilizing social capital', *Probation Journal*, *55*(1): 9–24.

Mills, A., Meek, R. and Gojkovic, D. (2011) 'Exploring the Relationship Between the Voluntary Sector and the State in Criminal Justice', *Voluntary Sector Review*, *2*(2): 193–211.

Mills, A., Meek, R. and Gojkovic, D. (2012) 'Partners, Guests or Competitors: Relationships between criminal justice and third sector staff in prisons', *Probation Journal*, *59*(4): 391–405.

MoJ (2010) *Breaking the Cycle: Effective punishment, rehabilitation and sentencing of offenders*. London: MoJ.

Moore, J. (2009) 'Penal Reform: A history of failure', *Criminal Justice Matters*, *77*(1): 12–13.

Morgan, R. (2012) 'Crime and Justice in the "Big Society" ', *Criminology and Criminal Justice*, *12*(5): 463–481.

Mythen, G., Walklate, S. and Kemshall, H. (2013) 'Decentralizing Risk: The role of the voluntary and community sector in the management of offenders', *Criminology and Criminal Justice*, *13*(4): 363–379.

Nash, S. (1984) 'Prostitution and Charity: The Magdalen Hospital, a case study', *Journal of Social History*, *17*(4): 617–628.

Neilson, A. (2009) 'A Crisis of Identity: NACRO's bid to run a prison and what it means for the voluntary sector', *The Howard Journal of Criminal Justice*, *48*(4): 401–410.

Newburn, T. (2003) *Crime and Criminal Justice Policy*. Essex: Pearson.

Neuberger, J. (2009) *Volunteering Across the Criminal Justice System*. London: The Cabinet Office.

NPC (2015) *Transforming Rehabilitation: The voluntary sector perspective*. Available at: www.thinknpc.org/publications/transforming-rehabilitation-the-voluntary-sector-perspective/. Accessed: 23 February 2016.

Paxton, W. and Pearce, N. (2005) 'The Voluntary Sector and the State', in Paxton, W., Pearce, N., Unwin, J. and Molyneux, P. (eds) *The Voluntary Sector Delivering Public Services*. York: Joseph Rowntree Foundation.

Phoenix, J. and Kelly, L. (2013) ' "You Have to Do It for Yourself" Responsiblization in youth justice and young people's situated knowledge of youth justice practice', *British Journal of Criminology*, *53*(3): 419–437.

Pope, A. (1969) *An Essay on Man*, 4 vols. Menston: Scolar Press.

Robinson, G. and McNeill, F. (2008) 'Exploring the Dynamics of Compliance with Community Penalties', *Theoretical Criminology*, *12*(4): 431- 449.

Rogers, H. (2014) 'Kindness and Reciprocity: Liberated prisoners and Christian charity in early nineteenth-century England', *Journal of Social History*, *47*(3): 721–745.

Rothman, D. J. (1980) *Conscience and Convenience*. Boston: Little, Brown and Co.

Rutherford, A. (1984) *Prisons and the Process of Justice: The reductionist challenge*. London: Heinemann.

Ryan, M. (2011) 'Counterblast: Understanding penal change: Towards the Big Society?' *The Howard Journal of Criminal Justice*, *50*(5): 516–520.

Senior, P. (2011) 'The Voluntary and Community Sector: The paradox of becoming centre-stage in the Big Society', *British Journal of Community Justice*, *9*(1/2): 37.

Silvestri, A. (2009) *Partners or Prisoners? Voluntary sector independence in the world of commissioning and contestability*. London: Centre for Crime and Justice Studies.

Smith, D., Paylor, I. and Mitchell, P. (1993) 'Partnerships Between the Independent Sector and the Probation Service', *The Howard Journal of Criminal Justice*, *32*(1): 25–39.

Spierenburg, P. (1984) *The Spectacle of Suffering*. Cambridge: Cambridge University Press.

Tarlow, S. (2007) *The Archaeology of Improvement in Britain, 1750–1850*. Cambridge: Cambridge University Press.

Tett, L., Anderson, K., McNeill, F., Overy, K. and Sparks, R. (2012) 'Learning, Rehabilitation and the Arts in Prisons: A Scottish case study', *Studies in the Education of Adults*, *44*(2): 171–185.

Tomczak, P. (2014) 'The Penal Voluntary Sector in England and Wales: Beyond neo-liberalism?' *Criminology and Criminal Justice, 14*(4): 470–486.

Tomczak, P. (forthcoming) 'The Voluntary Sector and the Mandatory Statutory Super-vision Requirement: Expanding the carceral net', *British Journal of Criminology*.

Vennard, J. and Hedderman, C. (2009) 'Helping Offenders into Employment: How far is voluntary sector expertise valued in a contracting-out environment?' *Criminology and Criminal Justice, 9*(2): 225–245.

Women in Prison (2006) *Response to 'Reducing Re-offending through Skills and Employment'*, London: Women in Prison.

Wolff, N. and J. Draine (2004) 'Dynamics of Social Capital of Prisoners and Community Reentry: Ties that bind?', *Journal of Correctional Health Care, 10*(3): 457–490.

Zedner, L. (2006) 'Policing Before and After the Police: The historical antecedents of contemporary crime control', *British Journal of Criminology, 46*(1): 78–96.

3 Actor-network theory and its application

3.1 A theoretical predicament

Scholars of crime and punishment have long faced a dilemma between producing detailed case studies specifying empirical particulars, or relying upon generalisations which may marginalise the particular and be oversimplifications (Garland, 2001: vii). For Garland, the solution to these difficulties is continued critique at different scales. He suggests that the individual author 'must go back and forth between the general and particular', until they discover the 'level of analysis that seems to offer the optimal vantage point' (2001: vii). It is, however, unclear how this 'optimal' vantage point can be found.[1] Indeed, perhaps Garland's 'optimal' vantage point does not exist for scholars aiming to integrate analyses of complex and messy criminal justice processes which operate at various scales. As a case study, the experience of imprisonment is directly mediated by an array of factors including macro level government policies and Prison Service instructions/orders, individual prison conditions, and relationships between prisoners and staff within specific parts of the prison. Amongst these diverse actors it is unclear which or *whose* vantage point is optimal.

There are two relatively discrete and discontinuous imprisonment research traditions. The micro social body (e.g. Bosworth, 1999; Sparks *et al.*, 1996) focusses upon the internal dynamics of institutions, such as the day-to-day routines and struggles within, to demonstrate what imprisonment is like for the kept and the keepers (Carrabine, 2000: 310). The macro social tradition (e.g. Durkheim, 1983; Foucault, 1977) illustrates what prison and punishment are for, by describing their external functions and links to broader social processes, economic relations, political structures, historical formations and cultural sensibilities (Carrabine, 2000: 310). Although established, these tendencies to analyse at just one scale are problematic and provide partial accounts. Focussing on macro level strategies of domination (e.g. Foucault, 1977) denigrates interactions at the micro scale, which could be where resistance or counter-trends to domination operate, but a purely microsociological account explains little about how the powerful are able to be powerful (Herbert-Cheshire, 2003; Carrabine, 2000).

This theoretical predicament is present when attempting to theorise the penal voluntary sector. Fully conceptualising this sector requires analysing the diverse activities of a complex and messy collection of heterogeneous voluntary organisations that interact with multiple levels of the criminal justice system (e.g. individual prisons, the Prison Service, the MoJ) and produce a range of outcomes. This task is complicated further because existing scholarship regarding non-state actors in punishment tends to divide along partisan and political lines, resulting in partial accounts. It is therefore especially important to avoid pre-judging the effects of charitable work.

Conceptualising the sector could be done in more than one way, but actor-network theory (ANT) is particularly helpful for solving this theoretical predicament.[2] ANT is a theory of agency, knowledge and organisation (Steins, 2001). It rejects a basic dualism which troubles the social sciences: that between micro and macro scale actors (or, in another form, nature and society), and insists that both can be examined in the same manner (Herbert-Cheshire, 2003: 460). It is therefore useful for bridging problematic analytic divides between the general and the particular, enabling scholars to examine local and national level, or macro and micro scale activities, on the same terms and to integrate these accounts (Pollack *et al.*, 2013: 1119). If the complex array of actor-networks which create relatively stable configurations such as punishment are black boxed in scholarship (Callon and Latour, 1981: 285) and associated with a single, apparently powerful actor such as the MoJ, it obscures *how governing is performed by networks of state and non-state actors*, whose activities are co-ordinated by shared objectives and understandings (Jessop, 1995: 317). By illustrating how the power of the state is dependent upon the stability of these actor-networks, or interactions between diverse actors, the act of governing is rendered far more precarious (Herbert-Cheshire, 2003: 460). As such, this approach is *politically enabling*, transforming power and politics into 'far more open-ended process(es) of contestation and engagement' (O'Malley, 1996: 312).

As noted in Chapter 1, I do not claim to provide a programmatic or comprehensive 'ANT approach' but anticipate that the approach I have assembled and applied here, which uses a range of techniques from the ANT toolkit, will be useful for future research. Applications include research involving multiple partner organisations in the increasingly complex, hybrid and privatised landscape of penal service delivery (such as in restorative justice programmes), and studying other parts of the voluntary sector at policy and practice level. ANT and its applications for criminological research are fully explained in the remainder of this chapter. I begin with the theory and then examine how these theoretical principles were translated into methodological practices in order to conceptualise the sector.

3.2 Actor-network theory and criminological research

> For sociology the era of exploration may start again, provided we keep reminding ourselves of this motto: *don't fill in the blanks*.
>
> (Latour, 2005: 246, emphasis in original)

ANT has much to offer to sociological analysis, although it has thus far been little used by criminologists and can appear impenetrable (this is certainly not the case!). ANT[3] is a method to investigate situations by tracing connections between actors, rather than a theoretical framework which imposes interpretation on a situation (Pollack *et al.*, 2013; Latour, 2005). It provides an intellectual toolkit, or set of sensibilities, aiming to sensitise researchers to complex and multiple realities that might otherwise have remained obscure (Nimmo, 2011: 109; Law, 2004: 157). It offers a framework to investigate power and organisation, by mapping the range of heterogeneous actors[4] involved in creating these effects (Pollack *et al.*, 2013; Latour, 1999). The ANT approach is to trace connections and 'learn from the actors without imposing on them an a priori definition of their world building capabilities'[5] (Latour, 1999: 20; see also Latour, 2005). But ANT is not a 'singular whole' and exists in various forms (Alcadipani and Hassard, 2010: 429), perhaps because it is not a programmatic theory but rather a general attitude and attempt to be sensitive to the multiple circulating forces that affect both each other and ourselves (Nimmo, 2011: 109; Hitchings, 2003: 100; Latour, 1999: 20).

ANT was developed in the field of Science and Technology Studies, and principally propagated by the work of John Law, Bruno Latour and Michael Callon (Law and Hassard, 1999). It has been applied to a range of case studies within multiple social science fields, principally to explain interactions between human and non-human actors (Alcadipani and Hassard, 2010: 419). Case studies include scallops and fishermen (Callon, 1986), the Portuguese spice trade to India (Law, 1986) and seatbelts (Latour, 1992). More recently, ANT has been used in a limited number of criminological studies (Martel, 2004; Carrabine, 2000). It gives as much attention to the agency of micro actors (e.g. a prisoner, local action group or scallop), as it does to the power of macro actors (e.g. the MoJ, the state), and considers the interactions between the two (Herbert-Cheshire, 2003: 459). Although macro actors do appear more powerful than micro actors (Law, 1992: 320), ANT holds that 'the difference between them is brought about by power relations and the construction of networks that will elude analysis if we presume a priori that macro actors are bigger than or superior to micro actors' (Callon and Latour, 1981: 280).

Callon's seminal 'much cited' 1986 study of a scientific research project to improve the aquaculture of scallops in St Brieuc Bay, Brittany, France (Alcadipani and Hassard, 2010: 420) demonstrates the interplay between falling scallop stocks in the Bay, the aims of three scientists who wanted to develop knowledge about scallop habitats and farming techniques, and the wider scientific community who were interested in crustacean farming techniques.

During a process of translation, the identity of the actors, the possibilities for their interaction and the margins of manoeuvre are negotiated and delimited (Callon, 1986). In this case, the scientists were the project sponsors[6] and formed a centre of calculation, claiming that consumer demands could be satisfied by studying the behaviour of scallops and developing farming techniques. In order to achieve their aim of developing scallop farming techniques, the scientists converted themselves into spokespersons for the local fishermen (who had overfished scallops), the global scientific community (who were interested in scallop farming techniques) and the scallops themselves (whose numbers increased during the scientists' experiments). In this process of translation, the scallops were micro actors but formed the boundary objects around which the interests of the fishermen, the three scientists and the wider scientific community aligned. The scallops acted by surviving and reproducing, thus increasing stocks, or failing to reproduce and dying.

ANT provides the capacity to efface modern analytical divisions, e.g. between macro and micro actors or agency and structure, by focussing on how power relations between heterogeneous actors are constructed and maintained (Nimmo, 2011; Carrabine, 2000; Law, 1992; Callon and Latour, 1981). Following ANT, concepts such as institutions, organisations and states are rejected as vague and 'too global', (Latour, 1996: 369). ANT's ontological position is that social relations such as power, hierarchies and organisation are the precarious effects of the assembly and ordering of heterogeneous materials (Law, 1992: 390). Rather than insisting that we are 'already held by the force of some society' (Latour, 2005: 8), following ANT, all the heterogeneous elements in an organisation have some capacity to resist the ordering of the network and could be assembled anew (Law, 1992: 384). Size and power are thus treated as *effects* rather than givens, and demonstrating how structures of power and organisation are (re)produced challenges the status quo of power relations and supports politically enabling research. Although ANT is consistent with the Foucauldian tradition of investigating how power works through disciplinary strategies, it provides tools which address the absence of a coherent theory of scale and agency in traditional Foucauldian analysis (Herbert-Cheshire, 2003). Viewing power as an effect of interactions between heterogeneous actors enables macro and micro scale phenomena (e.g. penal policy and practice) to be examined on the same terms. This broadens the social scientific ontology and supports rich, integrated accounts by sensitising researchers to complex realities (Nimmo, 2011: 109; Law, 2004: 157).

ANT's clear tenets and the structured application that I present in this chapter have applications in the increasingly diverse and decentralised landscape of penal services, being particularly useful for analysis of the 'loose and baggy' penal voluntary sector. ANT underpinned my analysis of small charities and non-marketised charitable relationships with penal institutions, which feature in neither current policy discussions nor penal voluntary sector literature (Martin, 2013). ANT thus enables a step change in academic understandings of this increasingly significant sector, developing policy-centric, marketised accounts to illustrate how voluntary organisations mediate experiences of imprisonment and probation at the micro and macro levels, through (non-)marketised relationships with penal institutions. This entails understanding the sector as a 'hybrid' of diverse voluntary organisations which have varied relationships with criminal justice agencies, and thus mediate the operation and experience of punishment in multiple ways. Acknowledging that both enabling *and* controlling effects upon prisoners and probationers can result means that pathways to these outcomes can be traced, providing a more theoretically complete and politically enabling conceptualisation of the sector.

Two core techniques from ANT are applied here: the *principle of generalised symmetry* and the process of *translation*. The principle of generalised symmetry cross-cuts unhelpful analytical divides by approaching apparently disparate actors from the same analytical perspective, or *symmetrically*. This is based on the theoretical assumption that the large and powerful are no different in kind to the small and wretched (Law, 1992: 379–380). Powerful actor-networks are understood to have the same nature as weaker ones, but their scale and power results from being longer and more intensely connected (Latour, 1996: 371). The principle is most commonly applied to examine non-human actors, leading to more-than-human ontologies (e.g. including scallops) (Nimmo, 2011; Sage *et al.*, 2011; Latour, 2005), but can also be utilised to examine scale and agency (Nimmo, 2011; Carrabine, 2000). Although non-humans play an important role in the actor-network of punishment (e.g. prison buildings, courts, electronic offender databases, policy texts), the principle of generalised symmetry is most fruitfully applied in this case to examine the scale and agency of diverse voluntary and statutory organisations.

As explained in Chapter 2, recent literature has focussed on the effects of macro level policy reforms upon larger voluntary organisations that are atypical of the sector. It has not fully examined the heterogeneity of the sector's component organisations, nor the agency of voluntary organisations to influence and resist market policy reforms. I use the principle of generalised symmetry to broaden conceptualisations of the sector. Relatively small voluntary organisations are included in my account and studied on the same terms as larger ones, and I examine the agency of voluntary organisations rather than assuming the power of statutory criminal justice agencies (Carrabine, 2000: 312). This underpins an account of charitable involvement in macro level penal strategies, without assuming the subjugation of voluntary organisations by powerful statutory agencies or severely limiting understandings of how punishment and charitable work are experienced by prisoners and probationers in time and place (see Carrabine, 2000: 312).

The process of translation is used to study the construction of relationships and power (Gray *et al.*, 2009; Callon, 1986). It is a four-phase process illustrating how heterogeneous actors are integrated (or resist integration) into an actor-network with a common goal (Latour, 2005: 106–108; Callon, 1986: 196). This accessible and structured method shows how actors can impose themselves and their definitions of a situation upon other actors (Sage *et al.*, 2011; Callon, 1986). By mapping exactly how effects such as organisation and power are created (or fail), ANT 'demystifies the power of the powerful' (Law, 1992: 390). Using translation creates an understanding of interactions and organisation, while avoiding the analytical trap of starting out by 'assuming whatever we wish to explain' (Law, 1992: 380) and imposing a pre-determined structure and hierarchy of actors upon the account (Pollack *et al.*, 2013: 1119). This approach does not deny or overlook powerful actor-networks, nor reify resistances to them (Law, 1992). Rather, it emphasises that the scholarly focus should be on how power relations are constructed and maintained (Carrabine, 2000: 312). Because there are differences between the powerful and the wretched in practice, the task for scholars is to examine differences in the methods and materials that powerful and weak actors deploy to generate themselves and overcome the resistance of their component parts (Latour, 1996: 371; Law, 1992: 390). Studying translations thus moves away from analysis of organisation as 'a discrete structural entity and towards the study of processes and practices of organising' (Alcadipani and Hassard, 2010: 420).

I apply the process of translation to examine and illustrate how diverse relationships (e.g. informal, contractual, payment by results) are constructed between statutory criminal justice agencies and diverse voluntary organisations. This structured approach is particularly useful due to the heterogeneity of voluntary organisations and their varied relationships with statutory (and private) criminal justice agencies. Analysing these translations can be used to explain if and how voluntary organisations are involved in marketised, punitive, and expansionist agendas, whilst simultaneously exploring their resistances to these developments.

By following the tenets of ANT and utilising these two core tools, this account of the penal voluntary sector explores the agency of diverse voluntary organisations to resist neoliberal policy reforms and act as agents of state control. This conceptualisation does not seek to provide representative conclusions about the sector and charitable work with prisoners and probationers. Any such conclusions would be misleading, due to the variety of voluntary organisations and their diverse relationships with statutory criminal justice agencies. The aim of ANT is to develop theories as 'sensitising devices' to appreciate the complexity of the world, rather than positivist theory verification (Hitchings, 2003: 100; see also Law, 1994). As such, ANT is applied to conceptualise the sector more fully, by exploring the diversity of the sector's component organisations and relationships with statutory criminal justice agencies, and considering the complex and multiple effects of charitable work.

Without using ANT for this conceptualisation, these nuances might have remained obscure amid the macro level debate about marketising penal services (see Nimmo, 2011: 109; Law, 2004: 157). Although voluntary organisations play a role in macro level penal strategies of domination and control, at the micro level they can change the lived experience of punishment, e.g. by enhancing the social capital of prisoners and probationers, and enabling their desistance from crime. Examining these effects *alongside* macro level analyses of power and control creates a more theoretically complete and politically enabling conceptualisation of the sector, which illustrates exactly how voluntary organisations can exercise their agency amidst the penal service market and/or make a valuable contribution to prisoners and probationers. This provides a crucial counterpoint to recent literature highlighting voluntary organisations' inability to resist marketisation (e.g. Corcoran, 2012; Meek *et al.*, 2010; Neilson, 2009).

I now provide a detailed explanation of the ANT tools that I have combined to conceptualise the penal voluntary sector. First, the principle of generalised symmetry is explored and its applications for studying scale and agency in relation to the penal voluntary sector are explained. The four-phase process of translation and its applications are then detailed. Finally, the relationship between ANT and specific methodological practices is considered, to contextualise the findings presented in subsequent chapters and support future applications.

3.3 The principle of generalised symmetry

The principle of generalised symmetry is the crucial analytical move of ANT, dictating that apparently disparate actors should be examined on the same terms, or symmetrically (Nimmo, 2011: 111; Carrabine, 2000: 312; Latour, 1993: 94; Callon and Latour, 1981: 279). ANT conceptualises social relations (such as power, hierarchies, organisational arrangements, knowledge and information flows) as the precarious effect of the assembly and ordering of networks of heterogeneous materials (Law, 1992: 390). Networks are heterogeneous because they are the result of interactions between diverse human and non-human actors (such as texts, machines and architectures) at various scales (Law, 1992).

The principle is most often applied to bridge the analytical divide between human and non-human actors (Nimmo, 2011: 109; Sage *et al.*, 2011: 275; Law, 1986: 258; see also Latour, 2005), hence ANT has highlighted the importance of non-human actors in social life and illustrated that almost all human actions are mediated through objects (e.g. computers, printers), or hybrids of objects and people (e.g. the postal service) (Law, 1992: 381–382). Human actors and social relations exist in relations with multiple extra-social networks of humans and non-humans (Nimmo, 2011; Latour, 2005). Indeed, the social order depends on non-human actors, such as machines, clothes, texts and architectures, that contribute to the patterning of 'social' networks (Law, 1992: 382). For example, scientific knowledge is the product of an actor-network of heterogeneous materials: scientists, skilled hands, test tubes, reagents, journal articles, computers, microscopes and so on (Law, 1992: 381). These heterogeneous bits and pieces that 'would like to make off on their own' are instead organised into a patterned network (Law, 1992: 381). Knowledge thus has a material presence created by organising and ordering heterogeneous materials into an actor-network and overcoming the individual resistances of its component actors (Law, 1992: 381). Similarly, the organisation fits elements of the social, the technical, the conceptual and the textual together to create an ordered network of heterogeneous materials (Law, 1992: 381). The multitude of heterogeneous actors which (re)produce social order therefore ought to be recognised and made visible (Latour, 1993). ANT enables this through the idea of 'hybrids', or heterogeneous assemblages in which humans and non-humans are mixed up together (Nimmo, 2011: 109).

Although the principle of generalised symmetry is most commonly employed to cross-cut analytical divides between human and non-human actors, the idea of approaching apparently disparate bodies of actors symmetrically can also be applied to efface common analytical divisions such as between macro and micro scale actors, and between agency and structure (Pollack *et al.*, 2013: 1119; Nimmo, 2011: 111; Carrabine, 2000: 312; Law, 1992: 389). The applications for scale and agency are most important here. It is peculiar that the principle has been applied so frequently to non-human actors at the expense of applications for scale and agency, but this is perhaps why ANT is prominent in disciplines such as business studies, geography and architecture, but has so far had a limited presence in criminology where non-human actors may be less crucial in analyses. Applications for analysing scale and agency are now examined.

3.4 Analysing large and small organisations in the same way (or, scale and the principle of generalised symmetry)

In analysing structure, organisation and power, ANT suggests that 'we should start with a clean slate' (Law, 1992: 380) and seek to learn from the actors, rather than assuming a priori that certain actors have greater world building capacities (Latour, 1999: 20). Taking this approach, social theory is rebuilt on analysis of social networks, rather than social networks being an addition to social theory (Latour, 1996: 369). In order to move beyond the marketised account of the voluntary sector and build a more complete conceptualisation, two 'clean slates' will be adopted here, which pertain to scale and agency. The first 'clean slate' necessitates examining macro and micro scale voluntary organisations on the same terms (as both each other and statutory agencies), and then building a more complete conceptualisation of the sector out of this analysis. This entails setting aside the assumptions that statutory organisations drive voluntary action, and that large voluntary organisations, which tend to be heavily reliant on state funding, have the greatest world-building capacities and should therefore dominate research.

Just as ANT does not ontologically differentiate humans and non-humans and examines them on the same terms, it rejects distinctions between micro and macro scale actors. Following the principle of generalised symmetry, just as localised procedures of power are reproduced, adapted and transformed by global strategies, global strategies are modified and reshaped by local agents (Herbert-Cheshire, 2003: 459). This application has not been fully exploited by scholars of punishment, but its utility is demonstrated by Carrabine's study of the discourses influencing practices at HMP Strangeways, which fuses the discrete macro and micro social prison research traditions using ANT.[7] Carrabine insists that microsociological accounts of prison life should not be considered separately from the macrosociological roles that the institution performs in society (2000: 309). The principle of generalised symmetry provides a conceptual framework that can account for the diversity of micro levels of action, yet also examine how practices at the micro level relate to 'broader modes of regulation' (2000: 311). Carrabine's ANT-inspired approach provides a more theoretically comprehensive account of penal strategies of domination and transformation, without severely limiting understandings of how imprisonment is enacted or experienced in time and place (2000: 312). As such, his analysis can demonstrate what the prison is for (macrosociologically) and reveal what imprisonment is like (microsociologically), without privileging one level of analysis at the expense of the other (2000: 317).

Recent analysis of the penal voluntary sector has been located within the macro social research tradition and based on policy reforms. Smaller voluntary organisations are almost entirely absent from recent literature, being notable only as a result of concerns about their 'future viability' (Mills *et al.*, 2011: 195) due to their inability to participate in the market for penal services (Corcoran, 2011: 41; see also Chapter 2). This absence is perhaps because a 'vital array' of non-contractual prison and probation work does not feature in recent policy discussions (Martin, 2013: no pagination). Examples of the activities which are overlooked in policy and (perhaps consequently) in scholarship include: reading schemes; family support projects; arts work; faith based activities; prisoner listener programmes and resettlement support (Martin, 2013). Much of this work may be undertaken by the smaller voluntary organisations that we know very little about.

Working with relatively few service users, without a formal service delivery contract, or outside the boundaries of current policy discourse does not mean that small voluntary organisations are not worthy of scholarly interest (Tomczak, 2014). This approach denigrates interactions at the micro scale (see Carrabine, 2000) and means that potential positive effects of smaller organisations' work are not explored. For example, Martin argues that the vital array of voluntary organisation programmes which are not acknowledged in recent policy reforms and associated scholarship have effects that include: saving lives, promoting 'decent regimes and dynamic security' in prisons and also sometimes acting as precursors to 'a more challenging resettlement programme' (2013: no pagination). Following ANT, the penal voluntary sector can be understood as a 'hybrid' of small and larger charities, which build and are built into diverse relationships with statutory criminal justice agencies. This account considers the diversity of voluntary organisations and explores how punishment and charitable programmes are experienced in time and place, without overlooking the role of the sector in penal strategies of domination (see Carrabine, 2000). The second 'clean slate' relates to voluntary organisations' agency, which is now explored.

3.5 Analysing 'powerful' and 'weak' actors in the same way (or, agency and the principle of generalised symmetry)

> Seemingly entrenched and unchangeable power relations are dependent, to some extent at least, upon the performance of those small scale and everyday aspects of life which are frequently taken for granted.
>
> (Bosworth and Carrabine, 2001: 501–502)

Work within the sociology of imprisonment has demonstrated how prisoners, who are 'subjects' within the prison, exercise agency and 'actively engage in interpreting the legitimacy of their punishment' (Bosworth and Carrabine, 2001: 502; see also Sparks *et al.*, 1996). As such, 'power in prison is constantly contested', and prison life is characterised by ongoing negotiations of power (Bosworth and Carrabine, 2001: 501; see also Carrabine, 2000). It is therefore important to remember that the agency of individuals and groups can affect penal practices, even though prisoners (and charities) may appear to be almost powerless (Bosworth and Carrabine, 2001). For example, Bosworth and Carrabine describe an argument about hair between two female young offenders and a hairdresser visiting a prison, which led to the young offenders seeking to publicly humiliate the hairdresser and prove her wrong about the texture and length of black people's hair (2001: 510). Despite the offenders' 'actual relative lack of power', they were able to exercise resistance to their own satisfaction in this case. The 1990 Strangeways prison riots saw prisoners resisting power on a far larger scale, and exercising extreme violence in response to the severe breakdown of legitimacy caused by the implementation of their punishment (Carrabine, 2004, 2000).

Recent literature has emphasised the apparent financial imperative for voluntary organisations to participate in the market for penal services on the government's terms. This indicates that voluntary organisations are effectively forced to compete in the market for penal services, and overlooks their agency to resist or modify this imperative. However, ANT contests assumptions that one type of actor drives the other. Avoiding the analytical trap of positioning some actors as agents and others as subjects and thus imposing a normative hierarchy, ANT seeks to provide a politically enabling empirical sociology of power, by examining interactions between different actors (Clegg, 1989: 204). By illustrating how minute relations between heterogeneous actors bring about the world, the principle of generalised symmetry can also be applied to upset the common analytical division between agency and structure (Law, 1992: 389). Phenomena such as organisation, size and domination are not understood as inherent characteristics, but as effects continually generated by interactions between heterogeneous actors (Alcadipani and Hassard, 2010: 425; Carrabine, 2000: 313; Law, 1994: 11).

Rather than insisting that we are 'already held by the force of some society' (Latour, 2005: 8), ANT emphasises that effects such as size, inequality and domination exist 'more or less precariously', always remain open to challenge, and must be continually (re)produced in order for 'social' relations to endure (Law, 1992: 384; see also Carrabine, 2000: 313). All the heterogeneous elements in an organisation therefore have and retain some capacity to resist the ordering and reproduction of the network (Latour, 2005: 5; Law, 1992: 384). Network ordering (and thus social structure) take on the properties of verbs, because they always remain uncertain and contested processes of overcoming resistance, and never become the fait accompli that a noun suggests (Law, 1992: 380, 389). The pattern of accommodations, alliances and separations is always able to shift, as resistances and struggles over power are permanent features of social life (Carrabine, 2000: 319). The fact that order sometimes comes crashing down (e.g. the collapse of the USSR, or on a smaller scale in the 1990 Strangeways prison riots), demonstrates that even the masters of the universe are vulnerable (Law, 1992: 379; see also Carrabine, 2000). This approach challenges existing power relationships by highlighting that all the actors in a network have the opportunity to collude in or resist its reproduction, thus demonstrating that organisation always could be otherwise (Law, 1992: 379).[8]

As discussed in Chapter 2, recent literature regarding the penal voluntary sector and the market for penal services in England and Wales has not fully explored the agency and autonomy of voluntary organisations. In recent years, voluntary organisations have apparently been unable to resist policy reforms requiring their active involvement in the penal service market, despite the risks this market poses to a distinctive charitable ethos and campaigning work (e.g. Corcoran, 2011; Mills *et al.*, 2011). Statutory criminal justice agencies have been positioned as the voluntary sector's puppet masters, pulling its strings through policy reforms and funding for service delivery contracts. But ANT indicates that voluntary organisations should not be conceptualised a priori as subjects, but as actors who can exercise some influence over penality at the macro and micro levels. Although voluntary organisations may have a relative lack of power in comparison to statutory criminal justice agencies (see Bosworth and Carrabine, 2001), they should not be seen merely as passive recipients of penal policy agendas (see Latour, 2005: 10).

Conceptualising voluntary organisations as agents unable to resist neoliberal reforms or the 'magnetic pull' of state contract funding (Corcoran, 2009: 32) is too simplistic and overlooks the diversity and agency of voluntary organisations. The reduction of a highly variegated network of voluntary organisations into a unitary, homogeneous sector in political discourse works to render those organisations biddable and governable entities (Carmel and Harlock, 2008: 156). By failing to acknowledge resistances to the 'co-option' of the sector and the diversity of voluntary organisations therein, scholars of the sector are reinforcing that effect (Zedner, 2002; see also Chapter 8). A solution to this, following ANT, is to explore voluntary organisations' agency and resistance to market policy reforms and penal practices *alongside* analysing how statutory criminal justice agencies translate thought and action across time and space (see Carrabine, 2000: 319).

Carrabine's study of the Strangeways prison riots demonstrates that the dominant (macro level) alignments of discourse and practice which operate within penal institutions at any given time are both continually produced and open to contestation by heterogeneous actors in the penal system (2000: 317). This theorisation is politically enabling. The principle of generalised symmetry is applied here to explore if and how voluntary organisations exercise their agency to collude with, influence or resist penal policies that they do not agree with. The assumption that all voluntary organisations are being compelled to seek contract funding will therefore be tested. Adopting this approach supports an exploration of the dangers and harms posed by marketisation and can acknowledge the potential for net-widening to occur, without overstating the importance of marketisation and negating the agency of charities. It can therefore underpin analysis of the potential enabling *and* control effects of voluntary organisations' work, and illustrate the interactions through which these effects occur.

A more representative and complete account of the sector is thus provided, following ANT, by applying the principle of generalised symmetry to examine voluntary organisations' activities at the macro and micro scales, and considering the agency of voluntary organisations to resist market policy reforms. The questions of scale and agency considered in this section are addressed in the first analysis chapter, Chapter 4. This chapter scopes the voluntary sector and maps the heterogeneity of its component organisations, using data from the document analysis of charitable publications. It explores small voluntary organisations and assesses their agency. The principle of generalised symmetry is also applied in Chapters 5 and 6, which examine varied micro and macro level translations involving voluntary organisations and statutory agencies.

3.6 Translation, or analysing relationship building

3.6.1 Introduction

After applying the principle of generalised symmetry the next, overlapping stage of ANT analysis is to examine translations (Law, 1992: 380, 389). ANT conceptualises the task of sociologists as characterising 'the ways in which materials join together to generate themselves and reproduce institutional and organisational patterns in the networks of the social' (Law, 1992: 379). The process of translation is a central concept of ANT (Gray *et al.*, 2009; Callon, 1986) and provides a structured means of achieving this task. Mapping translations enables scholars to trace how actors translate phenomena into resources and those resources into powerful actor-networks (Clegg, 1989: 204), and to examine why some actor-networks are more successful than others at overcoming the resistance of individual actors. The four inter-related and overlapping phases of translation are: problematisation, interessement, enrolment and mobilisation, which are explained in full in subsequent sections.

Translation provides a specific and accessible framework (Sage *et al.*, 2011: 277) for understanding the diverse relationships between voluntary organisations and statutory criminal justice agencies (including contractual, payment by results and informal relationships), and considering how these relationships can impact upon prisoners and probationers. Applied to the penal voluntary sector, translation indicates that the power of the penal apparatus to regulate and/or transform the convicted comes from the actor-networks created through discursive and practical alignments (Carrabine, 2000: 319). State power works through the translation of thought and action from centres of calculation across time and space, and through the enrolment of agency within particular projects.

Actors can be either intermediaries or mediators of an actor-network (Latour, 2005; 1996). Intermediaries transport meaning or force without transformation and can be black-boxed in analysis, while mediators transform, translate, distort and modify the meanings and elements that they are supposed to carry (Afarikumah and Kwankam, 2013). The aim of ANT analysis is to multiply the 'mediating points between any two elements' rather than deleting and conflating mediators (Latour, 1996: 378). As such, each member of the penal system (state, charitable, private actor, individual) is *actively involved* in the translation of thought and action, giving rise to struggles, accommodations, alliances and separations (Carrabine, 2000: 319).

Translations can be used to demonstrate the roles voluntary organisations play in punishment and map exactly how voluntary organisations collude with, influence and resist the marketisation of penal service delivery. Mapping points of alliance and resistance between voluntary organisations and statutory criminal justice agencies can illuminate how power and control are extended, for example how macro scale policy reforms have translated thought and action across time and space and enrolled voluntary organisations. Translation can also explain how positive effects may result for prisoners and probationers (e.g. if charitable work improves their experience of punishment), and how voluntary organisations can modify or upset the operation of punishment. The four phases of translation (problematisation, interessement, enrolment and mobilisation) are now explored and illustrated. Callon's 1986 account of translation based on research to improve scallop aquaculture in St Brieuc Bay provides one of the more structured, accessible and easily definable perspectives on translation (Sage *et al.*, 2011: 279) and is therefore used to underpin this explanation.

3.6.2 Phase 1: problematisation

During the problematisation, the project sponsor seeks to define a problem, or set of problems, that is of concern to various other actors, whom the project sponsor determines (Afarikumah and Kwankam, 2013; Sage *et al.*, 2011). The sponsor attempts to interest other actors by defining a set of problems and indicating a means of resolving the shared problem, thus defining identities and associations between actors in discursive and practical terms (Sage *et al.*, 2011: 281; Gray *et al.*, 2009: 430). Problematisation entails the punctualisation of actors, in which actors with heterogeneous motives, aims and actions are simplified to mutually acceptable definitions (Callon and Law, 1982: 617–618). The links between actors may be based upon 'boundary objects', such as prisoners and scallops, which allow multiple actor-networks to partially align (Sage *et al.*, 2011: 284).

Powerful macro actors, or obligatory passage points, are constructed by the project sponsor during the problematisation. These actors become indispensable to other actors in the actor-network (Sage *et al.*, 2011: 281; Callon, 1986: 202). At the problematisation stage, the entities and relationships have been identified and envisaged but not yet tested. A series of trials of strength between actors follow, which test whether the actors adopt, negotiate or refuse their assigned roles. The outcome of these trials ultimately determines the solidity of the problematisation (Callon, 1986).

For example, in Callon's scallops study (1986), the problematisation saw a group of scientific researchers who were interested in scallop reproduction defining and disseminating problems shared between fishermen, scallops and the wider scientific community. The researchers held a conference in 1972 with representatives of the fishing community, aiming to increase scallop stocks by increasing their reproduction. They presented themselves as interested in advancing knowledge about how scallops anchor. The scallops were the boundary objects allowing the interests of different actors to align. Through their investigation, the researchers sought to improve the stock of scallops in St Brieuc Bay by increasing their chance of growth, survival and reproduction, thus also improving profitability for the fishermen and advancing wider scientific knowledge about scallops. The researchers then indicated that the shared problems could be resolved if all the relevant actors co-operated with their proposed programme of investigation and accepted the roles assigned by the researchers. The researchers thus became the obligatory passage point for solving the shared problems. A series of human and non-human actors were interested in the research project, and the identities of and links between actors were established.

3.6.3 Phase 2: interessement

The interessement involves the project sponsor attempting to stabilise the identities of the other actors, as defined in the problematisation (Callon, 1986: 203). The claims of the problematisation are tested through trials of strength. Actors enlisted by the problematisation can either submit to integration into the initial plan, negotiate the terms of their integration, or refuse the transaction by defining their interests differently (Gray *et al.*, 2009: 430; Callon, 1986: 203). Actors can only define their identities 'through their relations with other actors in action' (Sage *et al.*, 2011: 282). While the problematisation is the front end of project planning, the interessement involves ongoing negotiations through which the claims made in the problematisation are tested and modified (Sage *et al.*, 2011: 282). Through these negotiations, social structures composed of heterogeneous actors are shaped and consolidated (Callon, 1986).

In Callon's study (1986), the interessement involved the researchers seeking to lock other actors into proposed roles. The researchers held meetings and debates for the fishermen to explain reasons for declining scallop stocks, created graphs to illustrate this decline and presented spectacular results from a Japanese experiment that they would draw on in St Brieuc Bay. For the interessement of scientific colleagues, the researchers published articles and solicited interest through conferences. The researchers argued that their exhaustive literature review indicated nothing was known about the anchoring process of scallops, which formed an issue of increasing economic importance for St Brieuc Bay and France. The researchers used a towline and collectors for the interessement of the scallops, allowing them to anchor, grow and produce larvae. This was based on a technique invented in Japan, which involved towlines made up of collectors being immersed in the sea. The collectors carried fine-netted bags which supported the anchorage of larvae. These bags allowed free flow of water, prevented young scallops from escaping and protected the larvae from various predators. The devices of interessement were the towlines and collectors immersed in St Brieuc Bay (for the scallops) and the texts and conversations which supported the researchers' project (for the fishermen and the scientific community).

3.6.4 Phase 3: enrolment

Enrolment is the successful translation of interests within an actor-network and occurs when interessement successfully leads to alliances: the other actors accept the roles and interests defined by the project sponsor through the process of multilateral negotiations, bargaining and making concessions (Afarikumah and Kwankam, 2013: 79; Sarker *et al.*, 2006: 55; Callon, 1986: 206, 211). The power and influence of an actor-network can be expanded by increasing the number of actors enrolled into it (Latour and Woolgar, 1986: 271) and increasing its durability and mobility (Law, 1992: 387). Inscription often occurs during enrolment, and the commitments that have been negotiated are recorded, or inscribed, into the shared social or textual memory and stabilised through a process of artefact creation (Afarikumah and Kwankam, 2013: 79; Sarker *et al.*, 2006: 55). Inscription can include creating texts, e.g. contracts or manuals, and creating technical artefacts such as security systems (Sarker *et al.*, 2006: 55). Embodying relationships in durable materials such as texts suppresses resistance and stabilises the actor-network (Law, 1992: 387). Materials and processes of communication such as writing, electronic communication, banking systems and trade routes create mobility, or the means for networks to act at a distance (Law, 1992: 387).

However, translation always remains a process and never becomes stable because enrolment is not permanent (Callon, 1986). De-inscription or betrayal may occur if an actor previously associated with an actor-network goes on to sever their ties (Sarker *et al.*, 2006: 55). Actors may use anti-programs to leave or achieve de-inscription from an actor-network, e.g. by performing actions which conflict with the interests of the actor-network they have previously been enrolled into (Sarker *et al.*, 2006: 55; Callon, 1986: 219). Actors can also exert dissidence, which works against the enrolment strategies of opposing actor-networks (Callon and Law, 1982).

In Callon's study (1986), the scallops enrolled by anchoring to the towlines. This involved the researchers negotiating tidal currents, parasites and the materials which composed the scallop collectors. The fishermen were enrolled without any resistance and were prepared to accept the researchers' conclusions without discussion. The scientific colleagues were enrolled because they accepted the principle that scallops would anchor to the towlines and collectors. This definition and distribution of roles was a result of multilateral negotiations which determined the identity of the actors. The outcome was that the scallops anchored themselves, the scientific colleagues believed in the principle of anchorage and the fishermen were persuaded that the researchers' collectors could boost scallop stocks in the Bay.

3.6.5 Phase 4: mobilisation

Mobilisation is the point at which an actor becomes the spokesperson for an actor-network, being able to speak in the name of other actors (Sage *et al.*, 2011: 286). Spokespersons are powerful macro actors who can translate the interests, roles and relations of the entire actor-network (Sage *et al.*, 2011: 286; see also Callon and Latour, 1981). Examining translations thus provides an understanding of 'all the negotiations, intrigues, calculations, acts of persuasion and violence, thanks to which an actor or force takes, or causes to be conferred on itself, authority to speak or act on behalf of another actor or force' (Callon and Latour, 1981: 279). Size is therefore shown to be 'the consequence of struggle' (Carrabine, 2000: 312).

In Callon's study (1986), the scallops express absolutely nothing, yet gain a credible spokesperson by anchoring to the collectors and being counted by the researchers, who then register these results and convert them into tables for use in scientific papers and articles. If these results are judged significant by scientific colleagues, the researchers can speak legitimately for the scallops of St Brieuc Bay. The researchers became influential spokespeople because they assembled and then spoke on behalf of crustaceans, fishermen and experts. The scallops, fishermen and scientists were initially dispersed but the researchers were successful and came to speak on behalf of these entities, legitimately claiming that the scallops did anchor and that the fishermen wanted to restock the Bay.

3.6.6 Translation and the penal voluntary sector

My conceptualisation of the penal voluntary sector was informed by analysis of two translations, which illustrate that penal voluntary organisations interact with statutory criminal justice agencies in a variety of ways. Recent scholarship provides some understanding of how voluntary organisations gain access to prisoners and probationers through commissioning processes in penal service markets (e.g. Corcoran, 2011; Neilson, 2009). But where a commissioning process does not operate and there are no plans to introduce this mechanism, it is unclear how relationships are constructed between charities and criminal justice agencies. As such, we have a limited understanding of how the 'vital array' of charitable work which does not feature in recent policy reforms (Martin, 2013) is facilitated and undertaken.

The first translation, informed by the principle of generalised symmetry, was principally bottom up and examined multiple small scale translations between voluntary organisations and statutory criminal justice agencies. These relationships were sponsored by local statutory criminal justice agencies *and* individual voluntary organisations. These relatively small relationships may have important and valuable effects upon prisoners and probationers which are not understood because these relationships have not yet been studied elsewhere. This translation is presented in Chapter 5 and draws on data from interviews and document analysis.

The second, principally top-down, translation provides a more specific understanding of how some voluntary organisations were translated into a practical and discursive macro scale network of marketised penal service delivery. Chapter 6 maps the process of translation beginning with the publication of *Breaking the Cycle*, which formed a problematisation by the MoJ (MoJ, 2010). Chapter 6 considers how this translation affected, and was affected by, voluntary organisations. This chapter demonstrates how the MoJ translated the phenomena of voluntary organisations' engagement with prisoners and probationers into a biddable and governable resource which the MoJ mobilised to shore up the further marketisation of criminal justice services. This illuminates how the MoJ imposed themselves, and their definition of the appropriate role for the voluntary sector in punishment, upon some voluntary organisations. This translation ultimately extended the network of carceral control, resulting in a new statutory supervision requirement for short-sentence prisoners, who were previously unsupervised post-release (Tomczak, forthcoming).

Chapter 7 considers the effects of charitable work upon prisoners and probationers. This chapter assesses the potential value of charitable work, alongside its role in extending social control and net-widening, which is enabled by the understanding that there is no singular social order, but rather orders and resistances (Law, 1992: 379, 386). The mediating roles of the penal voluntary sector are drawn out and the concepts of social control and net-widening are problematised using the idea of mediation. The next section describes how these theoretical ideas were translated into methodological practice in order to conceptualise the sector.

3.7 Theory into practice

3.7.1 Introduction

ANT is often regarded as an essentially theoretical approach without a methodological repertoire as such (Nimmo, 2011: 109). While this is not necessarily the case, the relationship between ANT and specific methodological practices has received less discussion than the overall theoretical approach (Pollack *et al.*, 2013; Nimmo, 2011).[9] In order to support future applications of ANT, the selected methodological practices and analytical process are now explained.

3.7.2 Limiting the research site

The 'highest ethical standard' for ANT analysis is to be 'irreductionist' (Latour, 1996: 378). Accounts should multiply the 'mediating points between any two elements' rather than deleting and conflating actors (Latour, 1996: 378), or black-boxing actors as intermediaries who do not transform meaning or force (Afarikumah and Kwankam, 2013). A good account is therefore a description in which all the actors do something and do not transport effects without transforming them (Latour, 2005: 128). But, ANT could lead to analysing 'endlessly interconnected networks of association' (Pollack *et al*., 2013: 1121), particularly in the case of exploratory research such as this. It is therefore necessary to make conscious boundary choices in order to create coherent knowledge in a textual format (Pollack *et al*., 2013: 1121; Latour, 2005: 148).

My boundary choices affected the voluntary organisations and relationships studied. I foregrounded relationships between voluntary organisations and statutory agencies, and did not specifically explore relationships between voluntary organisations and private companies who run prisons and deliver prison/ probation services. Private companies are undeniably significant actors in punishment and the alliance between Serco, Catch 22 and Turning Point is examined in Chapter 6, but there is a limited body of existing commentary and secondary data about partnerships between private companies and voluntary organisations. Specifically analysing these relationships would have required a significant investment of time and resources, which were not available here.

As explained in Chapter 1, I studied formally constituted voluntary organisations that had been registered as charitable organisations with the Charity Commission in England and Wales for at least a year, and so had documents to include in the first stage of data collection. I limited the sample to voluntary organisations whose principal focus was (ex-)offenders and/or their families in England and Wales. This excluded victim-focussed organisations, organisations with a different geographical focus which are nested within a different policy context (e.g. Penal Reform International, Families Outside (Scotland)). It also excluded voluntary organisations for whom (ex-)offenders and/or their families form one of multiple client or interest groups, but not the principal focus e.g. The Fawcett Society (campaign for women's equality); Barnardo's (support for young people); ACEVO/Association of Chief Executives of Voluntary Organisations. All of these decisions deleted actors from the resultant account of the sector (see Latour, 1996: 378) and some of the excluded organisations are significant penal service providers. However, this project meets the criteria for a 'good ANT account' as it substantively broadens understandings of the sector and multiplies the mediating points previously acknowledged in relationships between voluntary organisations and statutory criminal justice agencies. In addition to macro level policy reforms, I explore the role of small voluntary organisations, the agency of voluntary organisations and non-contractual relationships between voluntary organisations and statutory criminal justice agencies.

3.7.3 Data collection and analysis

Data collection and analysis in this case were overlapping processes, which were guided by ANT throughout. Table 3.1 at the end of this section summarises how the tenets of ANT were applied to conceptualise the sector in four overlapping stages. Data were collected from three sources: (a) the financial accounts and annual reports of over forty voluntary organisations for the tax year 2009–2010, (b) policy documents, and (c) semi-structured interviews with eleven voluntary organisation staff and two statutory sector staff. The documents were all in the public domain and provided a large amount of freely accessible data which informed and supplemented the interviews. Using these multiple methods and different sources to collect data greatly increased the breadth and depth of the inquiry and enabled analysis of multiple mediating points in the translations (Latour, 1996: 378).

The first stage of data collection aimed to 'scope' diversities within the sector and explore the heterogeneity of the research site, which is known as deploying uncertainties or deploying controversies. Deploying uncertainties provides the opportunity to discover unexpected actors and resources, and enable them to emerge on their own terms (Latour, 2005: 16). Scoping the heterogeneity of voluntary organisations was particularly valuable because of the 'loose and baggy' nature of the sector. An obvious place to begin was by examining policy documents and publications relating to the *Breaking the Cycle* Green Paper (e.g. MoJ, 2013a, 2012, 2011a, 2011b, 2010), along with voluntary organisations' responses to the Green Paper (e.g. Action for Prisoners' Families, 2011). In order to uncover a broader range of voluntary organisations and deploy uncertainties, I undertook an extensive web-based search for voluntary organisations.[10]

The Charity Commission website was particularly useful, having an 'advanced search' function allowing keywords such as 'prison', 'offenders' and 'probation' to be searched. This website provided the annual accounts for all voluntary organisations with an income in excess of the Commission's £25,000 reporting threshold, and the annual reports for many organisations. Documents for the tax year 2009–2010 were reviewed, which were the most recent documents available at the time of data collection in late 2011. Other websites also 'signposted' further organisations, whose documents were then found via the Charity Commission. As a result of these searches, a working sample of over forty voluntary organisations was created. Although not a comprehensive review of voluntary organisations in England and Wales, the sample included diverse organisations with a variety of income ranges, funding sources and objectives. In order to handle the large volume of information and create an overview of the data, I constructed a series of databases from the sample. These databases listed voluntary organisations' functions, geographical scope and income sources. The findings generated from the process of deploying uncertainties are presented in Chapter 4.

I then approached over twenty voluntary organisations by email to request an interview. The sampling method was purposive, so participants were approached because their specialist knowledge would facilitate an investigation relevant to the research. I was particularly interested in voluntary organisations which were not dependent on state funding because I was surprised by the number of these organisations that emerged during the document analysis, given that they were largely absent from existing literature. Of the eleven interview participants from voluntary organisations, nine represented organisations that were not dependent on state funding. This provided a substantive amount of data about this 'silent' group for whom relatively little published information was available. All eleven participants worked for organisations whose principal function was service delivery, three of which were female-only projects. Two further interviews were with recently retired, senior-ranking statutory sector staff who had significant involvement with voluntary organisations during their careers. One of these interviewees had worked in prisons, the other in probation.

These in-depth semi-structured interviews enabled further investigation of questions raised by the document analysis and provided rich, wide-ranging data. Ethnography has been used for ANT research (e.g. Law, 1994) and would also have provided useful insights into the sector. However, gaining a breadth of responses from a larger number of voluntary organisations was more appropriate for this exploratory research seeking to conceptualise the sector. Interviews were undertaken between January and April 2012. The semi-structured technique meant emergent unanticipated topics could be pursued in the interview. Participants were allowed to 'ramble' as this fitted the ANT approach of learning from the actors (Latour, 1999: 20). Five interviews were conducted face-to-face and the remaining eight were conducted over the telephone at participants' choice. Telephone interviewing provided a highly efficient technique, enabling collection of a large volume of data and inclusion of a larger number of geographically dispersed participants than solely using face-to-face interviews would have. Some of the telephone interviews were more revealing than those carried out face-to-face, echoing the finding that telephone interviews increase respondents' perception of anonymity (Greenfield *et al.*, 2000). Furthermore, the potential to use telephone interviewing provided access to busy individuals, whose views and experience would not otherwise have been included (Miller, 1995), which meets the ANT aim of multiplying mediating points in translations. All interviews were digitally recorded (with permission) and transcribed as soon as possible after completion.

Data analysis began during data collection, as the initial findings informed (without determining) subsequent stages of data collection and I began developing themes. Ethnographic content analysis of the documents and interview transcripts was undertaken by initially distilling themes from the data and revising these themes as new data and understandings emerged (Bryman, 2012: 559). I explored the data by reading and re-reading the published documents and interview transcripts, and gathering data under each theme. This thematic analysis was carried out using word processing software and by constructing tables and maps of translations.

After deploying uncertainties, the next analytical stage is applying the principle of generalised symmetry to analyse specific uncertainties and cross cut analytical divides (Nimmo, 2011: 109; Latour, 1993: 94). Here, this involved the uncertainties of scale and agency in relation to voluntary organisations. Small charities and charitable agency were examined alongside macro scale policy reforms and the scales of statutory action were also problematised by categorising the 'criminal justice system' into agencies operating across a spectrum from individual prisons up to the MoJ. Interactions between the spectrum of statutory agencies and heterogeneous voluntary organisations are illustrated in Chapters 4–7. Agency was investigated by considering voluntary organisations' ability to resist participating in the expanding market for penal services (see Chapter 4).

The next analytical step involves examining translations (Law, 1992: 380, 389) and tracing associations between actors (Latour, 2005). This entailed 'scoping' the range of interactions between charities and statutory criminal justice agencies, using data from MoJ publications (e.g. MoJ, 2013a, 2012, 2011a), voluntary organisation publications and the interviews; and then tracing translations between these actors. The findings of the 'scoping' process (described in Chapter 4) informed the translations presented in Chapters 5 and 6. This involved comparing the data to Callon's four-phase process of translation (1986) and existing applications thereof (principally Sage *et al.*, 2011; Gray *et al.*, 2009; Carrabine, 2000). Small scale processes of translation were mapped in the same way as macro scale policy translations, following the principle that apparently disparate actors should be examined symmetrically.

Mapping smaller processes of translation which were instigated both by voluntary organisations and statutory criminal justice agencies provides an understanding of small scale charitable activity, about which very little is known (see Chapter 5). This enables the agency of voluntary organisations to be investigated at the macro and micro level, whilst simultaneously considering how power works through disciplinary strategies (Herbert-Cheshire, 2003: 458–459). Chapter 6 demonstrates that the MoJ's texts acted to discursively define the role for voluntary organisations in marketised penal delivery to some extent, and explores how the resultant discourse affected practices at the micro level.

ANT was then applied to consider the effects of charitable work by undertaking thematic analysis of the publications and interview transcripts, and considering the analysis of translations. This involved identifying further data which dealt with the effects of charitable work (e.g. Fine Cell Work, 2010), and then coding these effects as 'mediator' or 'intermediary'. ANT was useful here because, in line with the aim of multiplying mediating points, it supported a novel integrated account of the range of effects of charitable work which may otherwise have remained obscure (see Nimmo, 2011: 109; Law, 2004: 157). Chapter 7 considers how the diverse actions of voluntary organisations affect prisoners and probationers, or how voluntary organisations can act as intermediaries and mediators of punishment. Table 3.1 summarises how the sector was conceptualised in these four overlapping stages, but this is necessarily a simplification of the continuous analytical process.

My sample of over forty voluntary organisations' documents, thirteen interviews and policy-related documents does not speak for the estimated 1,500 voluntary organisations that work with prisons and probation (Meek *et al.*, 2010: 3). However, this research used multiple methods and gathered complementary findings about a range of diverse voluntary organisations, to create a *richer* understanding of the sector. This chapter has detailed the study's theoretical framework and methodology, rendering the research process as transparent as possible and maximising the potential for future applications of ANT. The next chapter presents the findings of the scoping stage of analysis, or deploying uncertainties.

Table 3.1 An ANT research process[a]

Stage 1: Deploying uncertainties
→ WHAT? Exploring the heterogeneity of the research site. Actors are allowed to emerge on their own terms by refusing to restrict analysis of the categories and materials used by actors in their relationships (Latour, 2005: 16).
→ HOW? Scoping the diversities found among penal voluntary organisations by undertaking extensive web searches for organisations[b] (Chapter 4).

Stage 2: Applying the principle of generalised symmetry
→ WHAT? Examining heterogeneous actors on the same terms. The principle can be applied to overcome common analytical divides between the social and the natural, macro and micro scale actors, and agency and structure (Carrabine, 2000: 313; Law, 1992: 389).
→ Stage 1 informs Stage 2, because deploying uncertainties illustrates which application(s) of the principle are most appropriate for the research case. The principle was applied here to examine scale and agency in relation to voluntary organisations and their interactions with statutory criminal justice agencies.
→ HOW? Collecting and analysing interview and document data. I developed thematic codes for scale and agency and coded all the data (Chapters 4 and 5).

Stage 3: Analysing translations
→ WHAT? How interactions between actors generate effects such as size, power and organisation (Law, 1992: 380). Here macro and micro level translations are analysed. This two-pronged approach was informed by the principle of generalised symmetry.
→ HOW? Coding the interview and document data, then mapping two four-phase processes of translation (Chapters 5 and 6).

Stage 4: Mediating punishment
→ WHAT? The effects of actors' work. Actors can be either intermediaries or mediators of an actor-network. Intermediaries transport meaning or force without transformation while mediators transform and modify the meanings and elements that they carry (Afarikumah and Kwankam, 2013; Latour, 2005).
→ HOW? The interview and document data was analysed and coded to explore the intermediary and mediating effects of charitable work (Chapter 7).

Notes
a These phases guided the research but they are overlapping and inter-related. This table simplifies a complex process.
b Helpful websites were: Clinks, Charity Commission, Churches' Criminal Justice Forum, Criminal Justice Alliance, Third Sector.

Notes

1 N. B. Nelken (2009: 291–292) highlights the concurrent risks of comparative research being ethnocentric, so assuming that our ways of thinking about and responding to crime are universally shared, and relativist, so taking the view that we will never really be able to grasp what others are doing and cannot evaluate whether what they do is right.
2 For criticisms of ANT and a convincing rebuttal, see Alcadipani and Hassard, 2010; Orlikowski and Baroudi, 1991.
3 ANT is sometimes referred to as a 'sociology of associations' (Latour, 2005) or a 'sociology of translation' (Carrabine, 2000: 312; see also Callon, 1986). Indeed, there is a debate over the suitability of the term 'actor-network theory' among some theorists (e.g. Law, 2004; Law and Hassard, 1999). For this analysis, the theoretical

principles are of greater importance than the terminology adopted. The terminology 'ANT' is used here, in line with a substantial body of scholarship (e.g. Nimmo, 2011; Sage *et al.*, 2011; Gray *et al.*, 2009; Sarker *et al.*, 2006).

4 Human and non-human actors can also be referred to as actants (Gray *et al.*, 2009: 425). This specialist terminology is not adopted here, in order to maintain clarity, accessibility and simplicity of expression.

5 This research was iterative: although largely exploratory and aiming to build theory, it was not purely inductive because existing literature shaped (but did not determine) the data collection process.

6 The term 'project sponsor' refers not to the funder, but the actor(s) who define and establish a common goal for the actor-network (Latour, 2005: 106–108; see also Gray *et al.*, 2009: 425).

7 Carrabine uses the alternative terminology 'a sociology of translation' (2000).

8 There are overlaps between this perspective and the work of Bordieu, but there are also significant differences. For a full discussion thereof, see Loughlan *et al.* (2014). Most fundamentally, Bordieu critiques how the state has buckled under economic pressures, while Latour denies that the state ever held much control.

9 This criticism is not limited to ANT methodology. In a review of project management research, Smyth and Morris (2007: 428) found that few authors were explicit about the methodology they adopted, although research methodology has a key role in generating knowledge about projects and their management.

10 Large datasets are available and have supported quantitative research, including the Charity Commission dataset, the 2008 National Survey of Third Sector Organisations, the Guidestar database and the Clinks Working with Offenders Directory (Gojkovic *et al.*, 2011: 6). These datasets were not exploited here as they did not provide the specificity required.

References

Action for Prisoners' Families (2011) *Response to Breaking the Cycle February 2011*. Available at: www.prisonersfamilies.org.uk/uploadedFiles/2010_Policy/Response%20 to%20Breaking%20the%20Cycle.pdf. Accessed: 6 October 2013.

Afarikumah, E. and Kwankam, S. Y. (2013) 'Deploying Actor-Network Theory to Analyse Telemedicine Implementation in Ghana', *Science*, 1(2): 77–84.

Alcadipani, R. and Hassard, J. (2010) 'Actor-Network Theory, Organizations and Critique: Towards a politics of organizing', *Organization*, 17(4): 419–435.

Bosworth, M. (1999) *Engendering Resistance: Agency and power in women's prisons*. Aldershot: Ashgate.

Bosworth, M. and Carrabine, E. (2001) 'Reassessing Resistance: Race, gender and sexuality in prison', *Punishment and Society*, 3(4): 501–515.

Bryman, A. (2012) *Social Research Methods*. Oxford: Oxford University Press.

Callon, M. (1986) 'Some Elements of a Sociology of Translation: Domestication of the scallops and the fishermen of St Brieuc Bay', in Law, J. (ed.) *Power, Action and Belief: A new sociology of knowledge?* London: Routledge.

Callon, M. and Latour, B. (1981) 'Unscrewing the Big Leviathan: How actors macrostructure reality and how sociologists help them to do so', in Knorr-Cetina, K. and Cicourel, A. V. (eds) *Advances in Social Theory and Methodology: Toward an Integration of micro and macro-sociologies*. Boston: Routledge and Kegan Paul.

Callon, M. and Law, J. (1982) 'On Interests and their Transformation: Enrolment and counter-enrolment', *Social Studies of Science*, 12(4): 615–625.

Carmel, E. and Harlock, J. (2008) 'Instituting the "Third Sector" as a Governable Terrain: Partnership, procurement and performance in the UK', *Policy and Politics*, *36*(2): 155–171.

Carrabine, E. (2000) 'Discourse, Governmentality and Translation: Toward a social theory of imprisonment', *Theoretical Criminology*, *4*(3): 309–331.

Carrabine, E. (2004) *Power, Discourse, and Resistance: A genealogy of the Strangeways prison riot*. Aldershot: Ashgate.

Corcoran, M. (2009) 'Bringing the Penal Voluntary Sector to Market', *Criminal Justice Matters*, *77*(1): 32–33.

Corcoran, M. (2011) 'Dilemmas of Institutionalization in the Penal Voluntary Sector', *Critical Social Policy*, *31*(1): 30–52.

Corcoran, M. (2012) 'Be Careful What You Ask For: Findings from the seminar series on the Third Sector in criminal justice', *Prison Service Journal*, *204:* 17–22.

Clegg, S. (1989) *Frameworks of Power*. London: Sage.

Durkheim, E. (1983) 'The Evolution of Punishment', in Lukes, S. and Scull, A. (eds) *Durkheim and the Law*. Oxford: Martin Robertson.

Fine Cell Work (2010) *Trustees' Report and Unaudited Accounts for the Year Ended 31 December 2010*.

Foucault, M. (1977) *Discipline and Punish: The birth of the prison*. London: Allen Lane.

Garland, D. (2001) *The Culture of Control: Crime and social order in a contemporary society*. Chicago: University of Chicago Press.

Gojkovic, D., Mills, A. and Meek, R. (2011) 'Scoping the Involvement of Third Sector Organisations in the Seven Resettlement Pathways for Offenders', *TSRC Working Paper 57*. Southampton: Third Sector Research Centre.

Gray, D., Graham, A., Dewhurst, Y., Kirkpatrick, G., MacDougall, L., Nicol, S. and Nixon, G. (2009) 'Scallops, Schools and Scholars: Reflections on the emergence of a research-oriented learning project', *Journal of Education for Teaching*, *35*(4): 425–440.

Greenfield, T. K., Midanik, L. T. and Rogers, J. D. (2000) 'Effects of Telephone versus Face-to-Face Interview Modes on Reports of Alcohol Consumption', *Addiction*, *95*(20): 277–284.

Herbert-Cheshire, L. (2003) 'Translating Policy: Power and action in Australia's country towns', *Sociologia Ruralis*, *43*(4): 454–473.

Hitchings, R. (2003) 'People, Plants and Performance: On actor network theory and the material pleasures of the private garden', *Social and Cultural Geography*, *4*(1): 99–114.

Jessop, B. (1995) 'The Regulation Approach and Governance Theory: Alternative perspectives on economic and political change?' *Economy and Society*, *24*(3): 307–333.

Latour, B. (1992) 'Where are the Missing Masses? The sociology of a few mundane artefacts', in Bijker, W. E. and Law, J. (eds) *Shaping Technology/Building Society: Studies in sociotechnical change*. Cambridge, MA: MIT Press.

Latour, B. (1993) *We Have Never Been Modern*. Harlow: Pearson.

Latour, B. (1996) 'On Actor-Network Theory. A few clarifications plus more than a few complications', *Soziale Welt*, *47*(4): 369–381.

Latour, B. (1999) 'On Recalling ANT', in Law, J. and Hassard, J. (eds) *Actor-Network Theory and After*. Oxford: Blackwell.

Latour, B. (2005) *Reassembling the Social: An introduction to Actor-Network Theory*. Oxford: Oxford University Press.

Latour, B. and Woolgar, S. (1986). *Laboratory Life: The construction of scientific facts*. Princeton, NJ: Princeton University Press.

Law, J. (1986) 'On the Methods of Long-Distance Control: Vessels, navigation and the Portuguese route to India', in Law, J. (ed.) *Power, Action and Belief: A new sociology of knowledge?* London: Routledge.

Law, J. (1992) 'Notes on the Theory of the Actor-Network: Ordering, strategy, and heterogeneity', *Systems Practice*, 5(4): 379–393.

Law, J. (1994) *Organising Modernity*. Oxford: Blackwell.

Law, J. (2004) *After Method: Mess in social science research*. Abingdon: Routledge.

Law, J. and Hassard, J. (1999) *Actor Network Theory and After*. Oxford: Blackwell.

Loughlan, V., Olsson, C. and Schouten, P. (2014) 'Mapping', in Aradau, C., Huysmans, J., Neal, A. and Voelkner, N. (eds) *Critical Security Methods: New frameworks for analysis*. Abingdon: Routledge.

Martel, J. (2004) 'Policing Criminological Knowledge: The hazards of qualitative research on women in prison', *Theoretical Criminology*, 8(2): 157–189.

Martin, C. (2013) *Dazzled by the Fireworks: Realising detail in the overwhelming scale of reform*. Clinks Blog Post. Available at: www.clinks.org/community/blog-posts/dazzled-fireworks-realising-detail-overwhelming-scale-reform. Accessed: 25 May 2013.

Meek, R., Gojkovic, D. and Mills, A. (2010) 'The Role of the Third Sector in Work with Offenders: The perceptions of criminal justice and third sector stakeholders', *TSRC Working Paper 34*. Birmingham: Third Sector Research Centre.

Miller, C. (1995) 'In-depth Interviewing by Telephone: Some practical considerations', *Evaluation and Research in Education*, 9(1): 29–38.

Mills, A., Meek, R. and Gojkovic, D. (2011) 'Exploring the Relationship Between the Voluntary Sector and the State in Criminal Justice', *Voluntary Sector Review*, 2(2): 193–211.

MoJ (2010) *Breaking the Cycle: Effective punishment, rehabilitation and sentencing of offenders*, London: MoJ.

MoJ (2011a) *Lessons Learned from the Planning and Early Implementation of the Social Impact Bond at HMP Peterborough*. Available at: www.gov.uk/government/uploads/system/uploads/attachment_data/file/217375/social-impact-bond-hmp-peterborough.pdf. Accessed: 16 October 2013.

MoJ (2011b) *Breaking the Cycle: Government response*. Available at: www.gov.uk/government/uploads/system/uploads/attachment_data/file/186345/breaking-the-cycle-government-response.pdf. Accessed: 16 October 2013.

MoJ (2012) *Findings and Lessons Learned from the Early Implementation of the HMP Doncaster Payment by Results Pilot*. Available at: www.catch-22.org.uk/Files/hmp-doncaster-payment-by-results-pilot.pdf?id=275e92a7-3ce6-4604-8760-a118010ebb54. Accessed: 18 October 2013.

MoJ (2013a) *Statistical Notice: Interim re-conviction figures for the Peterborough and Doncaster payment by results pilots*. Available at: www.gov.uk/government/uploads/system/uploads/attachment_data/file/206686/re-conviction-results.pdf. Accessed: 17 October 2013.

Neilson, A. (2009) 'A Crisis of Identity: NACRO's bid to run a prison and what it means for the voluntary sector', *The Howard Journal of Criminal Justice*, 48(4): 401–410.

Nelken, D. (2009) 'Comparative Criminal Justice: Beyond ethnocentrism and relativism', *European Journal of Criminology*, 6(4): 291–31.

Nimmo, R. (2011) 'Actor-Network Theory and Methodology: Social research in a more-than-human world', *Methodological Innovations Online*, 6(3): 108–119.

O'Malley, P. (1996) 'Indigenous Governance', *Economy and Society*, 25(3): 310–336.

Orlikowski, W. J. and Baroudi, J. J. (1991) 'Studying Information Technology in Organizations: Research approaches and assumptions', *Information Systems Research*, *2*(1): 1–28.

Pollack, J., Costello, K. and Sankaran, S. (2013) 'Applying Actor-Network Theory as a Sensemaking Framework for Complex Organisational Change Programs', *International Journal of Project Management*, *31*(8): 1118–1128.

Sage, D., Dainty, A. and Brookes, N. (2011) 'How Actor-Network Theories Can Help in Understanding Project Complexities', *International Journal of Managing Projects in Business*, *4*(2): 274–293.

Sarker, S., Sarker, S. and Sidorova, A. (2006) 'Understanding Business Process Change Failure: An actor-network perspective', *Journal of Management Information Systems*, *23*(1): 51–86.

Smyth, H. J. and Morris, P. W. (2007) 'An Epistemological Evaluation of Research into Projects and their Management: Methodological issues', *International Journal of Project Management*, *25*(4): 423–436.

Sparks, R., Bottoms, A. E. and Hay, W. (1996) *Prisons and the Problem of Order*. Oxford: Clarendon Press.

Steins, N. A. (2001) 'New Directions in Natural Resource Management: The offer of actor-network theory', *IDS Bulletin*, *32*(4): 18–25.

Tomczak, P. (2014) 'The Penal Voluntary Sector in England and Wales: Beyond neoliberalism?' *Criminology and Criminal Justice*, *14*(4): 470–486.

Tomczak, P. (forthcoming) 'The Voluntary Sector and the Mandatory Statutory Supervision Requirement: Expanding the carceral net', *British Journal of Criminology*.

Zedner, L. (2002) 'Dangers of Dystopias in Penal Theory', *Oxford Journal of Legal Studies*, *22*(2): 341–366.

4   Mapping a loose and baggy monster

Scoping the sector

4.1 Introduction

ANT analysis starts with a clean slate and then entails learning from the actors, so researchers must begin analysis by fully exploring the heterogeneity of the research site (Latour, 2005, 1999; Law, 1992). This guards against the analytical trap of imposing a pre-determined structure and hierarchy of actors upon the account (Pollack *et al.*, 2013: 1119) and 'assuming whatever we wish to explain' (Law, 1992: 380). Although essential, scoping diversities was difficult for this study as the voluntary sector is notoriously difficult to define (Paxton and Pearce, 2005: 6). As noted in Chapter 1, it contains a 'bewildering variety of organisational forms, activities, motivations and ideologies' and has been characterised as an 'inherently messy ... loose and baggy monster' (Kendall and Knapp, 1995: 66).

Recent analysis of the sector has been located within the macro scale penal research tradition and has tended to emphasise the effects of the growing market in penal services. Although commentators have acknowledged that organisations within the sector are 'highly differentiated' (Corcoran, 2011: 40; see also Mills *et al.*, 2011: 204), the factors which create this heterogeneity and their importance have not been fully explored. This chapter presents preliminary analysis and illustrates diversities found amongst penal voluntary organisations. It problematises questions of scale and agency in relation to the penal voluntary sector, assessing a wider range of voluntary organisations and a wider set of their interactions with statutory criminal justice agencies than those included in recent marketised scholarship. Following ANT, the analytical process began by exploring the 'loose and baggy' nature of the sector and the heterogeneity of organisations within it, or 'deploying uncertainties' in ANT terms (Latour, 2005). This process illustrated that a plethora of (often relatively small) voluntary organisations operate alongside prisons and probation without a contract, although such work has thus far received very limited attention from scholars.

The material presented in this chapter comes from document analysis of charitable publications. As explained in Chapter 3, the first stage of data collection involved reviewing the financial accounts and reports of over forty diverse charities with a variety of funding sources and objectives, in order to move beyond policy documents and the discourse of marketisation. Organisations in the sample were sorted into a series of databases illustrating their functions, geographical scope and income sources. While some loose categorisations were made, the aim was simply to understand the diversities amongst charities. This chapter has four overlapping and related components which mirror the ANT analytical process:

1   scoping heterogeneities among penal voluntary organisations (or deploying uncertainties). Section 4.2 sets out the key variables of organisational functions, scale of operations, the relative role of volunteers, focus on employing ex-service users, and incomes.

2   considering scale in relation to the penal voluntary sector (using the principle of generalised symmetry). Sections 4.2 and 4.3 explore the scales at which voluntary organisations operate and are funded by statutory criminal justice agencies.

3   considering agency in relation to the penal voluntary sector (using the principle of generalised symmetry). Sections 4.3 and 4.4 assess how voluntary organisations exercise their agency and pursue their organisational objectives amid the penal service market.

4   scoping how relationships between charities and criminal justice agencies are instigated (deploying uncertainties in relation to translations). Section 4.5 scopes the formation of multiple charitable projects and contextualises the translations examined in Chapters 5 and 6.

4.2   Scoping diversities among voluntary organisations

4.2.1   Functions

The primary and secondary functions of organisations in the sample were compared to Kendall and Knapp's typology of voluntary organisation functions (1995: 67), namely service delivery, policy advocacy, mutual aid and co-ordinating functions. This typology was not imposed upon the sample and the categorisations were illustrative rather than deterministic. Every voluntary organisation in the sample delivered a direct service to its clients, either in kind or in the form of information and support (Kendall and Knapp, 1995: 67), but the services offered and service users varied. For example, Fine Cell Work offered prisoners the opportunity to train in paid, skilled, creative needlework (Fine Cell Work, 2010: 2). The Apex Trust provided 'employment-related advice and support services' to jobless (ex-)offenders and probationers living in the community (Apex Trust, 2010: 4). Among other functions, NEPACS owned two caravans which were used to provide prisoners' families with a one-week respite holiday (NEPACS, 2010: 7).

Numerous organisations undertook campaigning or 'policy advocacy' work, which involves collecting information about a specific interest and utilising this information to put public pressure on decision makers through direct action,

campaigning, lobbying and advocacy work, aiming to change policy and practices (Kendall and Knapp, 1995: 67). Fourteen organisations in the sample cam-
paigned as one of their functions and four were principally campaigning
organisations (e.g. the Prison Reform Trust and the Howard League). By way of
illustration, the Prison Reform Trust aimed to create a 'just, humane and
effective penal system' by 'influencing Parliament, Government and officials
towards reform' (Prison Reform Trust, 2010: 4). Their key campaign was to
ensure prison is reserved for those whose offending is so serious that they cannot
serve their sentence in the community (Prison Reform Trust, 2010: 3, 4). Similarly, the Howard League for Penal Reform worked for 'less crime, safer communities and fewer people in prison' (Howard League, 2010: no pagination).
Again, client groups varied between organisations. Action for Prisoners' Families was not principally a campaigning organisation, but their mission included
representing the issues affecting prisoners' families to government and policy
makers (Action for Prisoners' Families,[1] 2010: 4).

Eight organisations provided 'mutual aid', which entails self-help and
exchange around a common need (Kendall and Knapp, 1995: 67). For example,
the Apex Trust run the ACT4 Women Project in Merseyside, a women-only peer
support project which offered opportunities for project beneficiaries to support
their peers in building self-confidence and self-reliance (Apex Trust, 2010: 4).
Although the Samaritans had a broader remit and were not a *penal* voluntary
organisation, their Prison Listener Scheme was another important example of
mutual aid. Under this scheme, prisoners were trained by the Samaritans to listen
to fellow prisoners in confidence. The scheme aimed to reduce prison suicides
and self-harm, and alleviate the feelings of prisoners in distress.

Five voluntary organisations were involved in 'co-ordinating' or umbrella
functions, providing services to other voluntary sector bodies (Kendall and
Knapp, 1995: 67). Clinks was one such organisation, supporting voluntary and
community organisations who worked 'with or for offenders and their families'
(Clinks, 2010: 2). Clinks' activities included 'sharing good practice' between
their member organisations (Clinks, 2010: 2). Action for Prisoners' Families was
also an umbrella organisation, whose primary objective was to work with their
members to 'ensure that real improvements are made that increase the likelihood
of families maintaining wellbeing during and following imprisonment' (Action
for Prisoners' Families, 2010: 4). Their work included producing specialist publications for member organisations working with the families of prisoners
(Action for Prisoners' Families, 2010: 4).

This section has illustrated variations in voluntary organisations' functions.
Although all four of Kendall and Knapp's functions (1995) feature in this analysis, the service delivery and policy advocacy functions are most important for
this discussion. The next section scopes further significant variables amongst
voluntary organisations, which are analysed in subsequent sections.

4.2.2 Further significant variables

The *geographical reach and scale* of voluntary organisations varied significantly. The sample included national voluntary organisations, those operating over several counties and local organisations. For example, Nacro operated nationally and actively engaged over 90,000 individuals with their services during 2009–2010 (Nacro, 2010: 8). AFFECT (Action For Families Enduring Criminal Trauma) operated across Dorset, Hampshire, East Sussex and West Sussex.[2] Community Resettlement Support Project provided befriending and support to male prisoners preparing to leave only HMP Bedford, and engaged with 218 (ex-)offenders during 2009–2010[3] (Community Resettlement Support Project, 2010: 4, 7). Although these significant variations in the scale of voluntary organisations and their activities are challenging to conceptualise, it is important that relatively small charities are not overlooked in analyses (following the principle of generalised symmetry). Section 4.3 provides more detail about such organisations.

The *relative role of paid staff and volunteers* differed. Some organisations operated on an entirely voluntary basis, e.g. AFFECT was run from volunteers' private homes and had no paid workers.[4] Fine Cell Work, however, worked with 300 inmates in twenty-nine prisons during 2009–2010, supported by both paid and volunteer staff (Fine Cell Work, 2010: 1). They had six full and two part-time staff with staffing costs of £248,333, and engaged with 286 volunteers over the accounting year, forty-five of whom trained prisoners to a professional standard in quilting and embroidery (Fine Cell Work, 2010: 1, 14). Pact were a large organisation who supported 'thousands of families who have experienced the imprisonment of a loved relative' and 'thousands of prisoners during their first night and the early days of custody' (Pact, 2010: 5). This organisation had much higher staffing costs of £2 million, but worked with a relatively few 268 volunteers (Pact, 2010: 11, 28). As a relative anomaly at the largest end of the scale, the national organisation Nacro had staffing costs in excess of £37 million, 1,350 paid full-time equivalent staff, and additional agency and temporary staff (Nacro, 2010: 23–24). The number of volunteers was not directly specified in the 2009–2010 accounts, but the 2011 accounts reported a team of 1,500 staff and volunteers, 1,331 of whom were paid staff (Nacro, 2011b: 8, 25). Volunteer numbers in 2010–2011 were therefore just 169. These examples of AFFECT, Fine Cell Work, Pact and Nacro show that proportions of volunteer and paid staff varied significantly across the penal voluntary sector. The accounts data used here has enabled only a crude comparison of volunteer numbers, so it is not clear whether volunteers worked for an hour per year or an hour per week, nor whether they engaged with basic service delivery or were involved at a higher level, e.g. with service design. However, larger organisations seemed to draw on the volunteer workforce significantly less than smaller organisations.

A small number of organisations stated that they had an *emphasis on employing ex-service users*. St Giles Trust aimed to employ a 'substantial proportion' of their workforce from ex-service users, who formed 38 per cent of the 2009–2010 staff team, with one being appointed to the Board of Trustees (St Giles Trust, 2010: 4). Storybook Dads formally employed two ex-prisoners following their release from HMP Dartmoor (Storybook Dads, 2010: 11). Clean Break also stressed the role for women (ex-)offenders in their work, noting that three of their eleven volunteers had an offending background, one of whom participated whilst released from prison on temporary licence (Clean Break, 2010: 6). These variations in the proportion of paid and volunteer staff within voluntary organisations and the employment opportunities for ex-service users are likely to influence the effects of voluntary organisations' work with prisoners and probationers, which are explored in Chapter 7.

Two organisations in the sample indicated that their work was run on an entirely *voluntary and non-proselytising* basis, although this is unlikely to be true for all charitable programmes. Pact ran the Basic Caring Communities scheme at HMP Wandsworth, which offered befriending support for men leaving the prison and provided 'the experience of "community"' (Pact, 2010: 10). Pact's working principle was to 'accompany people, rather than "saving" them' (Pact, 2010: 10). The Prison Phoenix Trust aimed to encourage 'prisoners in the development of their spirituality and sense of personal responsibility, through the disciplines of meditation and yoga' (Prison Phoenix Trust, 2010: 2). Prisoners took the initiative in making contact with the Trust, which was 'careful not to impose our recommendations without an invitation' (Prison Phoenix Trust, 2010: 12). Again, the degree to which prisoners and probationers engage with charitable programmes voluntarily is likely to influence their effects.

Voluntary organisations' *incomes* spread over an enormous range. Nacro had the highest income by far in the sample, at £61 million (Nacro, 2010: 8), with Langley House Trust second at £8.8 million (Langley House Trust, 2010: 4). The organisation with the lowest income was AFFECT, who were exempt from the Charity Commission's reporting and regulatory process as their income was below the threshold. AFFECT provided their accounts following an e-mail request, which showed an income of £3,500. Funding is explored further in the next section.

This section has outlined the variables of organisational functions, scale of operations, the relative role of volunteers, focus on employing ex-service users, and income range. These brief examples illustrate the diversities found among penal voluntary organisations and reflect the 'bewildering variety of organisational forms, activities, motivations and ideologies' reported among the general voluntary sector (Kendall and Knapp, 1995: 66). It is important to at least acknowledge this diversity when referring to the penal voluntary sector, otherwise accounts will be reductionist and misleading.

This diversity also raises important questions pertaining to scale and agency. Regarding scale: is it possible to analyse the 'Big Players'/corporate-style voluntary organisations such as Nacro alongside smaller, volunteer-led or volunteer-run organisations? All voluntary organisations must demonstrate their pursuit of some charitable objectives to comply with the requirements of the Charity Commission. However, voluntary organisations may have more points of difference than similarities, as indicated in this section. This reflects Armstrong's assertion that 'the "non-profit" descriptor is very powerful; it encourages us to think of nonprofit status as the most important means of categorizing extremely diverse organisations' (2002: 356). Regarding scale and agency: what are the smaller voluntary organisations which form the vast majority of the sector (Corcoran, 2011: 40) doing amid the market for penal services? How are their relationships with statutory criminal justice agencies being affected? Is the future viability of smaller charities which cannot compete in the penal service market under threat as claimed (see Mills *et al.*, 2011: 195)? Does their 'dependence' on state sources of funding require them to become proactively competitive (see Chapter 2)? These questions are considered in the remainder of this chapter, in which small voluntary organisations are analysed on the same terms as the 'Big Players' in the sector (following the principle of generalised symmetry).

4.3 Charitable funding sources

4.3.1 Introduction to funding

Funding is highly significant in recent penal voluntary sector literature (Tomczak, 2014). Commentators have stressed that the sector is heavily reliant on state funding (Corcoran, 2011: 32; Gojkovic *et al.*, 2011: 18; Mills *et al.*, 2011: 193; Ryan, 2011: 519; Neilson, 2009: 401; Silvestri, 2009: 3) and its component organisations are thus considered highly vulnerable to 'being drawn into … marketised penal reform' to ensure their continued survival (Corcoran, 2011: 46; see also Corcoran and Hucklesby, 2013; Mills *et al.*, 2011: 195; Garside, 2004: 9). Charitable activities have allegedly been driven by the imperatives of policy reforms emphasising competitive commissioning. This is concerning because organisations could drift away from their original missions and social welfarist ethos in pursuit of contract funding, thus compromising their social-justice oriented campaigning and advocacy roles in favour of delivering services for statutory organisations (Mills *et al.*, 2011: 207; see also Chapter 2).

In this section, the principle of generalised symmetry is applied to test the argument outlined above and to challenge the agent/subject dichotomy between the MoJ and voluntary organisations. As detailed in Chapter 2, a significant amount of academic and policy commentary has emphasised the importance of the expanding penal service market, but there has been less consideration of how charities can exercise their agency to remain outside or modify this market. In order to examine the MoJ's policy reforms and voluntary organisations' agency on the same terms (as dictated by ANT), charitable agency requires significantly more consideration. The review of charity accounts indicated that their reliance on state funding has been overstated. Their funding came from a broad spectrum of state and non-state sources in the forms of donations, grants, contract funding and earned income. Voluntary organisations usually had multiple income streams, with many receiving different types of funding from both state and non-state sources. These varied income streams are now analysed, and the discussion is structured around scale.

4.3.2 State funding

Commentators have tended to present state funding as a unitary entity. However, the accounts showed that voluntary organisations were funded by a variety of statutory agencies, which operated within and outside criminal justice at a variety of scales. Sources of non-penal state funding used by voluntary organisations included: the Department of Health; Primary Care Trusts; the Department for Education; city and county councils; the Homes and Communities Agency; Supporting People and the European Commission. For example, the Department of Health awarded a grant of £300,000 to the Revolving Doors Agency in 2010 to support their work to influence policy (Revolving Doors Agency, 2010: 7, 23). While these funding relationships between voluntary organisations and non-penal statutory agencies are acknowledged, they are largely beyond the scope of this work.

Among state criminal justice funders, there were multiple agencies involved. State funding was provided by various criminal justice agencies, which operated at different scales and provided different types of funding. Examples of these funding agencies were: HM Prison Service, the National Probation Service, individual probation trusts, (NOMS) and the MoJ. Funder heterogeneities are now examined, to broaden the appreciation of charitable interactions with statutory criminal justice agencies (see also Chapter 1 regarding the levels at which the statutory criminal justice system operates).

At the macro scale, the MoJ provided a two-year restricted grant worth over £240,000 to Women in Prison to support their 'London Project' (Women in Prison, 2010: 3, 4, 13). This project provided services aiming to divert women from custody in prisons, magistrates' courts and women's centres (Women in Prison, 2010: 3, 4, 13). As explained in Chapter 2, the imperative for voluntary organisations to participate in marketised service delivery has apparently increased because competitive service commissioning has expanded alongside reductions in government grant funding (Maguire, 2012: 485; Meek *et al.*, 2010: 7). Grants are the old-style government funding source for voluntary agencies, and are significantly more open ended than the contracts introduced more recently (Maguire, 2012: 485). Grants can be restricted, i.e. subject to donor-imposed restrictions on their expenditure, or unrestricted, i.e. available for use at the discretion of the trustees in furtherance of the general objectives of the charity (Women in Prison, 2010: 12). This data demonstrates that state grant funding may have reduced, but was still used by voluntary organisations in addition to competitive contract funding at the time of the research.

Moving down the scale of statutory agencies, NOMS made a restricted grant of £48,386 to FPWP Hibiscus (FPWP Hibiscus, 2010: 10) and the National Probation Service made a restricted grant of £197,235 to Clean Break in 2010 (Clean Break, 2010: 34).[5] HM Prison Service provided 'generous' restricted grant funding to New Bridge to support their project work with prisoners (New Bridge, 2010: 22). Funding was also provided by individual prisons and probation trusts. For example, Greater Manchester Probation Trust made a restricted grant of £36,516 to POPS in 2010 (POPS, 2010: 18). HMP Downview made an unrestricted grant of £21,000 to Women in Prison (Women in Prison, 2010: 14). 'State funding' is therefore not a monolithic entity and comes with varying degrees of restriction. These ranged from the unusual unrestricted grant made by HMP Downview to Women in Prison, to highly specified contracts which firmly tied down the voluntary organisations' roles and responsibilities as contractors. Grants from statutory criminal justice agencies of various sizes were clearly still available to voluntary organisations. While money from any funder is usually accompanied by some exercise of influence on the recipient (Ellis Paine *et al.*, 2012), the idea that funding will now only follow voluntary organisations that adapt their priorities to fit those of marketisation and the criminal justice system (Mills *et al.*, 2011: 195) is too simplistic. Not all state funding is contractual and funders' priorities are a complex product of the structures and aims of multiple agencies.

There was certainly a group of voluntary organisations who were 'highly dependent' upon a plurality of state funding sources (Corcoran, 2011: 41). Examples were Nacro and St Giles Trust (Neilson, 2009: 403; St Giles Trust, 2010: 3). Nacro's state funders included the MoJ, the Department of Health, the Learning and Skills Council, NOMS, local authorities and primary care trusts. Likewise, the majority of St Giles Trust's income (c. 74 per cent) came from a plurality of state sources in the form of both grants and contract income. Sources included Kent County Council, Kent Probation Trust, London Probation Trust, London Councils, London Borough of Southwark, London Development Agency and NOMS (St Giles Trust, 2010: 3, 21). The very largest voluntary organisations with the highest incomes were particularly dependent on state funding. These organisations are most capable of bidding for service delivery contracts and could be argued to have the greatest impact among the sector, in terms of number of service users. However, this impact should not be assumed. Indeed, and as pointed out in Chapter 2, the smaller and possibly volunteer-led charities which are more typical of the sector may be the most worthful, arguably being 'more likely to bring the so-called "added value" to their work with offenders, particularly the building of social cohesion through their connections to the local community' (Mills *et al.*, 2012: 401; see also Corcoran, 2011; Benson and Hedge, 2009). As such, there may be an inverse relationship between voluntary organisations' scale and impact, with smaller organisations making disproportionate positive impacts upon prisoners and probationers. While there is a limited evidence base for any claims relating to the effects of charitable work, if Mills *et al.* (2012) are correct, perhaps little is actually at stake through market reforms involving the few 'Big Players' among the sector?

In order to more fully conceptualise the penal voluntary sector and thoroughly investigate the effects of diverse charitable work, non-state funding and the activities it sustained are now examined. Following the principle of generalised symmetry, these activities were studied on the same terms as programmes run with state contract funding.

4.3.3 Non-state funding

The accounts indicated that the apparently 'unpopular nature of work with offenders' (Mills *et al.*, 2011: 207; see also Maguire, 2012: 491) did not preclude the possibility of voluntary organisations fundraising from non-state or non-contractual sources. In fact, charities used a plurality of non-state funding sources to sustain their operations. Grants from charitable trusts and foundations, donations from individuals and organisations, social enterprise and corporate support were also vital to the continuing existence of many voluntary organisations and their work with prisoners, probationers and their families. Grant-making trusts played a particularly important role (Joseph Rank Trust, 2012: 5).

Indeed, a large number of voluntary organisations were not dependent upon state sources of funding, or even in receipt of it. Funding ran across a spectrum ranging from charities that were heavily dependent on state funding, e.g. Nacro and St Giles Trust, to self-proclaimed independent organisations which operated without any state funding, e.g. Inquest,[6] Unlock (Unlock, 2010: 2) and the Howard League (Howard League, 2010). Between these extremes of the funding spectrum, there were three other key configurations. First, there was a group of organisations that did not receive state income without necessarily being ideologically opposed to it, e.g. AFFECT[7] and Birth Companions (Birth Companions, 2010: 6). Second, there were organisations which depended on grants from trusts and charitable foundations but also earned some income from state sources. For example, the principal funder of Action for Prisoners' Families was grants from charitable trusts and foundations (including the Nationwide Foundation, the Linbury Trust and the John Paul Getty Junior Trust), but they also received two substantial restricted grants from the MoJ, for infrastructure and running the Prisoners' Families Helpline (Action for Prisoners' Families, 2010: 5, 8, 12). Finally, some organisations earned a percentage of their funds from social enterprise, e.g. Fine Cell Work (Fine Cell Work, 2010: 2) and Pact (Pact, 2010: 13).

Even organisations that delivered services under contract could simultaneously run other programmes funded from non-state sources. In addition to their MoJ contract to provide resettlement services at HM YOI Thorn Cross, the New Bridge Foundation ran a nationwide befriending service for prisoners that received no state funding (New Bridge, 2010: 21). New Bridge deemed their befriending service to have a potentially *transformative impact*, providing this example of a life-sentenced prisoner: 'A letter, a visitor, a New Bridge befriender, changed this man's life completely. Somebody did care and that gave him hope and with hope came the willpower to better his life' (New Bridge, 2010: 3). Similarly, Contact Cheshire Support Group ran the visitor centre at HMP Styal[8] under contract to HM Prison Service, but concurrently employed a family link worker who worked with prisoners in the First Night Centre and their families, funded by the Westminster Foundation (Contact Cheshire Support Group, 2010). NEPACS operated five prison visitor centres in the North East of England, funded by the MoJ on a 'cost recovery' basis (NEPACS, 2010: 4).

NEPACS also established 'Visitors' Voice' advocacy groups at HMPs Durham, Low Newton and Frankland, and employed a co-ordinator to further this advocacy work, funded by the Joseph Rowntree Charitable Trust (NEPACS, 2010: 8). NEPACS had plans to employ a 'Family Support Worker at HMP YOI Low Newton' having secured financial support from the Lankelly Chase Foundation (NEPACS, 2010: 8). These examples show that voluntary organisations can extend the remit of their contractual work, in ways which might make a valuable impact. These effects are discussed further in Chapter 7.

There are certainly several truths in the marketisation literature. It is undeniable that state funding sources are important for some voluntary organisations, that the market in penal services is changing the practices of some voluntary organisations and that many voluntary organisations face financial difficulties. However, the argument that competing for service delivery contracts and accepting the associated operating parameters is the only means for voluntary organisations to survive (Corcoran and Hucklesby, 2013: no pagination; Corcoran, 2011: 46; Gojkovic *et al.*, 2011: 18; Mills *et al.*, 2011: 193; Ryan, 2011: 519; Benson and Hedge, 2009: 33; Neilson, 2009: 401; Silvestri, 2009: 3; Garside, 2004: 9) is partial and misleading. This section has examined non-marketised charitable work. It has taken care not to assume the importance and dominance of state contract funding, following the principle of generalised symmetry. The resultant analysis has shown that the sources of charitable funding are in fact multiple and varied. State grants may have reduced alongside the growth of competitive service commissioning, but they have not disappeared entirely. The availability of funds from grant-giving trusts may have reduced due to the harsh economic climate, but again they have not disappeared entirely. The accounts demonstrated that alternatives to state contract funding remained and were used by voluntary organisations. Not all organisations were heavily dependent on state funding and, as such, not all organisations were financially compelled to participate in the penal service market. Building on these findings and following the principle of generalised symmetry, the next section examines the agency of voluntary organisations and explores the limits of the penal service market.

4.4 Beyond the penal service market

The notion that voluntary organisations are either 'rolling over' to pressures to compete for service delivery contracts 'or going under' (Benson and Hedge, 2009: 35; see also Maguire, 2012: 485; Meek, *et al.*, 2010: 7) is misleading and reductionist. The proportion of penal voluntary organisations that receive state funding is unknown, but in general 'three quarters of charities receive no government funding' (Corcoran, 2011: 41). Nevertheless, recent commentary has emphasised how macro scale policy reforms have extended the penal service market and created an apparent financial imperative for voluntary organisations to compete within it (Corcoran, 2011: 32, 33; Gojkovic *et al.*, 2011: 18; Mills *et al.*, 2011: 193; Ryan, 2011: 519; Neilson, 2009: 401; Silvestri, 2009: 3; Garside, 2004: 9). While the agency of voluntary organisations ought not to be overstated, the scholarly focus upon how successive governments have shaped charities into biddable and governable entities (Carmel and Harlock, 2008: 156) is problematic. This focus has obscured how participating in contracted-out service delivery will only ever be a priority or even a possibility for a certain type of voluntary organisation (Unwin and Molyneux, 2005: 37). It has masked that the expanding penal service market has actually elicited a variety of responses from voluntary organisations. Those without the organisational capacity, infrastructure or funds required to participate in commissioning processes, those without the need or desire to compete, and those ideologically opposed to state sponsorship and marketisation will be largely unaffected and may retain their autonomy and survive on their own terms as long as other sources of funding can be found or created. The 'scoping' phase of analysis uncovered how capacity for and attitudes to contracting actually varied widely across the sector and provided awareness of what voluntary organisations do without a contract.

A recent review demonstrates that £53.7 million of large contracts were awarded to voluntary sector organisations in England and Wales between May 2010 and October 2012 by the MoJ, NOMS, the Youth Justice Board and probation trusts (Garside *et al.*, 2014: 20). This marketplace was dominated by just three voluntary organisations, who shared two thirds of the total £53.7 million large voluntary sector contracts (Garside *et al.*, 2014: 20). The penal voluntary organisation RAPt (The Rehabilitation for Addicted Prisoners Trust) was the prime contractor, with £8.6 million-worth of contracts, and Nacro was in third place with £5.6 million-worth of contracts (Garside *et al.*, 2014: 20). The general voluntary organisation Working Links was second, with £6.4 million worth of contracts (Garside *et al.*, 2014: 20). Although these figures exclude spends of under £25,000 and voluntary organisations acting as sub-contractors in consortia bids (Garside *et al.*, 2014: 20), they indicate that the government's apparent 'dramatically increased engagement with the sector' (Neilson, 2009: 408) is better conceptualized as economic engagement with a few corporate-style voluntary organisations (Garside *et al.*, 2014).[9] Attitudes to contracting actually vary widely across the sector, as outlined in the three case studies presented below.

Nacro were 'actively working with government to identify opportunities in our market sector where government has announced an intention to outsource services' (Nacro, 2010: 6). They were aligning themselves with the marketisation agenda by directly responding to increases in performance-related, PbR service delivery contracts and 'adapting our operational structures to address the monitoring of performance' (Nacro, 2010: 6). By contrast, Fine Cell Work made no mention of contracting or performance monitoring in their accounts, but were working differently to mitigate the risk of a funding drop in the difficult economic climate (Fine Cell Work, 2010). Their business plan 'seeks to expand the charity's product sales' of prisoners' needlework, aiming to construct 'a sustainable social business and charity with the prisoners as stakeholders in the enterprise' (Fine Cell Work, 2010: 2). During the economic recession, Fine Cell Work in fact saw an increase in voluntary income, with product sales increasing and donation income rising by 70 per cent (Fine Cell Work, 2010: 7). Fine Cell

Work were thus supporting their operations without participating in or aligning with the penal service market.

The Community Resettlement Support Project deemed attracting funding to be a 'significant challenge' (Community Resettlement Support Project, 2010: 14). This is because they were a small, young and local organisation working with an 'unpopular' client group; they could not bid for contracts alone or in partnership with other organisations as they had 'insufficient resources and capacity'; and their principal activity was befriending, which is often considered 'an ambiguous activity by many funders who are concerned with targets and outcomes' (Community Resettlement Support Project, 2010: 14). Nevertheless, they secured substantial restricted grant funding from Volunteering England and were thus 'in a good position to move forward and achieve (our) objectives' (Community Resettlement Support Project, 2010: 13, see also 19). Like Fine Cell Work, this organisation was completely outside the penal service market but found alternative means of survival.

These three concise examples indicate that, despite widespread and long-standing funding struggles amongst voluntary organisations, their capacity to pursue and secure sources of funding that match their organisational priorities and characteristics should not be overlooked. The following three case studies of the Apex Trust, Unlock and Revolving Doors Agency further demonstrate voluntary organisations' ability to resist the penal service market and subvert associated threats to their ethos and campaigning. Amid the expanding penal service market, the Apex Trust reduced its previous dependence on state funding and found a middle way between rolling over and going under (Benson and Hedge, 2009). Unlock rejected all state funding and sustained their service delivery and campaigning work using funds from other sources. The Revolving Doors Agency introduced a new organisational focus on advocacy work amid marketisation.

The Apex Trust helped people with a criminal record obtain jobs through skills development and working to break down the barriers to their employment (Apex Trust, 2010: 3). In 2010 the organisation had experienced two extremely challenging years as a result of state funding agreements ending alongside reduced stock market values and dividend income due to the recession. In order to ensure the organisation's 'ongoing viability', the Trust designed and adopted a new strategy of developing 'services that are multi-funded, not dependent upon statutory contracting' (Apex Trust, 2010: 4). The Trust therefore successfully adapted to a challenging set of circumstances and reduced their vulnerability to state funding agreements not being renewed or changing in form, e.g. through the implementation of PbR. Recent accounts reiterate that they:

> are keen to sustain and develop our services in the long term and ... are pleased to confirm that ... grant making bodies have recognised the importance of the work that we have done and the Big Lottery has agreed to support us for a further three years.

(2014: 7)

Although state contract funding apparently exerts a 'magnetic pull' (Corc-oran, 2009: 32), the case of Apex Trust and further examples below indicate that the force of this magnetic pull has been overstated. Unlock (the National Associ-ation of Reformed Offenders) principally worked to empower 'reformed offend-ers to break down barriers to reintegration by offering practical advice, support, information, knowledge and skills' (Unlock, 2010: 3). Unlock had a clear policy of 'not seeking Government funding for service delivery' and instead sustained their activities by fundraising from grant giving trusts (Unlock, 2010: 14; see also 28). Unlock characterised participating in marketised service delivery as becoming an 'instrument of the state' (Bath, 2011: 16) and emphasised that 'the rhetoric of partnership in service delivery should not be confused with a relation-ship of equal partners' (Bath, 2011: 15). For Unlock, the contractual relationship between statutory agencies and voluntary organisations was that of: 'purchaser/ provider, master/slave' (Bath, 2011: 15). Unlock also had a campaigning role, giving a 'voice' to reformed offenders 'to influence discriminatory policies, behaviours and attitudes' (Unlock, 2010: 3). As such, Unlock engaged with stat-utory criminal justice institutions on a non-economic basis. They submitted a review of a draft leaflet for prisoners to the Parole Board, initiated a round table discussion with the Home Office and made submissions to the review of the Criminal Records Regime (Unlock, 2010: 20). The effects of these activities on policy-making are unknown, but it is notable that Unlock's service delivery and advocacy work have continued. Recent accounts illustrate that Unlock remains 'an independent charity that does not seek or receive money from government for delivering contracted services' and 'its strategic direction is determined by user need rather than statutory contract availability' (Unlock, 2014: 24).

Mills *et al.* (2011) provide a relatively optimistic analysis of voluntary organ-isations' ability to maintain their advocacy work amidst burgeoning involvement in the penal service market. The authors acknowledge the tension between receiving government funding and maintaining autonomy, but point out that 'despite the lack of funding for such activities, service provision organisations have found time and space to engage in advocacy' work (2011: 207). However, the case of the Revolving Doors Agency indicates that even this positive ana-lysis overstates the threat marketisation poses to voluntary organisations' cam-paigning roles. The Agency worked across England to improve services for people with multiple problems, including poor mental health, who are in contact with the criminal justice system. They established a new organisational model in 2010, the year that *Breaking the Cycle* was published, giving a 'greater focus in our work to influencing policy' by representing service users' views (Revolving Doors Agency, 2010: 7). The Agency obtained significant 'new model funding' from grants and trusts to enable them to carry out this advocacy work alongside service delivery (Revolving Doors Agency, 2010: 7, 11). This work to change systems and policy has continued and expanded, and the organisation's strategy is now 'focused on building understanding and commitment among political leaders and officials at national level and among a wide range of local leaders who have the power to change services in their area' (Revolving Doors Agency,

2014: 6). This is facilitated by their position of independence from 'any particular provider interest' (Revolving Doors Agency, 2014: 4).

Revolving Doors' shift towards campaigning and advocacy work may have been triggered by the tension between receiving state contract funding and campaigning to change penal practices, but has been in an unexpected direction. The well-versed risk of goal distortion involves organisations moving away from their original mission in the pursuit of contract funding, and compromising their campaigning and advocacy roles in favour of delivering services under contract to statutory organisations (Mills *et al.*, 2011: 207; Neilson, 2009: 407; Kendall, 2003: 78). Conversely, the Revolving Doors Agency's campaigning role has survived and flourished. It is therefore important to note that the expanding penal service market is not suffocating all organisations' campaigning roles. Although plausible for the few 'Big Players' such as Nacro (Neilson, 2009), this is not necesssarily true across the sector.[10]

Failing to explore counter-examples to voluntary organisations' subjugation through marketisation results in a partial and politically disabling account of the sector. Furthermore, it focusses discussion on the corporate-style 'Big Players' which may not be typical of the sector (Silvestri, 2009: 4; see also Corcoran, 2011: 41). These organisations have relatively large numbers of service users, but are few in number. Smaller voluntary organisations form the vast majority of the sector but are largely absent from existing literature (see Chapter 2). However, remaining outside the penal service market (either by choice or necessity) and having fewer service users neither renders these organisations extinct nor unworthy of scholarly attention. They should be examined on the same terms as the 'Big Players' (following the principle of generalised symmetry), and conclusions about their impacts should be drawn from evidence. The next section contextualises the following two analysis chapters by illustrating three different forms of relationship building between voluntary organisations and statutory criminal justice agencies.

4.5 Charitable relationships with statutory agencies

Preliminary analyses suggested that marketised, contractual relationships with the MoJ are not the only means through which voluntary organisations interact with statutory criminal justice agencies. After applying the principle of generalised symmetry, the subsequent, overlapping stage of ANT analysis involves analysing translations (Law, 1992: 380, 389). Reviewing policy and MoJ publications illustrated how macro level policy reforms can stimulate relationships between voluntary organisations and statutory criminal justice agencies. For example, the voluntary organisation Catch 22 participated in the PbR pilot scheme at HMP Doncaster (MoJ, 2012: 1). This pilot was influenced by *Breaking the Cycle*, which heavily promoted the use of PbR (MoJ, 2010). This translation is considered in detail in Chapter 6. However, it was less apparent how non-contractual relationships between voluntary organisations and statutory criminal justice agencies were built and operate.

It is unknown how the substantive funding from charitable trusts and foundations (as described in Section 4.3.3) translates into work with prisoners and probationers. As explained in Section 4.4, Fine Cell Work make no mention of intention to contract in their accounts, but produce needlework products with prisoners and their volunteers enter prisons (Fine Cell Work, 2010: 2–9). Document analysis does not explain how these interactions are facilitated, but the interview data demonstrated that relationships can be driven by:

- a smaller statutory criminal justice agency (e.g. an individual prison or probation trust) approaching a voluntary organisation;
- voluntary organisations approaching a statutory criminal justice agency.

Becoming aware of the range of interactions between charities and statutory criminal justice agencies through scoping the sector (or deploying uncertainties) enables these different interactions to be acknowledged and then examined symmetrically.[11] Following the principle of generalised symmetry, Chapter 5 analyses these smaller processes of translation on the same terms as the policy translation presented in Chapter 6. The significance of these different relationships for the effects of charitable work is then considered in Chapter 7.

This chapter has argued that a broader approach to studying the sector is required. It has moved beyond a marketised account and macro scale focus on policy reforms involving large voluntary organisations by applying the ANT principle of generalised symmetry to examine diverse charities on the same terms. This principle has been applied to consider charitable agency, the activities of relatively small voluntary organisations and non-marketised aspects of their work, in addition to involvement in macro scale market policy reforms. Key themes in this chapter have been charitable heterogeneity, scale, and agency, which are developed in the remainder of this book. Exploring these themes has demonstrated that the importance of marketisation for voluntary organisations across the penal voluntary sector has been overstated, and that voluntary organisations can still exercise their agency and pursue their organisational objectives. Moving beyond a macro scale, marketised account by assessing a wider range of voluntary organisations and their interactions with various statutory criminal justice agencies has laid the foundations for a more complete and politically enabling understanding of the sector (see also Hart, 2002; Zedner, 2002).

Notes

1 Action for Prisoners' Families ceased to trade on its own account on 30 September 2014 and its assets and liabilites were taken over by Family Lives, which will use remaining funds for the furtherance of the objectives of Action for Prisoners' Families (Action for Prisoners' Families, 2015). Family Lives work to improve outcomes for children and their families across the UK (not just prisoners' families) and have delivered the Offenders' Families Helpline since their merger with Action for Prisoners' Families (Family Lives, 2015).

2 There is a limited amount of published information available about this small organisation, but details can be found through the website: http://affect.org.uk/. Accessed: 19 October 2015.

3 Community Resettlement Support Project ceased to exist on 23 February 2016.

4 See http://affect.org.uk/about-u/. Accessed: 19 October 2015.

5 The purposes and restrictions of grants were not always explained in the accounts so this information cannot be included here.

6 See: www.inquest.org.uk/support. Accessed: 4 January 2013.

7 See http://affect.org.uk/about-u/. Accessed: 20 October 2015.

8 Contact Cheshire Support Group ceased to exist on 17 June 2015. The visitor centre at HMP Styal is now run by POPS.

9 This may be similar in the USA, where charities/non-governmental organisations cannot rely only on Department of Corrections funding because a small number of charities are granted most of the contracts for correctional services. Charities receive funds from many other governmental and private funding sources as well (Kaufman, 2015: 539).

10 Some further charitable lobbying will be affected by new rules on the spending of government grant funding which came into effect in May 2016. The new rules mean that grant funds from central government must not be used to lobby government and Parliament, although privately raised funds can still be used for campaigning.

11 Accounts cannot possibly examine every heterogeneity of the actor-networks that they analyse. However, even briefly acknowledging diversities can produce broader accounts and flag avenues for future research.

12 Voluntary organisations' documents were found through the Charity Commission website, where there is a 'Charity Search' function.

References[12]

Action for Prisoners' Families (2010) *Directors' and Trustees' Reports and Accounts for the Year Ended 31 March 2010.*

Action for Prisoners' Families (2015) *Directors' and Trustees' Reports and Accounts for the Year Ending 31 March 2015.*

Apex Trust (2010) *Trustees' Report and Unaudited Accounts for the Year Ended 31 March 2010.*

Apex Trust (2014) *Trustees' Report and Unaudited Accounts for the Year Ended 31 March 2014.*

Armstrong, S. (2002) 'Punishing Not-For-Profit: Implications of nonprofit privatization in juvenile punishment', *Punishment and Society*, 4(3): 345–368.

Bath, C. (2011) 'What Lies at the Heart of an Effective Relationship Between the Voluntary and Community Sector and Government?' in *Civil Dialogue: Ideas for better working between government and civil society*. London: Civil Exchange.

Benson, A. and Hedge, J. (2009) 'Criminal Justice and the Voluntary Sector: A policy that does not compute', *Criminal Justice Matters*, 77(1): 34–36.

Birth Companions (2010) *Trustees Annual Report and Financial Statements 31 March 2010.*

Carmel, E. and Harlock, J. (2008) 'Instituting the 'Third Sector' as a Governable Terrain: Partnership, procurement and performance in the UK', *Policy and Politics*, 36(2): 155–171.

Clean Break (2010) *Annual Report and Financial Statements.*

Clinks (2010) *Accounts for the Year Ended 31 March 2010.*

Community Resettlement Support Project (2010) *Trustees' Report and Annual Accounts 2009–2010.*

Contact Cheshire Support Group (2010) *Report of the Trustees and Unaudited Financial Statements for the Year Ended 31 March 2010 (Including annual report 2009–2010).*

Corcoran, M. (2009) 'Bringing the Penal Voluntary Sector to Market', *Criminal Justice Matters*, *77*(1): 32–33.

Corcoran, M. (2011) 'Dilemmas of Institutionalization in the Penal Voluntary Sector', *Critical Social Policy*, *31*(1): 30–52.

Corcoran, M. and Hucklesby, A. (2013) 'Briefing Paper: The third sector in criminal justice'. Available at: www.law.leeds.ac.uk/assets/files/research/ccjs/130703-thirdsec-crimjust-briefing-2013.pdf. Accessed: 12 August 2013.

Ellis Paine, A., Taylor, R. and Alcock, P. (2012) 'Wherever There is Money There is Influence: Exploring BIG's impact on the third sector'. *TSRC Working Paper 75*. Birmingham: Third Sector Research Centre.

Family Lives (2015) *Annual Report and Accounts for the Year Ended 31 March 2015.*

Fine Cell Work (2010) *Trustees' Report and Unaudited Accounts for the Year Ended 31 December 2010.*

FPWP Hibsicus (2010) *Report of the Trustees and Financial Statements for the Year Ended 31 March 2010.*

Garside, R. (2004) 'Who Delivers and Why it Matters', *Safer Society*, *21*: 7–9.

Garside, R., Silvestri, A. and Mills, H. (2014) *UK Justice Policy Review: Volume 3, 6 May 2012 to 5 May 2013*. London: Centre for Crime and Justice Studies.

Gojkovic, D., Mills, A. and Meek, R. (2011) 'Scoping the Involvement of Third Sector Organisations in the Seven Resettlement Pathways for Offenders'. *TSRC Working Paper 57*. Southampton: Third Sector Research Centre.

Hart, G. (2002) 'Geography and Development: Development/s beyond neoliberalism? Power, culture, political economy', *Progress in Human Geography*, *26*(2): 812–822.

Howard League (2010) *Annual Report 2009–2010.*

Joseph Rank Trust (2012) *Collaboration or Competition? Cooperation or Contestability?* Available at: http://theosthinktank.co.uk/research/theos-reports. Accessed: 7 June 2012.

Kaufman, N. (2015) 'Prisoner Incorporation: The work of the state and non-governmental organizations', *Theoretical Criminology*, *19*(4): 534–553.

Kendall, J. (2003) *The Voluntary Sector*. London: Routledge.

Kendall, J. and Knapp, M. R. J., (1995) 'Boundaries, Definitions and Typologies: A loose and baggy monster', in Davis Smith, J., Rochester, C. and Hedley, D. (eds) *An Introduction to the Voluntary Sector*. London: Routledge.

Langley House Trust (2010) *Annual Report and Financial Statements for the Year Ended 31 March 2010.*

Latour, B. (1999) 'On Recalling ANT', in Law, J. and Hassard, J. (eds) *Actor-Network Theory and After*. Oxford: Blackwell.

Latour, B. (2005) *Reassembling the Social: An introduction to Actor-Network Theory*. Oxford: Oxford University Press.

Law, J. (1992) 'Notes on the Theory of the Actor-Network: Ordering, strategy, and heterogeneity', *Systems Practice*, *5*(4): 379–393.

Maguire, M. (2012) 'Response 1: Big Society, the voluntary sector and the marketisation of criminal justice', *Criminology and Criminal Justice*, *12*(5): 483–505.

Meek, R., Gojkovic, D. and Mills, A. (2010) 'The Role of the Third Sector in Work with Offenders: The perceptions of criminal justice and third sector stakeholders'. *TSRC Working Paper 34*. Birmingham: Third Sector Research Centre.

Mills, A., Meek, R. and Gojkovic, D. (2011) 'Exploring the Relationship Between the Voluntary Sector and the State in Criminal Justice', *Voluntary Sector Review*, 2(2): 193–211.

Mills, A., Meek, R. and Gojkovic, D. (2012) 'Partners, Guests or Competitors: Relationships between criminal justice and third sector staff in prisons', *Probation Journal*, 59(4): 391–405.

MoJ (2010) *Breaking the Cycle: Effective punishment, rehabilitation and sentencing of offenders*, London: MoJ.

MoJ (2012) *Findings and Lessons Learned from the Early Implementation of the HMP Doncaster Payment by Results Pilot*. Available at: www.catch-22.org.uk/Files/hmp-doncaster-payment-by-results-pilot.pdf?id=275e92a7-3ce6-4604-8760-a118010ebb54. Accessed: 18 October 2013.

Nacro (2010) *Report and Financial Statements Year Ended 31 March 2010*.

Nacro (2011b) *Report and Financial Statements Year Ended 31 March 2011*.

Neilson, A. (2009) 'A Crisis of Identity: NACRO's bid to run a prison and what it means for the voluntary sector', *The Howard Journal of Criminal Justice*, 48(4): 401–410.

NEPACS (2010) *Report of the Trustees and Financial Statements for the Year Ended 31 March 2010*.

New Bridge (2010) *Annual Report 2010*.

Pact (2010) *Report and Financial Statements for the Year Ended 31 March 2010*.

Paxton, W. and Pearce, N. (2005) 'The Voluntary Sector and the State', in Paxton, W., Pearce, N., Unwin, J. and Molyneux, P. (eds) *The Voluntary Sector Delivering Public Services*. York: Joseph Rowntree Foundation.

Pollack, J., Costello, K. and Sankaran, S. (2013) 'Applying Actor-Network Theory as a Sensemaking Framework for Complex Organisational Change Programs', *International Journal of Project Management*, 31(8): 1118–1128.

POPS (2010) *Trustees' Report and Financial Statements for the Year Ended 31 March 2010*.

Prison Phoenix Trust (2010) *Financial Statements for the Year Ended 31 March 2010*.

Prison Reform Trust (2010) *Financial Statements 31 March 2010*.

Revolving Doors Agency (2010) *Trustees' Annual Report and Financial Statements for the Year Ended 31 March 2010*.

Revolving Doors Agency (2014) *Trustees' Annual Report and Financial Statements for the Year Ended 31 March 2014*.

Ryan, M. (2011) 'Counterblast. Understanding penal change: Towards the Big Society?' *The Howard Journal of Criminal Justice*, 50(5): 516–520.

Silvestri, A. (2009) *Partners or Prisoners? Voluntary sector independence in the world of commissioning and contestability*. London: Centre for Crime and Justice Studies.

St. Giles Trust (2010) *Financial Statements for the Year Ended 31 March 2010*.

Storybook Dads (2010) *Annual Report 2010*.

Tomczak, P. (2014) 'The Penal Voluntary Sector in England and Wales: Beyond neo-liberalism?' *Criminology and Criminal Justice*, 14(4): 470–486.

Unlock (2010) *Report of the Trustees and Financial Statements for the Year Ended 31 March 2010*.

Unlock (2014) *Report of the Trustees and Financial Statements for the Year Ended 31 March 2014*.

Unwin, J. and Molyneux, P. (2005) 'Beyond Transfer to Transformation', in Paxton, W., Pearce, N., Unwin, J. and Molyneux, P. (eds) *The Voluntary Sector Delivering Public Services*. York: Joseph Rowntree Foundation.

Women in Prison (2010) *Report of the Trustees and Financial Statements for the Year Ended 31 March 2010.*

Zedner, L. (2002) 'Dangers of Dystopias in Penal Theory', *Oxford Journal of Legal Studies*, 22(2): 341–366.

5 Charitable innovations in punishment

5.1 Introduction

Macro scale analyses of penal policy reforms and 'corporate-style' voluntary organisations that provide penal services under contract are undeniably important in conceptualising the penal voluntary sector. Some 'corporate-style' voluntary organisations have been greatly affected by recent penal policy reforms, as discussed in Chapters 2 and 6. But, macro scale analyses cannot provide an understanding of many charitable activities. It is unclear how relationships between charities and statutory criminal justice agencies are created when government procurement processes are not applied, e.g. where there is no contract funding provided for a service by the MoJ or another statutory agency. Given that the majority of contracts awarded to the voluntary sector appear to be held by a very small number of large organisations (Garside *et al.*, 2014; see Chapter 4), the mysterious process of how non-contractual relationships are built represents a significant gap in understanding.

This chapter addresses this gap, providing an analysis of how charitable programmes became established *on a small scale and informal basis* in prison and probation settings. These relationships are largely 'below the radar', featuring neither in recent policy discussions nor scholarship, thus meaning that an array of prison and probation work is not currently understood (Armstrong, 2002). But these small scale relationships could be where the sector undertakes some of its most valuable and innovative work (Martin, 2013; Mills *et al.*, 2012), with potential effects that include building social cohesion (Mills *et al.*, 2012), improving the experience of imprisonment (Liebling, 2004) and supporting desistance from crime (Burnett and McNeill, 2005). This chapter supplies a broad account of how relationship building (translation[1]) involving voluntary organisations and statutory criminal justice agencies could play out, both successfully and unsuccessfully. It illustrates the diversity of charitable interactions with prisoners, probationers and statutory criminal justice agencies, though it does not claim to be a representative account of these interactions. It depicts a range of relationships and analyses multiple translations, initiated both by local criminal justice agencies and individual voluntary organisations. It draws on data gathered from interviews with voluntary and statutory sector staff working in prisons and probation, and charitable publications and accounts documents. These different sources yielded different amounts and types of data, and case studies have been selected because there were substantive data available to illustrate them.

This chapter presents two key arguments. First, the MoJ was not the only statutory agency that initiates relationships with charities in relation to criminal justice. Smaller statutory criminal justice agencies also sponsored such relationships. Second, voluntary organisations were not merely being shaped to the demands of the penal marketplace by policy reforms, nor being appropriated by punitive and security agendas (Corcoran, 2012, 2011). Although this may be occurring for certain voluntary organisations, this chapter demonstrates that charities also affected the operation and experience of punishment in individual and local contexts, and had some impact on macro level agendas. Table 5.1 provides an overview of how the process of relationship building, or translation, could play out between voluntary organisations and statutory criminal justice agencies.[2] The four phases of this process are briefly explained in each section of this chapter and full details were provided in Chapter 3. While the four phases have been used to structure this chapter, it is important to note that the phases overlap and are interrelated.[3]

Helyar-Cardwell has pointed out that 'the issue of who delivers criminal justice services is important' (2012: 7). I would add that it is important to consider who delivers *which* penal services, and *who pays* for their delivery. Although a few larger charities are now involved in delivering core penal services under contract in England and Wales (e.g. Meek *et al.*, 2010; Neilson, 2009), the charitable work described in this chapter was principally optional *enrichment* rather than core custodial work (i.e. that required by Prison Service Orders, Prison Service Instructions and Probation Instructions). However, enrichment work can feed into core requirements. This analysis highlights what charities were doing, and were able to do, with prisoners and probationers in England and Wales in 2011–2012. This was shaped by various factors which operate at different scales and can change over time, e.g. the attitudes and needs of individual prison governors and probation gatekeepers, discourses about the roles of the penal voluntary sector, penal policies and the vision and initiative of individual charities. NOMS's benchmarking programme has recently introduced tighter specifications of which services should be provided, where, how, for whom and at what cost (Le Vay, 2015; Ludlow *et al.*, 2015). It is possible that there will be less local flexibility in penal service provision in future, particularly in core healthcare, education and resettlement services, due to the emerging new contractual model which has increased contracting through NOMS and the MoJ (Le Vay, 2015). However, custody contracts are expected to remain small and local (Le Vay, 2015), and, in the context of recent significant cuts to penal services and the resultant stretched prison systems (Ludlow *et al.*, 2015), it seems unlikely that the sort of charitable enrichment work described in this chapter will become undesirable to prisons and probation.

Table 5.1 Key events in translations

Phase[a]	Event	Description
Problematisation	Identification of the problem and actors *by a charity.*[b]	*Charity contacts* Prison/Probation.[d] Charity tries to interest the statutory agency and enable the charity to work with prisoners/probationers. The charity may try to interest the statutory agency in funding their work.
	Identification of the problem and actors *by a statutory criminal justice agency.*[c]	*Prison/Probation make contact* with a charity and try to interest them in the proposed project. The statutory agency may offer funding to interest the charity.[e]
Interessement	Interested actors submit to being integrated, negotiate the terms of the problematisation, or refuse the transaction.	Negotiations take place between charities and criminal justice agencies. The problematisation may be modified.
Enrolment	Elaboration of roles and responsibilities.	i) Relationship embedded in a *formal* contract, service level agreement or working protocol. ii) *Informal* agreement of protocols to be followed, roles and responsibilities.
Mobilisation	Reporting about charitable work with prisoners/probationers.	Publication of charities' annual reports and accounts.

Source: Gray *et al.*, 2009: 431.

Notes

a These phases guided the research but they are overlapping and inter-related. This table simplifies a complex process.

b Consortia of voluntary organisations may produce problematisations.

c The agencies of criminal justice may operate in partnerships e.g. the Police and Probation under MAPPA.

d This means all agencies running prisons and supervising (ex-)offenders on a statutory basis: there are private prisons and privatised prison services, and the Probation Service has recently been part privatised (MoJ, 2013b).

e External funders, e.g. charitable trusts and foundations, may also act in the translation, either alongside the problematisation or at an earlier stage of project development.

5.2 Defining shared problems: the problematisation phase

5.2.1 Introduction

Relationship building is analysed here using the ANT process of translation (see Chapter 3). This process begins with problematisations, in which project sponsors seek to define a set of problems that are of concern to various other actors

(Sage *et al.*, 2011; Callon, 1986). The research found two principal forms of problematisation: (i) statutory criminal justice agencies approaching voluntary organisations, and (ii) voluntary organisations approaching statutory criminal justice agencies, defining a problem of criminal justice and their proposed solution. The first set of relationships are broadly in line with the existing literature emphasising how statutory organisations drive charitable action, but the second set are notably different from current understandings of the sector, and show that voluntary organisations could instigate and implement programmes of work with prisoners and probationers.

5.2.2 Relationships initiated by statutory agencies

Three interview participants explained how they were approached with a problematisation or proposal sponsored by different local probation trusts (Kylie, Stan and Jane[4]). Each of these proposals resulted in successful translations, which saw three voluntary organisations coming to provide specific services for probationers. All three of the problematisations defined what the Trusts considered to be a problem with criminal justice, what the Trusts wanted the charities to do to resolve this problem (see Gray *et al.*, 2009: 430), and offered funding enabling the voluntary organisation to deliver this resolution for an initial period. This process is illustrated through the quotations below. In Kylie's case, the problem was the lack of support for high risk (ex-)offenders following release from prison. The proposed solution was for the probation trust and a local business organisation to fund Kylie's charity to deliver specific services. This was successfully translated and the charity began delivering services to support this 'problem' group. In Stan's case, the problem was the poor compliance of female probationers with the terms of their licences. The solution was to develop an alternative supervision environment for women on the charity's premises, encouraging compliance by removing barriers to their attendance. The charity was interested through funding to support the development of their project:

KYLIE: [Area] probation and the [area] Chamber of Commerce, they approached [our charity] at our head office, because there was a massive gap in provision for support for high risk ex-offenders. So initially we were jointly funded by Probation and the Chamber to provide ETE service, which is employment, training and education service, to high risk ex-offenders.

(Regional project manager)

STAN: I'm actually involved with a women's organisation in [area] and it's been partly set up by Probation.... They've given about £25,000.... How it started off initially is that Probation wanted a women-friendly centre from which to supervise their clients, because they'd identified a problem with the compliance of female offenders.... Basically women were feeling quite intimidated about coming in. You know what it's like, 8 out of 10 offenders are male, ... so women found it quite difficult. So they took a decision to say: 'well if we can support you in developing this women only-type centre, you allow us to supervise our female offenders there'.

(Statutory staff)

Stan's existing charity was supported and developed with funds from the local probation trust, in exchange for providing an all-female centre for supervision. Kylie's and Jane's charities were established with full state funding from local probation trusts, so these Trusts sponsored the problematisations both in terms of defining the problems to be solved and in financial terms. In both cases, this state funding was not renewed after the initial term, but both charities continued to operate by securing funds from other sources. Like Kylie's experience, Jane's charity also worked with high-risk (ex-)offenders following their release into the community. Jane's charity was initially fully funded by the local probation trust, but the charity were fully aware that this was one-off seed money. The condition that initial funding was only 'a start up' had been made 'clear' by the sponsoring probation trust. As such, the charity had focussed on securing other sources of funding to continue their work and had achieved this by the time that Probation funding ended. For Kylie's charity, the transition was less smooth. When the initial funding ran out, the specific employment, training and education services they had been delivering were put out to tender and subsequently taken over by a private company. The charity then withdrew their services for probationers entirely and shrank significantly due to the loss of funding, to the extent that their continued existence was in jeopardy. However, the charity ultimately secured lottery funding to continue working in that region and the organisation managed to survive, albeit working with a different group of (ex-)offenders:

JANE: When we first started in [year], [area] Probation ... gave us some, sort of, seed money to start. The first two years, [area] Probation gave us money, but they were clear that this was a start up. So from day one we started looking for other forms of funding. What we do is we go out and fundraise from other charities.... And we've just found out now, we've just been successful, we've had our funding extended for another three years.

(Regional project manager)

KYLIE: So that continued until [year] and then that contract ended and they didn't continue with that. So that was the end then of [our charity] working in this region with high-risk offenders. And there was uproar. You know, the probation officers had no-one to refer to, other organisations we dealt with were saying 'well, who's going to work with them?' and we were saying 'we're sorry but it's not our problem now, as much as we want to be doing it, if we're not being funded, then we can't do it'. And at that stage, I was on my own then. You know, staff had to be let go, another member of staff left because her job, there was no security really.... I was always aware that, if I didn't win more funding, that could be the end of [our charity] in this region, but then we won the lottery funding.

(Regional project manager)

The data presented in this section demonstrate that relationships with charities could be initiated and problematisations undertaken by statutory agencies other than the macro level MoJ, with these three examples relating to individual probation trusts. Stan, Jane and Kylie's charities also exemplified Garland's responsibilisation theory (2001; 1996) to some extent. In these three cases, charities were given a limited amount of state funding, which they supplemented or replaced with funds from non-state sources in order to continue delivering services to probationers. All three charities delivered services that were requested by their sponsoring probation trusts. For Stan, the state funding developed his charity rather than initiating it, but Jane and Kylie's charities were established using state funding and then had to find other funding to support their work. Both survived this complete withdrawal of state funding, but continued delivering the services requested by their respective probation trusts at their inception (but to a different client group in Kylie's case). This indicates that responsibility for crime control services was spread from the statutory probation trusts to these charities, which came to operate outside the criminal justice state and without state funding (Garland 2001: 124–125; see also Phoenix and Kelly, 2013: 422; Ilcan and Basok, 2004: 129–130; Garland, 1996: 454). However, many examples of charitable innovation which could not be explained by the responsibilisation thesis were also found. These are now explored.

5.2.3 Relationships initiated by charities

In contrast to the relationships explained in the last section, four interview participants explained that their charities successfully initiated relationships and sponsored problematisations by approaching individual prisons to 'offer their services' (Solomon, Holly, Sandy, Karen). These charities all provided enrichment activities for prisoners. The charities sought out and presented their individual problematisations to key actors in the prisons, *defining* specific 'problems' of criminal justice as the charities saw them and attempting to *interest* the prisons in enabling the charities to carry out their work with prisoners. The specific details of the problematisations and the means of interesting prisons varied across charities.

Solomon characterised his charity's approaches to prisons as 'a fishing expedition'. This process of 'fishing' often involved the charity's representatives approaching several different members of staff within one prison and repeatedly presenting their problematisation, in order to try to build a relationship with prison staff to enable their enrichment activity with prisoners, which could align with the objectives of various prison departments. Holly also referred to the persistence initially required to establish their charity's work in prisons and overcome prisons' resistance to allowing access:

SOLOMON: Erm, it's quite erm, ad hoc, how it is that we manage to work in different prisons. Some of the time [the charity's work is] run through the chaplaincy, some of the time through the education department, or the P.E. department or the drug rehab programme.... We know that there are certain positions that *we can go to*: head of learning and skills, or head of offender outcomes, sometimes the governor himself or herself. We can go to these people but we're not, *it's always a bit of a fishing expedition* (emphases added).

(Charity director)

INTERVIEWER: So, how are the links with the individual prisons established?
HOLLY: To begin with, [the charity's chief executive], [they] need a knighthood or something, because [they] really ... [they] kept on going until someone said yes. And without [their] dedication, you know, [the charity's work in prisons] wouldn't have happened.

(Central office project staff)

Although Solomon's charity had previously held larger ambitions about implementing their programme across the prison estate, their strategy then targeted individual prisons. Although this approach involves 'fishing', the charity found it was more likely to enable their work in individual prisons.

SOLOMON: We write, erm, periodically to [politicians], erm, and also to various MPs. Not so much any more expecting them to help us set up any kind of pilot project and then roll the whole thing out across the system because I don't think it works that way. In fact, somebody from the ... Trust told us that that idea of trying to develop a pilot project, a sort of model programme and then rolling it out just doesn't work, it isn't how things work,[5] it's sort of piecemeal and organic and word of mouth.

(Charity director)

The problematisations of different charities (and different projects run by the same charity) contained varying stakeholder *identities* and varying proposed *relationships between stakeholders* (see Sage *et al.*, 2011: 281; Gray *et al.*, 2009: 430). Although statutory criminal justice agencies do fund charitable work, this was not the case for any of the four charities described in this section. As such, these charities also had to present their problematisations to non-state funders in order to carry out their work (see also Chapter 4). In these problematisations, the identity of the prisons was not to fund the charity's work, but to enable it. This enabling role entailed providing charitable staff and/or volunteers with access to the prison and its prisoners, and in some cases, allowing charitable staff to take specific equipment inside prisons.

The prisons submitted to the terms of the charities' problematisations and enabled them to work with prisoners because of the benefits that charitable work offered to the prisoners and prison regimes. In the problematisations and proposed service delivery relationships, these benefits were offered to prisons without requiring a high investment of financial or human capital. For example, Sandy discussed how their charity could address prisons' family resettlement pathways[6] for them, without requiring a substantial financial investment from the prison. Similarly, Karen explained that her charity's activities were 'ideal' for prisons, as they contributed towards regime targets and improved order, again with minimal investment required from the prisons. These potential benefits and low costs encouraged prisons to allow charities access to prisons and prisoners, despite the inconvenience and security risks this posed:

SANDY: Actually one of the pathways that the Prison Service erm have to consider, because they've got 7 pathways that they're supposed to be addressing. You know there's drugs and, erm, money and budgeting and housing and things like that, and one of them is families. So for a lot of prisons, we are the, you know, we're addressing that pathway for them, without them having to invest a lot of money in it.

(Charity director)

KAREN: What they like is that we provide purposeful activity and they have certain targets to fill.... They have reducing reoffending targets, rehabilitation targets, purposeful activity targets and they need to meet them.... People who work in prisons know very well that if their prisoners have purposeful activities, then they behave themselves better.... We as a charity, virtually provide it for free, and obviously for prisons to do that for themselves costs them a lot of money.... If they just have a third sector partner coming in and doing it, all they have to do is agree to us having the [equipment] in, agree to us having volunteers and you know we basically run it for them. So for them it's ideal.

(Manager, central office)

This section has used interview data to illustrate that it is not only statutory criminal justice agencies that initiate relationship building: charities also act as *project sponsors*, defining shared problems that were of concern to both their charity and individual prisons. Examples of these shared problems were providing purposeful activity for prisoners and maintaining prisoners' family ties. Charitable work provided a means of resolving these shared problems and could offer benefits such as improving prisoner behaviour. The identity of the prisons in these problematisations was to allow the charities to carry out their work with prisoners, but not necessarily to fund it. In these four examples, the problematisations all ultimately led to working relationships (and successful translations) with one or more prisons, which, along with the financial support of nonstatutory funders, enabled the charities to carry out their work with prisoners. A more detailed 'case study' exploration of a problematisation sponsored by the charity Clean Break follows, which draws on data from their published documents.

5.2.4 Problematisation sponsored by a charity – the case of Clean Break

Clean Break is a charity working to reduce the unequal treatment of women compared to men in the criminal justice system. At the time of the research, they did this by providing a theatre production company and independent education programme, which aimed to support and empower female (ex-)offenders (Clean Break, 2010: 9). Their work was funded from a variety of state and non-state grants and contracts (Clean Break, 2010: 22). These included two large contracts from London Probation, an award from the Department for Business, Innovation and Skills, an Arts Council England Sustain Grant, and grants from charitable trusts and foundations (Clean Break, 2010: 22, 33, 34). This case study relates to one of their specific programmes of work: the Miss Spent programme, an arts-based education and training programme which was one of the only projects specifically designed for young women (ex-)offenders (14–21 years) available nationally at the time of the research (Clean Break, 2010: 11, 20).

Clean Break was established in 1979 by two women prisoners who 'believed that theatre could bring the hidden stories of imprisoned women to a wider audience' (Clean Break, 2010: 9). Clean Break defined a specific problem with criminal justice (unequal treatment of women) and constructed a specific solution to it (theatre and education). They noted that 'first-time women offenders are twice as likely as men to be sent to prison' and the prison population of black and minority ethnic women was three times greater than their proportion in the general population (Clean Break, 2010: 9). The charity worked to address these inequalities and created change directly, by empowering women who participated in their theatre and education programmes which 'develop personal, social, professional and creative skills leading to education and employment' (Clean Break, 2010: 9). This work was therefore deemed to effect 'profound and positive change in the lives of women offenders' (Clean Break, 2010: 10).

Clean Break also worked in the broader political context, campaigning for 'policies which recognise that the advancement of women's equality is advantageous for society as a whole' (Clean Break, 2010: 14). They stated that this advocacy work is 'at the core of (our) mission and embedded in our artistic and educational activity' (Clean Break, 2010: 11). Their campaigning work involved conference and research participation, media articles, contributions to policy development and government research into social inclusion and the arts (Clean Break, 2010: 11).

Clean Break presented this general problematisation to interested actors through different means. Particularly important actors were funders, gatekeepers in custodial settings and policy makers (Clean Break, 2010: 13, 20). Clean Break described presenting their problematisation through their theatre productions and running funders' breakfast events (Clean Break, 2010: 13). These events aimed to *interest* important actors by providing them with a better understanding of the charity's work, the role it could play in delivering high quality education and training for women (ex-)offenders, and its role in advancing the debate about the treatment of women by the criminal justice system (Clean Break, 2010: 13).

Clean Break also presented more specific problematisations which are of particular interest here. In 2010 the charity designated rolling out its Miss Spent programme into custodial settings as a *priority goal* (Clean Break, 2010: 20). The Miss Spent programme filled 'an important gap in gender-specific provision, leading to skills (and) qualifications' (Clean Break, 2010: 11). The charity trialled the programme in the community, undertook development work and contacted a range of custodial settings, such as juvenile units and Young Offenders Institutes, setting out this specific problematisation and attempting to interest gatekeepers to adopt the role defined for them by Clean Break (see Sage *et al.*, 2011: 281; Gray *et al.*, 2009: 430): i.e. enabling the Miss Spent programme to operate in custodial settings and funding it. This translation subsequently failed, because the gatekeepers in custodial settings did not submit to the terms set out by Clean Break, as is discussed in the following section.

5.3 Negotiating relationships and solutions: the interessement phase

5.3.1 Introduction

The second phase of the process of translation, interessement, is where the project sponsor attempts to standardise the identities of the other actors, as defined in the problematisation (Callon, 1986: 203). Actors enlisted by the problematisation can either submit to being integrated into the initial plan, or refuse the transaction by defining their interests differently (Callon, 1986: 203). The interessement entails trials of strength and refers to 'the on-going practical negotiations through which (the problematisation's) claims are tested, and almost always modified' (Sage *et al.*, 2011: 282). Data illustrating the negotiations and modifications involved in successful and unsuccessful interessements are explored in this section. An example of the unsuccessful Clean Break interessement is presented first, using data from the document analysis. This is followed by data from the interviews.

5.3.2 Unsuccessful interessement: Clean Break

The problematisation presented by Clean Break regarding its Miss Spent programme for young women was described in Section 5.2.4. This translation failed at the interessement phase. Clean Break reported 'considerable interest' from the custodial settings that they contacted (Clean Break, 2010: 20), so the professional curiosity of these actors was apparently engaged and they were interested in the problematisation to some extent (see Sage *et al.*, 2011: 281; Gray *et al.*, 2009: 430). However, 'many prisons' refused the transaction (Clean Break, 2010: 20, specific proportion not specified in the text) because of their inability to 'find full funding to buy into the programme ... largely due to cuts in prison education franchise contracts and the hours available for education activity for young offenders' (Clean Break, 2010: 20). The prisons did not submit to being integrated on the terms set out in the problematisation (which were to fund the programme, enable its operation in their setting and enable prisoners to participate) and so the translation failed at the interessement phase (see Callon, 1986: 203). Clean Break were, however, responding to this by continuing to work on securing 'interest and funding' to enable this programme to be rolled out (Clean Break, 2010: 21).

Clean Break subsequently had some success, obtaining a £41,000 grant from the Monument Trust which enabled the Miss Spent programme to run for ten young women in HMP Downview (Clean Break, 2011: 13, 15, 33). Although the programme achieved a 'strong' response, again Clean Break were 'unable to secure any funding towards Miss Spent from the prison as a result of reduced budgets for education activity in young offenders institutions', noting that 'ongoing financial pressures within custodial units, ... cuts to education provision and education staffing, (are) making it more difficult to support external course delivery' (Clean Break, 2011: 15). In 2011, Clean Break pledged to 'continue delivering (Miss Spent) in custodial settings wherever possible' and stated their intention to 'bring a version of the Miss Spent programme onsite to run alongside our adult women's programme' (Clean Break, 2011: 15).

In 2012 Clean Break again secured a restricted grant of £40,000 from the Monument Trust to deliver Miss Spent (Clean Break, 2012: 35). The year 2011–2012 saw the charity bring the course on site to their building in North West London (Clean Break, 2012: 2, 10). Although the programme was at that stage running in a revised form, this represents a modification of the original problematisation, which was for young women's custodial settings nationally to enable the Miss Spent programme to operate in their custodial settings and *fund it* (Clean Break, 2010: 11). Clean Break brought the course in-house following cuts within the prisons estate and subsequent difficulties in sustaining enrichment activities within it (Clean Break, 2012: 10). While the charity obtained limited funding, this was not from the custodial settings as planned and their aim of operating in custodial settings nationally was not achieved. In 2013 and 2014, Clean Break did not secure any income for Miss Spent or their relaunched young women's theatre programme, and failed to secure further funding from the Monument Trust (Clean Break, 2013: 7, 28, 29; Clean Break, 2014). Although Clean Break had significant success in other strands of their work from 2009–2014, the Miss Spent translation ultimately failed at the interessement phase because custodial settings did not agree to the terms set out in Clean Break's problematisation.

5.3.3 Successful interessements

None of the interview participants specifically referred to unsuccessful interessements, perhaps because participants were attempting to present their charities in a positive light. However, two interview participants (Solomon and Sandy) referred to successful interessements where they interested prisons, negotiated the terms of the problematisation, and ultimately carried out their work in prisons. The quotation from Solomon demonstrates how his charity lubricated the interessement process to support their work in prisons by building and maintaining relationships with prison staff, and trying to avoid inconveniencing staff who are gatekeepers for the institutions. Sandy's quotation explains that some initial difficulties were created by their equipment. This equipment was essential to carry out their enrichment work with prisoners, but posed a potential security risk. However, this obstacle was successfully negotiated by the charity and they gained access to prisons with their equipment:

SOLOMON: The work that we do in prisons is very much dependent on each individual prison saying: 'yes we'd like you to be running here and let us help you do it'.... We very much, you know, try to make the most of those personal relationships with prison staff that we have. And a big part of our work is about cultivating those relationships, you know, keeping friendly with them and trying to be sympathetic to the pressures that they're under, trying to offer what we offer in a way that doesn't cause disruption or headache to them, that fits in as smoothly, er, with them as possible.

(Charity director)

SANDY: At first it was quite difficult because of the nature of what we were doing, which was bringing in [specific] equipment into prisons ... you know, they're very security conscious. If you take a mobile phone in a prison you're in big trouble, because you can record on it.... I've got a good relationship with them now.... We do well and we abide by security, we've never caused any problems.

(Charity director)

Jacqui referred to a different trial of strength. Her charity provided enrichment activities to probationers, working in conjunction with the local probation trust. Jacqui explained how their engagement with Probation followed a trial of strength, in which her charity clearly expressed its principles about not directly participating in 'punishment' as they defined it. The charity saw their role as 'offering support' to women (ex-)offenders and prioritising their wellbeing, and refused to become directly involved with what they saw as the punitive and security aspects of Probation work. In practice, there is no bright line between punishment and wellbeing work. Services such as education, training and employment, in which (ex-)offenders' attendance is recorded and non-attendance can be reported to custodial or supervision staff, perhaps fall in the middle ground between punishment and wellbeing. But, Jacqui's charity had set and adhered to their own sphere of involvement in punishment:

JACQUI: We always work from the position that women's *wellbeing*, I guess, takes priority.... We've been very, erm, forthright I guess (laughs) is probably the word, in saying that: 'these are things that we will do and these are things that we won't do'.... As an organisation we've always said that we don't want to be part of the punishment. Erm, which is I guess why we don't do things like erm, like unpaid work and those kind of things. So we don't have anyone tidying our gardens (emphasis in recording).

(Regional project manager)

This section has outlined some of the negotiations and trials of strength which occurred during the interessement phases of relationship building between multiple charities and prisons/probation trusts. The interessement between Clean Break and various custodial settings failed because the prisons did not submit to Clean Break's requirement that they fund the work and the charity did not manage to find substantive alternative funding. By contrast, three interview participants explained how their charities successfully constructed relationships with a probation trust or prisons. The devices of interessement used by charities included: building relationships with prison staff, refusing to compromise on their required equipment but abiding by prison security procedures, and clearly stipulating the terms of their engagement with probationers before commencing relationships. The following section examines the next phase of relationship building – enrolment – in which different actors form a relationship and elaborate upon their various roles and responsibilities.

5.4 Forming relationships: the enrolment phase

5.4.1 Introduction

Enrolment occurs when multiple interests are successfully translated into an actor-network with a common goal (Callon, 1986: 206). This section considers the processes through which charities and statutory criminal justice agencies became enrolled into actor-networks with a common goal, by exploring the ultimate agreement and the negotiations which preceded it. This section illustrates that enrolment may occur either formally, e.g. where the relationship between statutory and voluntary sectors actors is embedded in a 'working protocol' or contract, or informally, through an informal agreement between charities and criminal justice agencies. The data presented below also demonstrate that charitable programmes may not be formalised (formally inscribed or stabilised) but nevertheless operate successfully over time. Data from the document analysis are explored first, followed by the interview data.

5.4.2 Formal textual enrolments

The published documents provided information about *formal* textual enrolments and inscriptions, such as service level agreements and contracts between charities and criminal justice agencies. Formal enrolments between prisons and the charities NEPACS and Pact are discussed in this section. NEPACS worked 'to provide excellent services for the children of prisoners', which are important because 'the maintenance of family ties is fundamental in any later process of rehabilitation and resettlement' (NEPACS, 2010: 7). Their accounts explained how the charity has 'developed *service level agreements* with the Prison Service ... in relation to the delivery of services to prisoners' families' (NEPACS, 2010: 3, emphasis added). NEPACS specifically referred to their service level agreements to provide Visitor Centres in five prisons in the north-east of England (NEPACS, 2010: 4, 5). These agreements formalised and *inscribed* the terms of the relationship between the charity and the prison, and represented the joint *enrolment* of these actors in an actor-network of service delivery. Following ANT, as this relationship has been formally inscribed in a textual agreement, its durability is increased and it is more likely to endure than a relationship which has not been inscribed into a shared social or textual memory (Sarker *et al.*, 2006: 55; Law, 1992: 387), at least until any break point or the enaction of any break clause in the textual agreement.

The service level agreements set out the terms of the enrolment, under which NEPACS operated the prison Visitor Centres on a 'cost recovery' basis (NEPACS, 2010: 4). However, this inscribed relationship was not entirely stable (see Sarker *et al.*, 2006: 55; Callon, 1986: 219). NEPACS noted that 'there are frequent delays in payments by the Prison Service (MoJ) during which time staff and suppliers have to be paid' (NEPACS, 2010: 4). Furthermore, the service was dependent upon volunteer workers, and any shortfall in volunteer numbers required NEPACS to meet the cost of employing paid staff in order to 'ensure continuity of provision' and comply with the terms of the service level agreement (NEPACS, 2010: 4). The Visitor Centres run by NEPACS were also likely to go out to tender in the future (NEPACS, 2010: 4). Although the charity was 'well placed to be awarded the contract', the uncertainty surrounding the outcome of the tendering process presented 'a threat' to their operations (NEPACS, 2010: 4). The potential competitive tendering for regional Visitor Centres remained a risk and an uncertainty for the charity over several years, although they continued to operate their Visitor Centres in the north-east of England (NEPACS, 2011: 8, 2012: 4, 2013: 3, 2014: 3).

None of the interview participants referred to enrolments which involved *formal* contracts being signed. However, Morris explained that his charity had drawn up a 'working protocol' to support their work with (ex-)offenders in the community. As most of these (ex-)offenders were released on licence, the charity had to have a working relationship with Probation. The charity also worked with high-risk sex offenders, so had a working relationship with the police. Although there was not a financial relationship between the charity and these statutory criminal justice agencies, the working protocol has similarities to formal and contractual relationships. Morris's charity works in a markedly different way to its statutory partner agencies, but had evidence that their approach was safe and successful. Drawing up the working protocol entailed a 'hard-ball' process of negotiation (or interessement), which then resulted in a relatively durable enrolment. This relatively formalised agreement and inscription of the relationship was, however, unique among the interview participants:

MORRIS: The model we have is to put a group of sex offenders in a house, so it's a therapeutic home.... What the police do is they consider that they will feed off each other's proclivities. But we see completely the opposite.... What we've done is we've got a working protocol. So we've acknowledged that we come from completely opposing positions.... We've run this successfully for 18 years.... Nobody then has committed a sexual offence as far as we know since they've left us.... We know that because of the records.... So they grudgingly said, 'Ok we'll work with you provided'. And it's the provisos that are listed in the protocols. Erm, it was quite an interesting *hard-ball* negotiation (emphasis in recording).

(Charity director)

An example of de-inscription was found in the secondary data from the charity New Bridge. De-inscription is when an actor previously associated with an actor-network goes on to sever their ties (see Chapter 3). New Bridge supported 'some of the most isolated and troubled men and women in our prisons' (New Bridge, 2010: 6) and in 'doing so they have saved lives, changed lives and restored hope where there was no hope' (New Bridge, 2010: 3). In their accounts, New Bridge explained that they had started working at HMP and YOI Swinfen Hall in 2004 (New Bridge, 2010: 17). Until August 2010, Swinfen Hall prisoners were offered support both in prison and upon release through New Bridge's 'Mentoring Service' (New Bridge, 2010: 17). However, this work ceased in August 2010 due to 'cuts in the prison budget' (New Bridge, 2010: 17). The prison withdrew their funding to support the mentoring service and so New Bridge withdrew it from the prison. This example illustrates that translation always remains a process (see Callon, 1986: 219), and even fairly long-standing relationships such as New Bridge's Mentoring Service may fail if an enrolled actor later rejects the identity set out for them in the problematisation (e.g. as a funder) and a new agreement cannot be reached. Enrolments other than formal textual enrolments are now considered.

5.4.3 Informal enrolments

The accounts of Pact indicated a *variety of enrolments* between the charity and statutory criminal justice agencies. Pact had formal contracts with the MoJ to run visitor centres at fourteen prisons, on a 'prison-by-prison basis' (Pact, 2010: 13, see also 30). Pact were also formally commissioned by NOMS to develop a 'new model of prison-based family support' which involved piloting Pact's 'Model Family Support Worker Programme' at HMPs Bristol, Belmarsh and Wandsworth (Pact, 2010: 8). There were further strands in the charity's operations in which the nature of the enrolment was not clear but appeared to be *informal*. Pact's accounts detailed their 'Play in Prisons' initiative, which was developed in conjunction with three Devon prisons (HMPs Channings Wood, Dartmoor and Exeter) and enabled by 'generous funding' from the Big Lottery Fund (Pact, 2010: 8). This initiative involved prison gyms being 'transformed into family play areas' and saw 'games and sports-based family visits' being introduced along with 'table-top activity schemes' (Pact, 2010: 8). The charity must have negotiated with these prisons and the Big Lottery Fund to gain access and funding for this initiative. However, the enrolments between the charity and these prisons do not appear to have been formally inscribed, although they may have gradually become inscribed in the institutions' social memories (see Sarker *et al.*, 2006: 55; Law, 1992: 387).

A variety of informal arrangements were found in the interview data. Four participants explicitly indicated that their working relationships with partner criminal justice agencies had not been inscribed in a formal arrangement. Solomon pointed out that his charity had no formal agreement with the Prison Service or individual prisons, and rather relied on informal arrangements with the individual prisons that they worked with. Stan's charity had a financial arrangement with a local probation trust (as explained in Section 5.2.2 above). Although probation's expectations of the charity had been communicated to them and discussed, their roles and responsibilities had not been inscribed in a text:

SOLOMON: There's, it's not, we don't have, er, any kind of formal agreement at, er, a national level, or a regional level with the Prison Service at all, erm the work that we do in prisons is very much dependent on each individual prison.

(Charity director)

STAN: It's not like a competitive tendering process. So Probation will expect us to deliver certain things, but it won't be written into some payment-by-results type contract. ... There are a number of projects that've been funded from a pot of money, I think about £15 million nationally that's gone to the voluntary sector, so that's quite structured.... We're doing it without any formal funding from the Corston pot.

(Statutory staff)

These relatively *informal enrolments* were echoed by Adrian and Sandy. Adrian explained that their charity worked in a prison as a 'small, local agency', without any financial input from the prison. The charity did not have an explicit or settled agreement (enrolment) setting out roles, responsibilities and monitoring/ assessment mechanisms for their work. Similarly, Sandy explained that their charity's work had expanded without ever establishing a formal contract or service level agreement with the prison. It was particularly interesting that both of these participants expressed uncertainty about the extent of such informal relationships between charities and prisons. Adrian suspected that similar arrangements might affect a number of small, local charities, but Sandy incorrectly assumed that their interaction was anomalous, being 'different from every other organisation that works in a prison' under a contract or service level agreement:

ADRIAN: They don't pay us, we don't have, like when you look at the sort of bigger agencies who have like contracts and things like that, they have very firmly tied down contracts which say 'we can do this, you do that, this is how it works', you know, 'we'll monitor it like this'.... As a small, local agency, I suspect we're not alone in that kind of relationship with the prison that we work in.

(Charity director)

SANDY: We're a bit of an anomaly ... we kind of grew without any *formal* arrangement being in place. Er, and it's been the way ever since.... We're different from every other organisation that works in a prison, whether it be drug projects, or families, you know, organisations that work with families, or whatever, they've got, they're contracted in and they've got a service level agreement and that's how they operate. And with us it's different, you know.... We don't have any formal real arrangements as such (emphasis in recording).

(Charity director)

Quantitative data about the extent of these relationships based on informal enrolments have not been gathered here. Such relationships may operate largely 'below the radar' of academic and policy awareness about charities' interactions with criminal justice agencies (and even charities' awareness, as in the case of Sandy). However, informal relationships could be the *modus operandi* through which these actors often engage (Martin, 2013). Although these interview data are not representative of the sector, only one of the thirteen participants (Morris) referred to formalising the enrolment following negotiations between actors (the interessement). Given that grant-making trusts may be 'the most significant funder – amongst charities working in the criminal justice system' (Joseph Rank Trust, 2012: 5), it is possible that many charitable programmes funded by grants are not formalised or inscribed in a service delivery contract or agreement.

Relationships based on informal enrolments may be considered more fragile than relationships which have been formalised or inscribed in contracts or texts. When relations are inscribed in inanimate materials such as texts they have more chance of lasting longer (Law, 1992: 387). Relationships can, however, also be inscribed in the social memory (Sarker *et al.*, 2006: 55) and habitual informal relationships can be relatively durable, e.g. as there is not a contract with an end date and as they can over time become accepted and unquestioned practice. The informal enrolments described in this section certainly have some durability. For example, Sandy stated that the charity's staff carried keys and thus could move relatively freely around the prison. The prison has therefore enrolled the charity's work to some extent by issuing the key and embodying the relationship in an inanimate object. Likewise, Adrian explained that their charity's staff had gate passes enabling them to access the prison, and some staff members also held keys:

SANDY: I mean I go out around the prison because we have to go and fetch them (prisoners) and bring them up to us, and because they can't get anywhere because of the keys.

(Charity director)

ADRIAN: You know, if we want to bring new people in we have to get a gate pass, if we want to do this, that or the other we have to get keys, some of our people hold keys so they can get round the prison.

(Charity director)

The lack of a formal contract or substantive agreement with the prison did also have some advantages, being linked to flexibility and autonomy for charities. Retaining informal relationships with the prisons offered benefits in terms of enabling the charity to innovate. For Sandy, their informal relationship with the prison had not caused problems so far, and the shared interests of both actors had sustained this relationship in an 'unspoken' way. This was different for Adrian, who explained that their charity's operations were not formalised in or protected by a contract. As such, their charity was relatively unprotected and their continued operations were 'left at the whim' of governing and lower level governors. This could make things 'quite difficult' for the charity if a disagreement or trial of strength occurred:

SANDY: There's such a lot of bureaucracy and red tape to do with prisons and it would have hampered our progress and our growth.... We've grown so fast and so efficiently.... I think that's because we've been able to do what we do without getting too involved with, you know, with the bureaucracy of the Prison Service.... I've got a good relationship with them (the host prison) now.... They just let us get on with what we're doing.... They just leave us alone. ... We're helping them to maintain family ties, which is what they wanna do. So it's kind of, it's sort of like an unspoken symbiosis.

(Charity director)

ADRIAN: And in some ways it means we can kind of say 'oh we'd like to do this', and, you know, we're not sort of tied down.... Bigger agencies who have like contracts and things like that, they have very firmly tied down contracts.... Which gives them a lot of protection in some ways.... What happens is the prison spots something or somebody sees something and goes 'oh I don't think I want that to happen', and then they just go, 'you can't do this any more', and that's the end of it.... You can kind of go 'well I think that's really important' and they go 'mmm well we don't' and that is pretty much the end of that.

(Charity director)

This section has explored both informal and formal enrolments and inscriptions that exist between charities and statutory criminal justice agencies. It was not clear from the data whether formal inscriptions such as service level agreements and working protocols were created at the request of charities or statutory agencies. Although formal enrolments had a relatively high durability in some ways, they retain some instabilities and the translations may still fail (see Callon, 1986). Informal arrangements may have drawbacks for charities, but can also provide flexibility and enough durability to endure. The extent of these informal relationships cannot be estimated from this data set but there are indications that they are not a rarity amongst charities working with prisons and probation (see also Martin, 2013; Joseph Rank Trust, 2012). These informal relationships are therefore deserving of recognition and further analysis.

It may be that operating 'below the radar' of academic and policy awareness enables charities to work with prisoners flexibly and operate relatively unhindered by prison bureaucracy. The same may be true for charities that work with probationers, although their base outside the secure and heavily regulated prison environment may mean this argument is less relevant. It is, however, also possible that the limited awareness of charitable work undertaken informally *limits awareness of possibilities for charitable resistance* to problematic penal policies. If, as Martin argues, 'there can *hardly be a prison in the country* that could continue to work as it does if there was a large scale collapse of voluntary, community and social enterprise services for people in custody' (2013: no pagination, emphasis added), charities potentially have significant capacity to challenge, modify and resist penal practices. If the power of the penal apparatus to regulate and/or transform the convicted *depends on and operates through* charitable work (see Carrabine, 2000: 319) to the extent that Martin suggests (2013), charities could have profound powers to protest and bargain for penal change. Charities may be self-censoring in order to maintain their access to prisons, or due to not being aware of their combined significance within prisons. However, the unrecognised significance of informal charitable work in prisons may offer the potential to express more dissent, particularly if done collectively by like-minded charities. Large scale or collective charitable resistance could potentially disrupt the translation of penal power (see Martin, 2013: no pagination re. the extent of charitable involvement in criminal justice; see Carrabine, 2000: 319 re. the translation of penal power) and stimulate penal reform in a way that smaller scale campaigning work cannot. However, this awareness should be 'handled with care', because another potential effect of increasing awareness of informal charitable work, particularly within prisons, could be making such work subject to greater regulation. This could hinder the operation of 'informally' run charitable enrichment activities for prisoners and probationers, which could negatively impact upon these already marginalised groups (see also Chapter 7). The next section expands this idea.

5.5 Being the spokesperson: the mobilisation phase

Mobilisation refers to an actor becoming the spokesperson for other actors in the network (Callon, 1986). The spokesperson is a powerful macro actor that can translate the interests, roles and relations of the entire network (Callon and Latour, 1981). Similarly, materials and processes of communication (e.g. writing) can order networks through space, creating mobile translations that act at-a-distance to translate the interests of an actor-network (Law, 1992: 387). This section considers how charities mobilised the actor-network of their operations, referring to two interview participants (Holly and Karen) and the case study of Storybook Dads from the secondary data.

Holly explained that their charity created mobile translations which acted-at-a-distance as it became more established, because non-human actors began to carry out the charity's problematisation on its behalf. The charity's website and items produced by prisoners through the enrichment activity increased the durability and mobility of the actor-network, embodying the charity's work in inanimate materials which went on to act on their behalf (see Law, 1992: 387). The charity's website and the material presence of prisoners' creations increased awareness of the charity's work amongst prison officers and further prisoners, and ultimately came to speak for the charity. As such, the durable materials of the website and products removed the charity's previous need to keep 'going until someone said yes', to interest prisons in their work and enable it to be carried out with prisoners (Holly; see also Section 5.2.3). Likewise, the work of Karen's charity gained mobility over time (see Law, 1992: 387). Awareness of their work compounded over their fifteen years of operation and 'word of mouth' now acts for the charity, meaning that they no longer have to undertake 'a lot of knocking on doors' to present their problematisation to prisons and enable their work with prisoners:

HOLLY: They (prisons) come to us. ... Now, I think it's much more that they see and we have a very good website, so they see what we produce, what individuals can achieve. ... So we have a profile that people would like to have.

(Central office project staff)

KAREN: I've been in the job a year and a half and in that time we've had about forty-five, forty-six requests from prisons who want us to start there. So, basically we (pause) don't need to approach them. It's kind of a word of mouth thing because we've been around for about fifteen years now. Erm, I know in the early days it involved a lot of knocking on doors.

(Manager, central office)

Turning to the secondary data, an interesting case study of mobilisation was provided by the charity Storybook Dads. Storybook Dads' programme addressed the damage that imprisonment does to the ties between parents in prison and their children in the outside world, enabling imprisoned parents to record stories and messages for their children which were then edited and presented as a gift (Storybook Dads, 2010: 4, 5). The charity had no direct campaigning or advocacy role. Their work was funded by 'grant giving trusts' (Storybook Dads, 2010: 12, see also 18) rather than individual prisons, NOMS or the MoJ. The idea for Storybook Dads was not an initiative from the MoJ, Prison Service or an individual prison but was developed by Sharon Berry when she was volunteering in HMP Channings Wood (Storybook Dads, 2010: 11). In 2002, she successfully operationalised the charity in HMP Dartmoor and became its chief executive (Storybook Dads, 2010: 11). HMP Dartmoor did not give direct financial support to the charity, but provided offices within the prison, which formed a base for its headquarters (Storybook Dads, 2010: 3, 12, 18).

The problem with punishment that Storybook Dads set out in their *problematisation* was the damage that imprisonment does to the ties between parent and child. They pointed out that 'half of all prisoners lose contact with their families completely' (Storybook Dads, 2010: 5). By way of solution, Storybook Dads' work enabled imprisoned parents[7] 'throughout the UK to maintain meaningful contact with their children', and provided 'the opportunity to reduce the damage done to their child as a result of the forced separation' imposed by imprisonment (Storybook Dads, 2010: 4). The charity *interested* actors by pointing out the value of their work in reducing the 'stress and trauma experienced by the children of imprisoned parents', and enabling imprisoned parents to help develop their children's literacy skills (Storybook Dads, 2010: 4). Prisoners could also gain valuable parenting, literacy and computer skills through producing and editing the recordings (Storybook Dads, 2010: 4).

As such, Storybook Dads' programme was argued to 'greatly increase outcomes' for parent and child (Storybook Dads, 2010: 4). These outcomes were improved through enhancing the literacy skills of both parent and child, and reducing children's feelings of 'abandonment, shame and isolation, which can in turn lead to anti-social behaviour and delinquency' (Storybook Dads, 2010: 4, 6). Improved family ties were also 'inextricably linked with reduced re-offending' when prisoners are released (Storybook Dads, 2010: 4), with prisoners that maintain family contact being 'up to *6 times less likely to re-offend*' (Storybook Dads, 2010: 5, emphasis in original). Overall, Storybook Dads deemed their work to provide 'social and financial benefits to society (which) are immeasurable' (Storybook Dads, 2010: 4). Their problematisation pointed out the consequences imprisonment can have for prisoner's families and explained the short and long term effects of these problems for society (e.g. by leading to anti-social behaviour). They also illustrated the value of their work with prisoners, in terms of improving their skills and reducing the likelihood of recidivism. These factors illustrated how the charity's work addresses a problem shared by, or relevant to, any actor concerned with preventing crime.

Storybook Dads mobilised their actor-network through their website, published annual report and accounts documents, and spoke on behalf of the prisoners and prisons that participated in their work. Storybook Dads explained that their work was enabled by a number of heterogeneous interested actors. These were cited as 'our loyal and hard-working team of Trustees, staff, volunteers and prisoners at our HQ in HMP Dartmoor'; and, at other prisons throughout the country, many ' librarians, prison officers, teachers, chaplains, civilian volunteers and prisoners' that supported the charity's work 'on top of an already busy schedule' (Storybook Dads, 2010: 3). 'Grant-giving Trusts' and 'members of the public' had financially supported their work, and 'publishers, authors and illustrators' had allowed the charity to use their books (Storybook Dads, 2010: 3).

Storybook Dad's annual report and accounts document went far beyond the minimum information needed to comply with the Charity Commission's regulatory requirements and acted to increase the durability and mobility of the actor-network. This document illustrated both the rationale for the charity's work and how it positively affects prisoners' children and broader society. These effects were explained through quotations from prisoners that have participated in the programme (Storybook Dads, 2010: 5, 7, 9) and prisoners' family members (Storybook Dads, 2010: 6). By pointing out the enabling roles played by all of the actors[8] which supported the charity in their website, published annual report and accounts documents, the charity became *spokesperson* for the heterogeneous actors that formed part of its actor-network of service delivery.

Through this document, the charity *identified and spoke for* all of the heterogeneous actors that enabled Storybook Dads' work. Charities cannot work to directly implement compulsory changes to penal regimes to the extent that the MoJ is able to. However, the extensive information provided in Storybook Dads' annual report and accounts publication spoke for and *translated* the interests, roles and relations of their entire actor-network of operations (see Carrabine, 2000; Callon and Latour, 1981). This document and the charity's website also acted to interest new actors that are affected by recidivism and interested in how its work could improve outcomes for prisoners, their children and broader society. Important 'new' actors were principally prison coordinators, who could support Storybook Dads' work without having to fund it (Storybook Dads, 2010: 10) and members of the public who could financially support the its work. Indeed, the charity expressed their hope that 'our increased PR will increase public donations' to fund further work (Storybook Dads, 2010: 12).

All charities have some sort of spokesperson role, which mobilises their work to some extent. Every charity with an income in excess of £25,000 must publish their accounts annually to meet the requirements of the Charity Commission, and charities also usually publish annual reports and have websites. These published documents contain varying levels of information. Some charities present very detailed accounts and reports, which furnish extensive information about their activities (as in the case study of Storybook Dads above). Others publish only minimal numerical accounts and do not speak for their work nor their actor-network of activities, beyond meeting the Charity Commission's minimum regulatory requirements. However, *the interests that charities are able to mobilise* in these individual publications and organisational websites, without compromising their service delivery operations, may be, or be perceived to be, limited.

For example, it is notable that the Storybook Dads publication did not criticise the practice of imprisonment, nor any aspects of the carceral regime (Storybook Dads, 2010). It focussed solely on the value of Storybook Dads' work as an *optional* regime enrichment activity, which would ideally spread further through the prison and young offender estate with the support of individual members of prison staff, donations from the public and income from *non-state* funders. There was no attempt to influence policy-making or practice at a level beyond *individual prison staff* (at the micro scale), who could choose to support the charity's work in addition to their already busy schedules (Storybook Dads, 2010: 3).

The interview data also supported this notion. For example, Adrian indicated that charities might only feel able to *mobilise certain aspects* of their organisational interests if they wished to maintain a service delivery relationship with prisons. This difficulty was not necessarily the result of the recent further marketisation of penal services nor the pursuit of contract funding (Mills *et al.*, 2011; Neilson, 2009). While the uncertainties associated with this contract culture may have increased general nervousness amongst charities, the inherent difficulty of gaining access to secure prison environments was deemed responsible. Adrian illustrated how attempting to mobilise a charity's campaigning interests could jeopardise their ability to continue delivering their services in prisons. Despite noting a plethora of concerns about the treatment of their women prisoner service users 'who have got really severe mental health problems and shouldn't be anywhere near a prison', Adrian's charity was unlikely to try to mobilise their campaigning interests in future:

ADRIAN: I don't think we'll be doing any kind of campaigning, because it's very, very difficult to campaign and work in a prison at one time, because prisons are very, very thin-skinned.... They get really, really, really twitchy if people criticise them.... People who deliver services,... while they may say: 'this is what we think and this is what's important', they don't do much actual full on campaigning.... As soon as you say there's a problem with it, *it's difficult*.... I think it is a very difficult environment for the Prison Service ..., so I think they are very touchy about the the charities that they, as they see it, let into their prisons, getting inside knowledge and then using it to criticise them publicly (emphasis in recording).

(Charity director)

This participant explained that the apparent conflict between campaigning and service delivery roles was particularly prominent for *penal* voluntary organisations. Adrian argued that it was easier for *voluntary organisations outside criminal justice* to mobilise their campaigning interests without compromising their service delivery activities. As such, she thought that the organisational model of undertaking both campaigning and service delivery activities was far less prominent within the penal voluntary sector than in the general voluntary sector:

ADRIAN: I think in this sector, because I've worked in a couple of sectors ... within the voluntary sector, there's a much bigger divide between erm (pause) campaigning organisations and service delivery organisations. So the campaigning organisations, people like the Howard League for Penal

Reform and people like that, they don't deliver *any* services. And people who deliver services, including people like us, but also quite big people like St Giles ... they don't do much actual full-on campaigning. And I think outside of the penal sector, you get much more combined (pause). So if you think of people like AdAction, they do a combination of campaigning and service delivery, as do people like the NSPCC. And I don't think that model exists so much within the criminal justice sector, because it's difficult. Because as soon as you, if you're gonna campaign about something, you're basically saying: 'it should be better' and as soon as you're saying it should be better, you're saying there's a problem with it (emphasis in recording).

(Charity director)

A similar sentiment was echoed by Jacqui, who described 'choosing their battles' with the statutory criminal justice agencies, but at a smaller scale than the campaigning work described by Adrian. Jacqui's ability to mobilise the interests of the charity, and the form of their general interactions with statutory staff, were constrained by the apparent need to maintain positive working relationships with all criminal justice agencies, in order to avoid potentially disadvantaging the charity's service users. In line with Adrian, Jacqui echoed the perceived need to behave particularly carefully with prison staff, due to their ability to remove prisoners' access to charitable support services and the uniquely restricted conditions of access to prisons. The delicate balances that charities created between their service delivery and campaigning interests could explain why informal charitable activity with prisons and probation remained 'under the radar', as described above:

JACQUI: For me to fall out with that person's probation officer, with that prison officer, with that prison health and advice worker, the only person who's gonna be affected is that woman. And particularly around prisons, you have to be very careful about choosing your battles with the prison. And how you respond to things or do anything, the worst thing really is to piss off that prison, to really piss off that prison governor, to the point where they can say 'actually, I don't want you in my prison any more'. It's just about making sure that you have those really positive working relationships and are able to think, maybe if I took this to prison, nothing's gonna get resolved, it's not kind of worth putting in actually. So we're quite careful.

(Regional project manager)

It therefore seemed that there is a 'service delivery paradox' for penal voluntary organisations. They saw a need for penal services but were unlikely to obtain state funding to provide them. They could not demand or realistically hope to initiate a large-scale roll out of their services. In order to be able to deliver services they felt unable to be too critical of punishment, although this could apply less to charities that work outside the secure environment of the prison and is potentially the result of limited awareness of the significance of informal charitable work in prisons. This apparent paradox created a very limited area of activity and constrained charitable campaigning activity. However, these constraints do not seem to be a problem of marketisation, as suggested by Neilson (2009: 406), but appeared to be a result of the closed prison environment. It is unclear whether this constrained campaigning activity is based on actual or perceived risks, i.e. whether charities are censored by custodial environments or they are self-censoring. As explained above, greater awareness of informal charitable presences in prisons may offer a powerful means of disrupting the translation of penal power. Nevertheless, despite the difficulties that charities experienced in increasing the durability and mobility of their translations involving statutory criminal justice agencies, charities did manage to continue engaging with prisoners and probationers through what they considered to be the most important means. Charities could even go on to significantly scale up their service delivery operations over time and win statutory support. This is illustrated in the next section, which provides a case study of a particularly successful translation which was sponsored by a charity.

5.6 Translation case study

Section 5.2 above explored relationships (or translations) which were initiated (or sponsored) by charities that approached a local criminal justice agency, such as an individual prison. This case study is also an example of a relationship initiated by a charity, but is particularly interesting because it began in one prison and then significantly increased in scale, gaining partial MoJ funding. This case study draws on data from an interview with Kelvin, a Manager based in the charity's central office. It demonstrates that charities should not be reduced to biddable agents of service delivery being shaped by penal policy reforms, as argued by Corcoran (2011) and Carmel and Harlock (2008, see also Chapter 2). This analysis illustrates that charities can affect macro level actors such as the MoJ.

Kelvin represented a charity whose work (and the problematisation that they present to interested actors) addressed a shared problem: the lack of employment opportunities for prisoners after release, which contributes to reoffending. This charity worked 'to reduce the rate of reoffending and to make sure that people get out (from prison) into work almost straight away and *don't come* back' to prison (Kelvin, emphasis in recording). They did this by providing training and education within the prison, followed by resettlement support post-release. The training and education was linked to a specific industry in which ex-prisoners had a relatively good chance of securing work. The charity's director sponsored the initial problematisation, approaching the host prison and seeking to interest them in the project by emphasising how the lack of effective work training in prisons links to recidivism:

KELVIN: It was the brainchild of [the charity's director] ..., [they] came up with the idea about seven or eight years ago ... [they] saw an opportunity, ... and decided it'd be a sort of fabulous opportunity to give the guys some serious training, doing something completely different where they actually get *proper* work that's more likely to actually get them off the streets, and keep them out of trouble, and get them high-level jobs (emphasis in recording).

The role of the prison set out in the initial problematisation was to host the project and enable the charity to work with prisoners approaching release. The charity's work was principally funded by grants and trusts, rather than the MoJ or the host prison: 'We don't get anything given to us, there's no government money spent in what we do.... We apply for grants here there and everywhere' (Kelvin). The project worked with prisoners approaching their release date, 'who have got six to eighteen months left to serve' and tried to'put them through as many of the qualifications as we can' (Kelvin). The charity had also established a successful partnership with a general employment charity that supported the prisoners' resettlement and worked to place them in jobs upon release:

KELVIN: We have engaged with [voluntary organisation] who will come in a month before any one person is due to be released, and try to get them an interview, and hopefully line them up with a job for when they are released. They will meet them at the gate, take them to their new accommodation should they require it and also take them to their new place of work.

An important feature of this charity's work was its sustained contact with prisoners after their release into the community. This work was carried out in partnership with their partner voluntary organisation and involved meeting with ex-prisoners 'weekly at their place of work to see how they're getting on' (Kelvin). Taking this approach meant problems could be identified quickly and dealt with, even finding alternative employment if required. Kelvin pointed out high reoffending rates: 'I think the current statistic is 70 per cent reoffend within the first year of release'. But, the 'graduates' of this project had a reoffending rate of less than 5 per cent: 'Out of the 75 people that we've had released since starting in [year], we've only had three reoffend. And the majority of them are still working'[9] (Kelvin). The continuing personalised support and interaction with prisoners after release was cited as a crucial and unique quality of the charity's work:

KELVIN: Basically the difference between us and everyone else is that we have the on-going aftercare. So a lot of the other things you can do, once you're released you're just left on your own with a list of contact numbers, you can call these people, these people'll help ..., but it's just all done by us from cradle to grave. And we stay in contact with them, and we bring them to our events to show success stories, we do write-ups on them, etcetera. And, yeah, that's why it's working.

The charity mobilised their actor-network through their website, published annual report and accounts documents, which included prisoner 'success stories' explaining how the charity had helped individuals turn their lives around. The charity had also gained significant press coverage, and had applied for and won a number of awards, which all expanded their spokesperson role. When the interviews were conducted in 2012, this charity had recently undergone a significant expansion from their original host prison onto two further prison sites and secured some funding from the MoJ:

KELVIN: We will be getting part-funding from the MoJ on the future sites, which will make life a little bit easier for us, but erm yeah, otherwise we'll still be raising a lot of the money ourselves and getting funding from various other sources.

By 2015 the charity had grown further onto a fourth prison site. This demonstrates that charities are not just affected by (or subject to) macro scale translations and the will of policy makers, but can make some impact at the macro scale, in this case undergoing a rapid and significant expansion of their operations enabled by MoJ support and funding.

The analysis presented in this chapter and in Chapter 4 has illustrated the independence and autonomy found amongst penal voluntary organisations. These charities must construct and maintain relationships with prisons and probation trusts, and their activities are bounded by penal protocols such as prison security procedures. It is however inaccurate to reduce charities to biddable subjects of macro level penal policymaking. This section has demonstrated how an enrichment programme initiated and designed by a charity was successful in tripling (and then quadrupling) its size and gaining some MoJ funding to support its work. Furthermore, voluntary organisations have previously lobbied and 'fought a hard battle' on behalf of prisoners' families (Silvestri, 2009: 4). As a result of these efforts, the needs of prisoners' families and their part in reducing recidivism 'have now been widely accepted and – to a degree – addressed by public policy' (Silvestri, 2009: 4). Charities therefore can make some impact at the macro level of penal policy and their work can be recognised by the MoJ. Following the principle of generalised symmetry, the next section explores the opposite effect, or how broader modes of regulation can affect practices at the micro level (Carrabine, 2000).

5.7 Broader modes of regulation

Data from three of the interviews indicated how macro level penal policy can affect charitable operations at the micro level. Kylie explained that funding could be easier to secure if working with a 'priority group', as identified by contemporary policy. Kylie detailed how she had seen policy makers identify a 'priority group', which was then often prioritised by 'other grant sources' such as grant-making trusts and foundations. Although there is a separation between state funding and the trusts and foundations, this shows how broader modes of regulation, such as policy identifying priority-recipient groups, can affect charitable work at the micro level. This 'trickle down effect' should not be assumed or overstated, however. Kylie explained how her charity had previously worked with male (ex-)offenders, but had lost funding for that work. They subsequently 'homed in' on the priority group of women, which enabled them to win funding in the aftermath of the Corston Report's emphasis upon the needs of females (Home Office, 2007):

KYLIE: What you find is, it will come from the Home Office, government, to say 'right, this is the priority that we want to work with now', so all the money seems to go to that priority group, whether it's young offenders, women offenders or whatever, and then the money's available from other grant sources, who say, 'right this is the priority group now'. So it's a case of homing in on that, and trying to get the applications in to win that funding.... The results from the Corston report gave us evidence and scope to have additional funding, to have more staffing hours just to concentrate on the women's centre, which we won earlier on in the year.

(Regional project manager)

Two interview participants also indicated that the macro level discourse of marketisation might be 'trickling down' to affect charitable work at smaller scale. Adrian explained that the charity had worked in only one prison for many years, but was now trying to expand its services into a further prison. Its work had previously been undertaken at no cost to the MoJ or host prison, and had been supported by charitable trust and foundations. However, if the charity did manage to expand its operations, it intended to stipulate that state funding must be provided in exchange for its services. This significant change to the prison's identity in the charity's problematisation could be *linked to the policy discourse* of further marketising penal services, e.g. in *Breaking the Cycle* (MoJ, 2010; see Chapter 6). This discourse has perhaps created the expectation that charitable work should involve a financial relationship with statutory criminal justice agencies. However, this quotation also illustrates another possibility for resistance. If charities are indeed 'giving prisons' substantial services 'for free' (Adrian), they are perhaps shoring up and financially supporting problematic carceral regimes. Withdrawing these services could therefore interrupt the translation of penal power, as explained in Section 5.4.3, but again this might have negative consequences for prisoners in terms of losing services:

ADRIAN: We are looking to potentially expand our services into either [names prison] or [names prison], but if we did that we'd make them pay. Partly because they're private prisons and partly because we can't just keep giving prisons all these things for free.

(Charity director)

Karen explained that her charity was seeking to build partnerships with other charities. The attempt to 'scale-up' operations by constructing relationships with a larger charity may simply make good business sense for a charity that believes in the value of its own work and wishes to benefit from economies of scale. However, it may also be linked to the policy discourse of marketisation, within which only large charities can hope to compete:

KAREN: We are currently building, you know, trying to build relationships with other organisations in the sector, because it seems like often we're doubling up the effort, and especially now that its harder and harder to get funding, if you can gang together with another organisation, especially if they're a bit bigger, then erm, you can achieve a lot more. Erm, for example, [name] Trust, I have good contacts there, good relationships there and we hope to do something with them. That kind of thing really, but yeah, we hope to do more of that in the future.

(Manager, central office)

Without negating the agency and heterogeneity of charities, or their diverse relationships with statutory criminal justice agencies, this section has illustrated some of the ways in which macro level modes of regulation (such as the privatisation of previously public services and the implementation of service delivery contracts involving consortia of private and voluntary sector organisations) may 'trickle down', to affect charitable activity at the micro scale. However, the degree of this impact should not be overestimated and it is important to note that the effects of marketisation upon many charities appear to be relatively limited.

5.8 Discussion

This chapter has demonstrated the limitations of a purely marketised account of the penal voluntary sector and illustrated how charities exercise their agency. Relationships between charities and statutory criminal justice agencies could be sponsored by individual criminal justice agencies, such as a single probation trust, approaching and subsequently responsibilising a charity to deliver a specific service. However, charitable work was not solely driven by statutory agencies. This chapter has examined how relationships between charities and statutory criminal justice agencies could be *initiated by charities*, by approaching individual statutory criminal justice agencies and sponsoring translations. While macro level reforms and discourses may 'trickle down' to affect charitable practices at the micro scale, the potency of the former should not be overestimated or assumed, and conversely charities can affect some change at the macro level, e.g. by gaining MoJ recognition for their work or affecting penal policy.

The extent of small scale and often informal relationships between charities and statutory criminal justice agencies appears to be significant, although such relationships seem to operate 'below the radar' of academic and policy awareness. Exploring smaller scale relationships in addition to the effects of macro level policy translations provides a more theoretically complete understanding of how charitable activities can affect the operation and experience of punishment in individual contexts. These smaller scale relationships may also facilitate valuable and innovative charitable work. In addition, gaining a better understanding of the extent of small scale charitable work raises possibilities for collective resistance to problematic penal practices, although the perceived conflict between service delivery and campaigning roles for penal voluntary organisations may constrain campaigning work. Following the principle of generalised symmetry, the next chapter considers how macro scale policy reforms can bring about relationships between charities and statutory criminal justice agencies.

Notes

1 Translation is the process through which multiple heterogeneous actors are integrated into a specific actor-network (Latour, 2005: 106–108). Chapter 3 provides a full description.
2 Private companies also run prisons, deliver prison and probation services and operate community rehabilitation companies alongside statutory criminal justice agencies. Relationships between voluntary organisations and private providers of penal services are not examined here, due to the research constraints of limited existing literature, time and resources. But this is not to suggest that such relationships do not exist. Indeed, future research could examine the relative presence, activities and funding of voluntary organisations in public and private prisons.
3 As noted in Chapter 1, the analytical approach applied in this chapter, i.e. using the four-phase process of translation, has far wider applicability for studying how different agencies work together. This could be utilised to study other criminal justice settings and programmes, e.g. the multi-level processes through which providers other than specific core prison authorities come to work in individual prisons. This approach may apply to charitable work in other areas, e.g. with local authorities. In addition, this approach offers a useful means of studying relationship building and negotiations between charities and statutory/private criminal justice agencies in other jurisdictions.
4 In the interview data, pseudonyms have been used and the names of individual agencies have been removed.
5 The receptiveness of prisons to pilot programmes of reform, and the importance of an evidence base indicating programme efficacy in determining its expansion both vary across jurisdictions and times.
6 There are seven resettlement pathways (Home Office, 2004): accommodation; education, training and employment; mental and physical health; drugs and alcohol; finance, benefits and debt; children and families; and attitudes, thinking and behaviour. Charities may be commissioned at a local and regional level to provide resettlement services (Gojkovic *et al.*, 2011) but state funding is not always available to charities whose work is relevant to the resettlement pathways.
7 The charity also worked with imprisoned women under the name 'Storybook Mums' (Storybook Dads, 2010: 12).
8 Non-human actors e.g. prison buildings, computers used for editing recordings and books containing stories also acted in this translation. Whilst this is acknowledged, the role of these non-human actors is not the focus of this analysis.
9 Reoffending rates vary between different groups of prisoners and are linked to multiple variables such as having accommodation, educational level and family contact and support (May *et al.*, 2008). It is important to note that prisoners that are selected for and participate in interventions such as this charitable programme are already likely to have characteristics associated with desistance from crime. This does not discount the value of the programme, but means that figures indicating its efficacy should be interpreted with caution.

References

Armstrong, S. (2002) 'Punishing Not-For-Profit: Implications of nonprofit privatization in juvenile punishment', *Punishment and Society*, *4*(3): 345–368.

Burnett, R. and McNeill, F. (2005) 'The Place of the Officer–Offender Relationship in Assisting Offenders to Desist from Crime', *Probation Journal*, *52*(3): 247–268.

Callon, M. (1986) 'Some Elements of a Sociology of Translation: Domestication of the scallops and the fishermen of St Brieuc Bay', in Law, J. (ed.), *Power, Action and Belief: A new sociology of knowledge?* London: Routledge.

Callon, M. and Latour, B. (1981) 'Unscrewing the Big Leviathan: How actors macrostructure reality and how sociologists help them to do so', in Knorr-Cetina, K. and Cicourel, A. V. (eds), *Advances in Social Theory and Methodology: Toward an integration of micro and macro-sociologies*. Boston: Routledge and Kegan Paul.

Carmel, E. and Harlock, J. (2008) 'Instituting the "Third Sector" as a Governable Terrain: Partnership, procurement and performance in the UK', *Policy and Politics*, *36*(2): 155–171.

Carrabine, E. (2000) 'Discourse, Governmentality and Translation: Toward a social theory of imprisonment', *Theoretical Criminology*, *4*(3): 309–331.

Clean Break (2010) *Annual Report and Financial Statements 31 March 2010.*

Clean Break (2011) *Annual Report and Financial Statements 31 March 2011.*

Clean Break (2012) *Annual Report and Financial Statements 31 March 2012.*

Clean Break (2013) *Annual Report and Financial Statements 31 March 2013.*

Clean Break (2014) *Annual Report and Financial Statements 31 March 2014.*

Corcoran, M. (2011) 'Dilemmas of Institutionalization in the Penal Voluntary Sector', *Critical Social Policy*, *31*(1): 30–52.

Corcoran, M. (2012) 'Be Careful What You Ask For: Findings from the seminar series on the Third Sector in criminal justice', *Prison Service Journal*, *204:* 17–22.

Garland, D. (1996) 'The Limits of the Sovereign State: Strategies of crime control in contemporary society', *British Journal of Criminology*, *36*(4): 445–471.

Garland, D. (2001) *The Culture of Control: Crime and social order in a contemporary society*. Chicago: University of Chicago Press.

Garside, R., Silvestri, A. and Mills, H. (2014) *UK Justice Policy Review: Volume 3, 6 May 2012 to 5 May 2013*. London: Centre for Crime and Justice Studies.

Gojkovic, D., Mills, A. and Meek, R. (2011) 'Scoping the Involvement of Third Sector Organisations in the Seven Resettlement Pathways for Offenders'. *TSRC Working Paper 57*. Southampton: Third Sector Research Centre.

Gray, D., Graham, A., Dewhurst, Y., Kirkpatrick, G., MacDougall, L., Nicol, S. and Nixon, G. (2009) 'Scallops, Schools and Scholars: Reflections on the emergence of a research-oriented learning project', *Journal of Education for Teaching*, *35*(4): 425–440.

Helyar-Cardwell, V. (2012) 'A Changing Landscape', in Helyar-Cardwell, V. (ed.) *Delivering Justice: The role of the public, private and voluntary sectors in prisons and probation*. London: Criminal Justice Alliance.

Home Office (2004) *The Reducing Re-offending National Action Plan*. London: Home Office.

Home Office (2007) *The Corston Report: A report by Baroness Jean Corston of a review of women with particular vulnerabilities in the criminal justice system*. London: Home Office.

Ilcan, S. and Basok, T. S. (2004) 'Community Governance: Voluntary agencies, social justice and the responsibilisation of citizens', *Citizenship Studies*, *(8)*2: 129–144.

Joseph Rank Trust (2012) *Collaboration or Competition? Cooperation or Contestability?* Available at: http: //theosthinktank.co.uk/research/theos-reports. Accessed: 7 June 2012.

Latour, B. (2005) *Reassembling the Social: An introduction to Actor-Network Theory.* Oxford: Oxford University Press.

Law, J. (1992) 'Notes on the Theory of the Actor-Network: Ordering, strategy, and heterogeneity', *Systems Practice*, 5(4): 379–393.

Le Vay, J. (2015) *Competition for Prisons: Public or private?* Bristol: Policy Press.

Liebling, A., with Arnold, H. (2004). *Prisons and Their Moral Performance: A study of values, quality, and prison life.* Oxford: Oxford University Press.

Ludlow, A., Schmidt, B., Akoensi, T., Liebling, A., Giacomantonio, C. and Sutherland, A. (2015) *Self-inflicted Deaths in NOMS' Custody Amongst 18–24 Year Olds.* Cambridge: RAND Europe.

Martin, C. (2013) *Dazzled by the Fireworks: Realising detail in the overwhelming scale of reform.* Clinks Blog Post. Available at: www.clinks.org/community/blog-posts/dazzled-fireworks-realising-detail-overwhelming-scale-reform. Accessed: 25 May 2013.

May, C., Sharma, N. and Stewart, D. (2008) *Factors Linked to Reoffending: A one-year follow-up of prisoners who took part in the Resettlement Surveys 2001, 2003 and 2004.* London: Ministry of Justice.

Meek, R., Gojkovic, D. and Mills, A. (2010) 'The Role of the Third Sector in Work with Offenders: The perceptions of criminal justice and third sector stakeholders', *TSRC Working Paper 34.* Birmingham: Third Sector Research Centre.

Mills, A., Meek, R. and Gojkovic, D. (2011) 'Exploring the Relationship Between the Voluntary Sector and the State in Criminal Justice', *Voluntary Sector Review*, 2(2): 193–211.

Mills, A., Meek, R. and Gojkovic, D. (2012) 'Partners, Guests or Competitors: Relationships between criminal justice and third sector staff in prisons', *Probation Journal*, 59(4): 391–405.

MoJ (2010) *Breaking the Cycle: Effective punishment, rehabilitation and sentencing of offenders.* London: MoJ.

MoJ (2013b) *Transforming Rehabilitation: A revolution in the way we manage offenders.* Available at: https://consult.justice.gov.uk/digital-communications/transforming-rehabilitation. Accessed: 17 October 2013.

Neilson, A. (2009) 'A Crisis of Identity: NACRO's bid to run a prison and what it means for the voluntary sector', *The Howard Journal of Criminal Justice*, 48(4): 401–410.

NEPACS (2010) *Report of the Trustees and Financial Statements for the Year Ended 31 March 2010.*

NEPACS (2011) *Report of the Trustees and Financial Statements for the Year Ended 31 March 2011.*

NEPACS (2012) *Report of the Trustees and Financial Statements for the Year Ended 31 March 2012.*

NEPACS (2013) *Report of the Trustees and Financial Statements for the Year Ended 31 March 2013.*

NEPACS (2014) *Report of the Trustees and Financial Statements for the Year Ended 31 March 2014.*

New Bridge (2010) *Annual Report 2010.*

Pact (2010) *Report and Financial Statements for the Year Ended 31 March 2010.*

Phoenix, J. and Kelly, L. (2013) ' "You Have to Do It for Yourself" Responsiblization in youth justice and young people's situated knowledge of youth justice practice', *British Journal of Criminology*, 53(3): 419–437.

Sage, D., Dainty, A. and Brookes, N. (2011) 'How Actor-Network Theories Can Help in Understanding Project Complexities', *International Journal of Managing Projects in Business*, 4(2): 274–293.

Sarker, S., Sarker, S. and Sidorova, A. (2006) 'Understanding Business Process Change Failure: An actor-network perspective', *Journal of Management Information Systems*, 23(1): 51–86.

Silvestri, A. (2009) *Partners or Prisoners? Voluntary sector independence in the world of commissioning and contestability*. London: Centre for Crime and Justice Studies.

Storybook Dads (2010) *Annual Report 2010*.

6 (In)voluntary control

6.1 Introduction

The publication of *Breaking the Cycle* Green Paper (MoJ, 2010) was the beginning of a macro level process of penal reform.[1] Among multiple reforms, this process expanded the *spatial and temporal reach of carceral power and control* through the introduction of a new twelve-month mandatory statutory supervision requirement (hereafter 'supervision requirement') for all prisoners sentenced to less than twelve months in custody (Tomczak, forthcoming). Short-sentence prisoners are now formally supervised 'for the first time in recent history' (MoJ, 2013c: 6), which is predicted to result in 13,000 additional offenders being recalled to custody annually at a cost of £16 million (Prison Reform Trust, 2013: 1). This chapter explores how charities acted as agents of social control, enabling and justifying this macro level process of penal reform through involvement in two prison-based PbR[2] pilots at HMPs Peterborough and Doncaster. These pilots initially emphasised voluntary participation, rehabilitation and resettlement, but led to significant expansions in carceral power and social control.

Analysing the process of translation[3] which followed *Breaking the Cycle* (MoJ, 2010) demonstrates how new marketised connections based upon PbR were created between the MoJ and penal voluntary organisations, resulting in expanded control. By studying the construction of connections, *processes of organising* can be grasped (see Porsander, 2005: 18). As such, this analysis illustrates some of the processes and interactions through which penal sevice delivery was reconfigured, control was expanded and the powerful MoJ was able to be powerful (see Carrabine, 2000: 313). It demonstrates how diverse members of the penal system (including voluntary organisations) were involved in translating thought and action through discourse and practice, but also the accommodations, alliances, struggles and separations that occurred (Carrabine, 2000: 319). While illustrating the critical role of voluntary organisations in extending the regulatory power of the penal apparatus, following the principle of generalised symmetry this chapter also explores how voluntary organisations affected and opposed certain developments and resisted the expansion of carceral control. These control effects are also problematised in Chapter 7.

In summary, *Breaking the Cycle* stressed the role for the voluntary sector in delivering 'more effective' penal services (e.g. MoJ, 2010: 10, 14, 15, 25, 27, 31, 35, 38, 41) and described a new mode of delivering 'more effective' (or marketised) penal services, via the PbR pilot scheme at HMP Peterborough, which was facilitated and legitimised by charities. This stimulated a further PbR pilot at HMP Doncaster, which was again facilitated and legitimised by charities. These pilots then both fed into the publication of *Transforming Rehabilitation: A Strategy for Reform* (MoJ, 2013c) which continued *Breaking the Cycle*'s trajectory, stressing that the market in penal services would be further opened up to public, private and voluntary sector providers, and assigning a central role to PbR as a means of improving competition, performance and effectiveness in penal service delivery (MoJ, 2013c). The process of reform culminated in the Offender Rehabilitation Act 2014, which introduced the twelve-month mandatory statutory supervision requirement for all prisoners sentenced to less than twelve months in custody.[4]

To map this translation, a series of MoJ publications were collated (MoJ, 2015a, 2015b, 2015c, 2013a, 2013b, 2013c, 2012a, 2011a, 2011b, 2010; see also Social Finance, 2011). Charitable responses to *Breaking the Cycle* and *Transforming Rehabilitation: A Strategy for Reform* were also examined (Howard League, 2013, 2011; Prison Reform Trust, 2013, 2011b; Nacro, 2011; St Giles Trust, 2011). This data was then compared to Callon's four-phase process of translation (as explained in Chapter 3) and existing applications thereof (principally Sage *et al.*, 2011; Gray *et al.*, 2009; Carrabine, 2000). Table 6.1 provides my overview of how this macro level process of relationship building, or translation, played out between statutory criminal justice agencies and voluntary organisations. The four phases of translation are briefly explained in each section of this chapter and full details were provided in Chapter 3. While the four phases have been used to structure this chapter, it is important to note that they overlap and are interrelated.

6.2 Defining shared problems: the problematisation phase

Translation begins with problematisations, in which project sponsors seek to define a set of problems and specific solutions that are of concern to various other actors (Sage *et al.*, 2011; Callon, 1986). *Breaking the Cycle* Green Paper was published on 7 December 2010 and represented a problematisation sponsored by the MoJ. The MoJ defined a shared problem in criminal justice, which was high rates of recidivism following release from prison, and detailed a specific solution, which was trialling PbR to pay penal service contractors drawn from the public, private and voluntary sector. This translation was principally a top-down initiative, operating from macro level national policy networks to affect organisation at a smaller scale.

High rates of recidivism following release from prison meant that 'most criminals continue to commit more crimes against more victims once they are released back onto the streets' (MoJ, 2010: 1). High rates of recidivism occured

Table 6.1 Key events in the translation[a]

Phase[b]	Event	Description
Problematisation	Identification of the problem and identification of actors.	The MoJ publish *Breaking the Cycle*.
Interessement	Interested actors submit to integration or refuse the transaction.	MoJ consultation on its proposals and publication of responses by interested public, private and voluntary sector organisations.
	Technology experimentation.	PbR pilot schemes (including HMPs Peterborough and Doncaster).
Enrolment	Elaboration of roles and responsibilities.	Contract negotiation and signing for PbR pilot schemes: roles and responsibilities specified, assessment mechanisms devised.
Mobilisation	Spokesperson reporting.	MoJ publish results of the interessement and PbR pilot schemes. MoJ publish *Transforming Rehabilitation* strategy.
		Extension of control through the new mandatory supervision requirement for short-sentence prisoners.

Source: Gray *et al.*, 2009: 431.

Notes

a In this chapter one translation was studied, whereas in Chapter 5 multiple translations were analysed.

b These phases guided the research but they are overlapping and inter-related. This table simplifies a complex process.

regardless of high criminal justice spending: 'despite a 50 per cent increase in the budget for prisons and managing offenders in the last ten years almost half of all adult offenders' and '75 per cent of offenders sentenced to youth custody' reoffended within a year of release from custody (MoJ, 2010: 1). As such, the MoJ characterised the criminal justice system as 'an expensive way of giving the public a break from offenders, before they return to commit more crimes' (2010: 1). The MoJ presented these high rates of recidivism as a shared problem, affecting individuals and groups across society by threatening the 'safety and security of the law-abiding citizen' who 'has a right to feel safe in their home and their community' (MoJ, 2010: 1). The apparent long term threat caused by young offenders was also emphasised: 'if we do not prevent and tackle offending by young people then the young offenders of today will become the prolific career criminals of tomorrow' (MoJ, 2010: 1). The MoJ connected these problems of criminal justice to the economic recession, stating the imperative to reduce the cost of punishment and emphasising their organisational commitment to 'playing its part in reducing spending to return the country to economic growth' (2010: 8). By focussing on the immediate and long term negative effects of recidivism and high criminal justice spending, the MoJ set out the problem of the expensive and failing criminal justice system in a way that other interested groups could (and should) relate to.

The MoJ proposed to rectify this shared problem through a 'rehabilitation revolution' in criminal justice (MoJ, 2010: 1). This revolution demanded that penal services were further marketised and decentralised, using the PbR contract mechanism to encourage offender rehabilitation. The situation of high spending yet enduring high rates of recidivism was explained by one fundamental failing of past criminal justice policy and practice: 'the lack of a firm focus on reform and rehabilitation' (MoJ, 2010: 1). As a result, 'significant amounts of money have been spent on punishing and rehabilitating offenders without properly holding providers to account for results' (MoJ, 2010: 38). PbR ostensibly offered the solution, by increasing accountability and incentivising service providers from all sectors to innovate and improve their effectiveness at 'reducing reoffending' (MoJ, 2010: 10, see also 6, 12, 38).

Actors implicated in solving the recidivism problem included 'everyone who can make a contribution' to the rehabilitation revolution (MoJ, 2010: 5). The voluntary sector was specifically implicated alongside the public and private sectors, and local partnerships of service providers, who all could and should 'compete in new markets' in criminal justice (MoJ, 2010: 2), thus playing their role in improving public safety and reducing the economic burden of criminal justice. In a powerful piece of rhetoric, these proposals were held to provide 'a once in a generation opportunity for providers from all sectors to work together to make a real difference' to both criminal justice and public safety (MoJ, 2010: 9), with the rehabilitation revolution promising to 'change those communities whose lives are made a misery by crime' (MoJ, 2010: 6). The Green Paper proposed a very specific means of resolving the shared recidivism problem (see Gray *et al.*, 2009: 430). In order to bring this revolution about, improve safety and generate 'savings to the taxpayer' (MoJ, 2010: 1), the MoJ called on the 'skills of the private sector and civil society' (MoJ, 2010: 2) to provide 'new rehabilitation programmes, delivered on a payment by results basis' (MoJ, 2010: 1). The inherent problems of short prison sentences and the role of broader social inequality in crime and recidivism were not discussed.

The problematisation that the MoJ presented in the Green Paper *defined the identities* of the interested stakeholders (see Sage *et al.*, 2011: 281; Gray *et al.*, 2009: 430), i.e. providers from all sectors who possessed the skills and expertise to work with prisoners and probationers to enhance rehabilitation. The problematisation also defined the *links* between these bodies, i.e. the social concerns of improving public safety and bringing about economic growth. Furthermore, the problematisation constructed an *obligatory passage point* (Callon, 1986: 202) to achieve these outcomes: competitive commissioning of penal services under the PbR mechanism, which must be routed through the

MoJ. As such, the problematisation constructed the MoJ as a macro actor that was *indispensable* to the other actors involved, in order to achieve the mutually desired outcomes of improved public safety and economic growth (see Sage *et al.*, 2011: 281; see also Callon and Latour, 1981).

At the time of publication in 2010, the proposals had a documentary materiality but represented a hypothetical problematisation which had yet to be tested in practice (Callon, 1986). The problematisation defined a set of shared problems and a set of solutions, and specified the roles of other interested actors. But these problems and solutions had not yet been accepted or adopted by other interested actors. If successfully realised, the proposals would create a new technology of penal service provision and funding using PbR. The Green Paper invited feedback on its proposals: 'we want to hear your views on the benefits and challenges posed by implementing them' (MoJ, 2010: 13). This aspect of the problematisation overlaps with the second phase of translation, which is now examined.

6.3 Negotiating relationships and solutions: the interessement phase

The second phase of the process of translation, interessement, is where the project sponsor attempts to standardise the identities of the other actors, as defined in the problematisation (Callon, 1986: 203). Actors enlisted by the problematisation can either submit to being integrated into the initial plan, or refuse the transaction by defining their interests differently (Callon, 1986: 203). The interessement entails trials of strength and refers to 'the on-going practical negotiations through which (the problematisation's) claims are tested, and almost always modified' (Sage *et al.*, 2011: 282).

The MoJ stimulated responses to the consultation from a range of interested organisations which published formal responses. These included G4S (G4S, 2011) and the Church of England (Mission and Public Affairs Council of the Church of England, 2011). Although the vast majority of voluntary organisations did not respond to the consultation, given the estimated 1,500 voluntary organisations working with prisons and probation in 2005 (Meek *et al.*, 2010: 3), *Breaking the Cycle* engaged the professional curiosity of at least twenty-eight voluntary organisations that invested the time and resources required to consider its proposals and write individual responses. Clinks (the umbrella organisation for penal voluntary organisations) also consulted its members and produced a collective response informed by over 500 professionals working in punishment (2011). Some charities were aligned with, or submitted to, the terms of the problematisation (see Callon, 1986: 203). For example, Nacro stated that *Breaking the Cycle* 'offers a real opportunity for positive reform', commending its victim focus and PbR's emphasis on outcomes (Nacro, 2011: 2), and St Giles Trust recommended outsourcing prison and probation services 'to specialist voluntary and community sector agencies' to deliver effective outcomes at less cost (St Giles Trust, 2011: no pagination). Other charities refused aspects of the problematisation and used this consultation opportunity to define their interests differently (see Gray *et al.*, 2009: 430; Callon, 1986: 203).

The Howard League's response expressed a dissident reaction (see Callon and Law, 1982) against enrolment into the actor-network of PbR and contractual penal service provision. They questioned the very premise of the Green Paper, and argued that a firm focus on reform and rehabilitation within the criminal justice system as currently constituted is not a mechanism that can bring about the envisaged rehabilitation revolution. They stressed that 'the underlying causes of local crime are best tackled through investment in public services beyond the criminal justice system, be it health, education or welfare' (Howard League, 2011: 41; see also Prison Reform Trust, 2011b) and argued that 'criminal justice, and imprisonment in particular, is a blunt tool which cannot in itself provide lasting solutions to the problem of crime' (Howard League, 2011: 4). More specifically, they voiced 'serious reservations about the payment by results proposals', pointing out that PbR has 'no track record of success' and could create 'inefficiencies' due to its complexity (Howard League, 2011: 17). They stressed that PbR could see service providers failing to engage with 'those who present the most need' and instead 'cherry-picking' offenders who are most likely to provide the desired 'results' (Howard League, 2011: 18).

Following the consultation period, the MoJ published *Breaking the Cycle: Government Response*, which explained that that the consultation had lasted twelve weeks and received over 1,200 written responses and feedback from eleven events run 'across the country' (MoJ, 2011b: 3). Four of these events were open to 'those with a policy interest, voluntary sector organisations and frontline staff from police, prisons and probation as well as members of the judiciary' (MoJ, 2011b: 3). The remaining seven events 'invited senior managers who deliver services to offenders to discuss the proposals' (MoJ, 2011b: 3). The MoJ stated that the consultation responses had helped them 'set a more intelligent course for delivering effective punishment and reducing reoffending in England and Wales' (2011b: 2). It is however difficult to find evidence of how dissident responses were taken into account or affected the proposals. The MoJ response underscored that PbR 'will underpin all our work on reoffending', stating: 'we are clear that we want to rapidly build on these pilots' (2011b: 7). There was neither acknowledgement of nor engagement with criticisms of this mechanism. As an alternative response to high recidivism rates, the Prison Reform Trust recommended drastically reducing short prison sentences, given their poor track record in reducing reoffending (Prison Reform Trust, 2011b: 4; see also Howard League, 2011: 8). The MoJ's response noted: 'we are not aiming to cut the prison population' (2011b: 2) and 'we will not push for community sentences to be used instead of prison' (2011b: 4). The next section considers the third phase of translation, during which the MoJ formally enrolled actors and experimented with PbR through pilot schemes.

6.4 Forming relationships: the enrolment phase

Enrolment occurs when multiple interests are successfully translated into an actor-network with a common goal (Callon, 1986: 206). This entails multilateral negotiations, bargaining and making concessions (Afarikumah and Kwankam, 2013: 79; Sarker *et al.*, 2006: 55; Callon, 1986: 211). This section examines the PbR pilots at HMPs Peterborough and Doncaster, illustrating how voluntary sector actors affected and were formally enrolled into the MoJ's translation alongside actors from the private sector. It considers the trials of strength and negotiations that occurred before contracts were signed and enrolment occurred.

Contracts for the first PbR pilot at Category B HMP Peterborough were signed in March 2010, and it launched in September 2010 (MoJ, 2011a: 1, 3). This pilot pre-dated the publication of *Breaking the Cycle* in December 2010 and featured significantly in it, with PbR pilots forming a critical aspect of the proposals therein (e.g. MoJ, 2010: 1, 10, 11). The Peterborough pilot entailed mentoring 3,000 adult, male, short-sentence prisoners[5] inside HMP Peterborough and following release, and linking them to services addressing offending behaviour (MoJ, 2012a: 2). Eligible prisoners were at least eighteen years of age when sentenced for a consecutive custodial period of under 365 days and discharged from HMP Peterborough during the pilot (MoJ, 2011a: 34; MoJ, 2015c: 13). The pilot's aim, or the *shared problem* addressed, was to reduce the high reconviction rates of short-sentence prisoners, of whom 60 per cent re-offended within the year following release (MoJ, 2011a: 3; Social Finance, 2011: no pagination).

The Peterborough PbR pilot formed the world's first trial Social Impact Bond, comprising a new mechanism for funding public services and a new technology of service delivery (MoJ, 2011a: 3). Investment funding from non-governmental investors was obtained upfront to provide this intervention aiming to improve social outcomes (MoJ, 2011a: 1). The non-governmental financial intermediary Social Finance raised £5 million from seventeen investors, who were 'mostly charitable trusts and foundations' (Social Finance, 2011: no pagination; MoJ, 2011a: 3). Around fifteen charitable trusts and foundations 'largely' provided the £5 million investment funding for the pilot, including the Esmee Fairburn Foundation and Lankelly Chase (MoJ, 2011a: ii, 5). The pilot's 'alignment with a charitable interest in criminal justice and offender rehabilitation' was a key attraction for investors (MoJ, 2011a: ii). If outcomes did not improve, the investors would lose their initial investment, but if the scheme succeeded and specific reductions in reconviction rates were achieved, the MoJ and the Big Lottery Fund would pay a return to investors (Social Finance, 2011). Reconviction rates of the pilot group in the eighteen months following release from custody would be compared to reconviction rates for the matched control group of prisoners (MoJ, 2011a; see also Cave *et al.*, 2012). The MoJ and the Big Lottery Fund would make an outcome payment if reconviction rates reduced by: a) 7.5 per cent or more across all 3,000 prisoners; or b) 10 per cent or more in all three cohorts of approximately 1,000 prisoners (MoJ, 2011a: 33–34; Social Finance, 2011) when compared to the matched comparison group. These thresholds were calculated by the MoJ's analytical team to reflect statistical levels at which the MoJ could be confident that improved outcomes had not occurred by chance (MoJ, 2011a: 33–34, 37). If successful, investors would receive increasing financial returns on their investment of up to 13 per cent per year over eight years (Social Finance, 2011). Although this investment offered the dual benefits of making a social impact and generating financial returns, all capital was at risk if outcomes did not improve (Social Finance, 2011).[6]

Social Finance (rather than the MoJ) had interested and enrolled a number of actors in this pilot before the Green Paper was published. Its prominence in the Green Paper illustrates the multiple circulating forces (Nimmo, 2011: 109; Hitchings, 2003: 100; Latour, 1999: 20) that affect macro level policy formation. Social Finance maintained responsibility for coordinating the pilot and commissioning service providers to support the pilot's aims (MoJ, 2015c: 11). Charitable actors were significant in the pilot as both investors and service providers. In the early stages of the pilot, three charities were enrolled as service providers to practically support prisoner resettlement: St Giles Trust, Ormiston Children and Families Trust and the YMCA (MoJ, 2011a). St Giles Trust was the principal service provider and other providers were appointed on an as-needs basis (MoJ, 2011a: 17). The model evolved in practice to include a different mix of commissioned charitable service providers: St Giles Trust provided case workers to deliver through-the-gate services and a peer advice trainer; Sova provided volunteers to support cohort members and a landlord liaison caseworker (Sova replaced the YMCA in the initial configuration, although the YMCA continued to provide gym access for cohort members); Mind supported cohort members with mental health issues; and Ormiston Families supported cohort members and their families in order to strengthen family relationships (MoJ, 2015c: 11–12). Social Finance also commissioned John Laing Training, a company which provided construction skills courses and was later recommissioned as a Community Interest Company (MoJ, 2015c: 12) and the pilot linked cohort members to local partner organisations in the community, including the police, probation, drug treatment, housing, Job Deal and Jobcentre Plus (MoJ, 2015c: 12).

The Peterborough pilot played a critical role in the translation which began with the Green Paper, but this pilot was not a 'typical' PbR scheme for four key reasons. First, the pilot was not initiated by the MoJ but by the non-governmental financial intermediary Social Finance, who approached civil servants with their novel concept (MoJ, 2011a: 10). This externally proposed idea was then incorporated into the MoJ's translation. Second, the pilot operated under a novel commissioning relationship, with unusual tasks being delegated to Social Finance. The government/MoJ had no direct relationship with the service providers, did not contract with them and had no control over their selection (MoJ, 2011a: iii). Such delegation would not occur under usual commissioning processes (MoJ, 2011a: iii, 15). Third, the pilot scheme was an expansion of existing statutory service provision, targeting short-sentence prisoners serving custodial terms of under twelve months, for whom there was previously no probation supervision (unless prisoners were under twenty-one years old) (MoJ, 2011a: 10). Fourth, the contract between Social Finance and the MoJ was not tendered through the usual competitive procurement process which enhances fiscal competitiveness (MoJ, 2011a: 14). The proposal brought by Social Finance was considered 'worth testing' and there was support for a 'proof-of-concept' pilot from a high level in the MoJ (MoJ, 2011a: 14). These four unusual conditions significantly affect the broader applications of this PbR pilot, yet it lent legitimacy to the later introduction of the PbR mechanism to pay service providers across criminal justice.

The complex dynamic between actors in this pilot involved six contractual relationships (MoJ, 2011a: 13, 15) that inscribed and stabilised actors' identities and commitments. The first enrolment, or contract was between the MoJ and Social Finance[7] to operate the pilot scheme (MoJ, 2011a: 13). As part of this negotiation, Social Finance undertook discussions with multiple interested statutory actors, including the MoJ, NOMS and HM Treasury, which resulted in agreed outcome measures and were translated into a contract and enrolment between the MoJ and Social Finance (MoJ, 2011a: 17). This contract was subject to ongoing amendments (MoJ, 2011a: 17), which may have entailed trials of strength between the actors. This contract also subsequently saw Social Finance and the participant charities enrolled into the MoJ's broader translation of penal reforms. Overall, the MoJ had three contracts: with Social Finance (which operated the pilot and secured investment), Peterborough Prison Management Limited (the consortium contracted for HMP Peterborough, with operation subcontracted to the private company Sodexo), and the independent results assessors (QinetiQ and the University of Leicester) (MoJ, 2011a: 3, 13, 17). Social Finance also had three sets of contracts: with their financial investors, voluntary sector service providers, and the Big Lottery Fund (which invested in the pilot and would pay an outcome return alongside the MoJ)[8] (MoJ, 2011a: 17).

While the Peterborough pilot may appear relatively independent, the MoJ was involved in its formation from a very early stage and significantly influenced its terms throughout. Social Finance identified the shared concerns of financial returns and social impact and approached the MoJ with this idea. Social Finance had originally focussed on short-sentence prisoners being discharged in another part of Cambridgeshire (MoJ, 2011a: 36). However, this group proved too small to be statistically significant (MoJ, 2011a: 36). Negotiations, or trials of strength, between the MoJ and Social Finance followed:

> It was a back and forth of changing the cohort terms and definition to be statistically significant, but then also assessing the operational feasibility of whether we could make that work, what the cost of delivering that would be.
>
> (Interview with the Director of Social Finance, in MoJ, 2011a: 36)

Ultimately, the MoJ's requirement that the pilot group of prisoners must be statistically significant proved critical and led to the alternative location of HMP Peterborough. Although Social Finance approached the MoJ with the problematisation, the final terms were determined through the interactions and negotiations between interested actors. Social Finance also made a confidentiality agreement with the MoJ before identifying and shortlisting potential investors, which were subsequently reviewed by the MoJ (MoJ, 2011a: 17). Following this review, investors signed a confidentiality agreement and then entered discussions with Social Finance (MoJ, 2011a: 17). Contracts were signed when the investment levels had been agreed between Social Finance and the individual investors (MoJ, 2011a: 17). Similarly, Social Finance negotiated with the Big Lottery Fund and agreed a payment structure with them, which was formalised and inscribed in a contract (MoJ, 2011a: 17). The Big Lottery Fund invested in the pilot through their national 'Replication and Innovation' funding programme that targets deep-rooted social problems (MoJ, 2011a: 13). Social Finance then negotiated with the individual voluntary organisations (and later, the company) which were to be involved in the pilot as service providers and drafted contracts with each of them, which were subject to ongoing amendments (MoJ, 2011a: 17).

The final contracts were between the MoJ and Peterborough Prison Management Limited, who are the consortium holding the contract to operate and maintain HMP Peterborough (MoJ, 2011a: 13). Peterborough Prison Management Limited subcontract the prison's operation to the private company Sodexo (MoJ, 2011a: 15). The MoJ negotiated a no-cost amendment to their contract with Peterborough Prison Management Limited, which enabled service providers to enter the prison, use prison premises and gain access to prisoners (MoJ, 2011a: 16). The sixth contract was between the MoJ and its independent assessors: QinetiQ and the University of Leicester (MoJ, 2011a: 13). These assessors were appointed through an MoJ procurement process and their role was to determine whether the pilot resulted in fewer reconvictions (MoJ, 2011a: 3, 17). The assessors had responsibility for identifying the comparison group and comparing reconviction rates of the pilot and comparison groups, using data from the MoJ extract of the Police National Computer (MoJ, 2011a: 33, 36).

This section has detailed how Social Finance set out a problematisation, identifying the shared concerns of financial returns and social impact for investors and participant charitable service delivery organisations, and then successfully interested and enrolled these actors and the MoJ in this project. The MoJ significantly affected the terms of the pilot and then enrolled this pilot (which was originally proposed by Social Finance) into its wider translation as a PbR pilot scheme. Trials of strength occurred during this process, e.g. in negotiations between actors and during the process of drawing up contracts. The problematisation which the MoJ presented in *Breaking the Cycle* successfully enrolled further non-state actors following publication. Subsequent PbR pilots included the Heron Unit/Project Daedalus in HMP Feltham, London,[9] and a significant resettlement pilot at the Serco-managed Category B HMP Doncaster (MoJ, 2012a: 1) which is now examined. The Doncaster PbR pilot operated within *Breaking the Cycle*'s context, embracing PbR in the delivery of penal services and addressing reoffending (MoJ, 2012a: 2). It involved an 'alliance' of service providers, comprising the private company Serco and voluntary organisations

Catch 22 and Turning Point. The contract was signed in April 2011, and the pilot commenced in October 2011 (MoJ, 2012a: 3).

Serco's contract to operate HMP Doncaster was due to expire in July 2011 (MoJ, 2012a: 3). As part of the MoJ procurement process for the new contract, which was run through the Prison Competition Programme, Serco submitted both core and variant bids (MoJ, 2012a: 3). The variant bid was ultimately successful, proposing a pilot scheme applying PbR principles to work with prisoners approaching discharge, and aiming 'to test the impact of replacing a multitude of process and output targets and performance monitoring with a single outcome-based target (to reduce the reconviction rate) with a strong financial incentive to achieve this' (MoJ, 2012a: 3). After bids were submitted, a process of negotiation and PbR contract design ensued between the MoJ, NOMS and the alliance, i.e. Serco, the penal voluntary organisation Catch 22 and the charity Turning Point (MoJ, 2012a: 3). Although this scheme was initially intended for all prisoners, the target group was reduced to short-sentence prisoners during the early stages of implementation, as: 'providing intensive case management in custody for all offenders was not the most efficient or appropriate use of resources' (MoJ, 2013a: ii).

The Doncaster pilot demonstrates the successful translation of the problematisation presented in the Green Paper. The alliance of Serco, Catch 22 and Turning Point was seduced (Callon, 1986) by the MoJ's problematisation and proposed a further PbR pilot scheme as part of Serco's bid to continue operating HMP Doncaster. The alliance also subsequently targeted short-sentence prisoners, mirroring the PbR pilot at HMP Peterborough and laying the foundations for enacting the supervision requirement. The next section examines the final stage of the MoJ's translation, illustrating how the MoJ became the principal spokesperson for the heterogeneous public, private and voluntary sector actors involved in these pilots, and ultimately mobilised all their diverse inputs to translate PbR contracting and the supervision requirement from policy rhetoric into practice.

6.5 Being the spokesperson: the mobilisation phase

Mobilisation refers to an actor becoming the spokesperson for other actors in the network (Callon, 1986). The spokesperson is a powerful macro actor who can translate the interests, roles and relations of the entire network (Callon and Latour, 1981). Materials and processes of communication (e.g. writing) can order networks through space, creating *mobile* translations that act at-a-distance to translate the interests of an actor-network (Law, 1992: 387). This section considers how the MoJ became the dominant spokesperson in the translation which followed the Green Paper, ultimately reporting for all the heterogeneous actors who responded to the consultations and participated in the PbR pilots. This group included some voluntary organisations in practice (as named above) and drew on a discursive 'voluntary sector' of biddable service providers. By defining a problem and solutions, deciding on outcome measures, signing contracts and generating results, the MoJ generated a series of intermediaries and equivalences (see Callon, 1986; Callon and Latour, 1981) that designated it the dominant spokesperson for all actors in the translation. By publishing proposals, running consultations, collating responses and running PbR pilots, the MoJ took primary responsibility for determining and publishing their results. The MoJ then mobilised and accumulated the inputs of heterogeneous voluntary and private sector actors. The MoJ's publications speak and act in both their own name and in the name of other actors from the private and voluntary sectors. The work of Social Finance in providing the stimulus for the HMP Peterborough pilot and the work of all the heterogeneous actors involved in the PbR pilots was ultimately most powerfully represented by MoJ.

The results of the PbR pilots at HMPs Peterborough and Doncaster were primarily determined and published by the MoJ (e.g. MoJ, 2013a), with analyses also provided by the independent assessors (e.g. Jolliffe and Hedderman, 2014) but mediated by the MoJ to some extent. The MoJ's analytical team had privileged access to the baseline reconviction data and determined both the time frame across which reconviction events would be measured and the statistical levels at which the pilots were judged to have achieved 'results' (MoJ, 2011a: 33, 36, 37). While the MoJ is not uniquely privileged in commenting on *Breaking the Cycle* and the PbR pilots, it is a powerful macro actor compared to weaker individual actors who publish their own publications, press releases and reports. The MoJ also became spokesperson for the prisoners' voices in this translation, although these voices sounded principally through statistics demonstrating prisoner reconviction rates (e.g. MoJ, 2013a). While there are a small number of quotations from prisoners to be found (e.g. MoJ, 2015b: 28, 30; MoJ, 2015c: 42–48), this is a very limited proportion of the MoJ's body of commentary. It is notable that prisoners formed the boundary objects[10] (Sage *et al.*, 2011: 284) which linked all actors and were the object of this policy reform, yet they 'speak' almost solely in terms of recidivism rates. Although prisoners retain their individual agency and capacity to resist co-operating or engaging with programmes, here the voices of those subject to the reforms were almost entirely eclipsed.

Drawing upon the externally proposed Peterborough Social Impact Bond, *Breaking the Cycle* interested and enrolled heterogeneous actors, including a small number of voluntary organisations, into further PbR pilots. The diverse inputs and discursive presence of these actors facilitated the pilots and were subsequently mobilised by the MoJ in the 2013 *Transforming Rehabilitation* programme. Following the format of *Breaking the Cycle* in 2010, the *Transforming Rehabilitation – a revolution in the way we manage offenders* consultation paper was published (MoJ, 2013b), followed by *Transforming Rehabilitation: A Strategy for Reform* (MoJ, 2013c).

The MoJ used *Transforming Rehabilitation: A Strategy for Reform* to reiterate that PbR was the best means to reduce reoffending and achieve socioeconomic benefits, stating: 'to make the biggest impact on reoffending rates, we want to give new providers, incentivised under 'payment by results', responsibility for rehabilitating as many offenders as possible' (MoJ, 2013c: 20). This is a clear example of Garland's responsibilisation theory, with non-criminal justice organizations becoming responsible for delivering crime control (2001) and illustrates how governing is increasingly performed by networks of state and non-state actors, whose activities are co-ordinated by shared objectives and understandings (Jessop, 1995: 317). Echoing the arguments of *Breaking the Cycle*, *Transforming Rehabilitation: A Strategy for Reform* emphasised that 'stubbornly high reoffending rates' persist despite high penal spending (MoJ, 2013c: 3). Under the new PbR mechanism, 'the taxpayer will only pay providers in full for those services that actually deliver real reductions in reoffending' (MoJ, 2013c: 3). PbR was again presented as the sole mechanism to control penal spending and the sole solution to current failures of punishment: '*only by doing this* will we bear down on the long term costs of the criminal justice system' (MoJ, 2013c: 3, emphasis added) and achieve the requisite 'relentless focus on rehabilitation' (MoJ, 2013c: 3). In *Transforming Rehabilitation: A Strategy for Reform* (MoJ, 2013c), PbR was presented as a mechanism that had been trialled, most notably through the prison-based pilots at HMPs Peterborough and Doncaster.

However, results for cohort one of the prison PbR pilots at Peterborough and Doncaster were not available until summer 2014, due to the time lag required for a twelve-month re-conviction measure (MoJ, 2013a: 1). Interim re-conviction figures for these pilots were published in a 2013 ad-hoc MoJ statistical bulletin as a result of 'the high level of public interest in these pilots, particularly in relation to the reforms set out in *Transforming Rehabilitation: A Strategy for Reform*' (2013a: 1). These interim results illustrated falls in re-conviction events for both pilots, but were incomplete and not statistically significant (MoJ, 2013a: 5–6). Despite these modest results and the Prison Reform Trust's faith that government would 'harness the lessons and evidence of success before rolling out a payment by results scheme nationally' (2011b: 3), the MoJ used *Transforming Rehabilitation: A Strategy for Reform* to reiterate the necessity and utility of PbR, without substantive empirical 'results' or evidence. For the completed Doncaster pilot, the first cohort (October 2011 to September 2012) had a reoffending rate 5.7 per cent lower than the 2009 baseline year, so the 5 per cent PbR target was met. The second cohort (October 2012 to September 2013) was 3.3 per cent lower than baseline, so the PbR target was not met (MoJ, 2015b: 2). Final Peterborough results are not due until summer 2016 (MoJ, 2015c), and all the available results are also based on voluntary rather than mandatory offender participation (MoJ, 2015b). Given that *Breaking the Cycle* stated the intention to roll out PbR across penal service commissioning by 2015 following pilots (MoJ, 2010: 11), the pilots were perhaps geared towards refining the PbR mechanism rather than testing its inherent suitability. In *Transforming Rehabilitation: A Strategy for Reform*, the MoJ at least acknowledged that the consultation had reported criticisms of the optimistic timetable for PbR implementation by 2015, significantly before full results from PbR pilots became available (2013c: 33). But the MoJ reiterated that PbR contracts would commence from autumn 2014 and justified this timetable because 'the need to reduce reoffending is pressing' and 'to achieve the reductions in reoffending rates we need, it is vital that we move ahead to put our new approach in place' (MoJ, 2013c: 33) They did ambiguously state that they 'will take a measured approach to implementation' (MoJ, 2013c: 33), but their position and implementation timescale remained unchanged.

Transforming Rehabilitation: A Strategy for Reform also proposed that 'statutory rehabilitation' be extended to short-sentence prisoners (MoJ, 2013c: 6). These prisoners were the object of the PbR pilots at HMPs Peterborough and Doncaster, which ran with voluntary organisation involvement. *Transforming Rehabilitation: A Strategy for Reform* explained the need to support prisoners 'through the prison gate' and deliver 'mentoring and rehabilitation support to get their lives back on track so they do not commit crime again' (MoJ, 2013c: 3). This 'support' was deemed particularly important for those released from short-sentences, who have the highest reoffending rates but 'currently do not get support they need' to resettle in the community, being 'typically left to their own devices on release' (MoJ, 2013c: 4). The document signalled a continuing role for the voluntary sector, noting that it: 'has an important contribution to make in mentoring and turning offenders' lives around' (MoJ, 2013c: 3). Although the need to reduce penal spending justified the introduction of PbR in *Breaking the Cycle* (MoJ, 2010: 8), the PbR mechanism then enabled the supervision requirement for short-sentence prisoners, which was funded by savings predicted from rolling out PbR for penal service providers (MoJ, 2013c: 4). Through the process of translation which began with *Breaking the Cycle*, an apparently natural link (Foucault, 1977: 232) was created between short-sentence prisoners and the need to supervise them in the community.

Nevertheless, individual actors still spoke on their own behalves. St Giles Trust stated that the interim results from the PbR pilots demonstrated 'a huge endorsement for the assessment modelling' and showed the pilot is both 'helping our clients turn their lives around and beginning to show savings for taxpayers by bringing down reoffending rates' (Pudelek, 2013: no pagination). St Giles Trust also 'believes charities can play a bigger role in future criminal justice services' and remained 'proud to be part of the first ever social impact bond' at HMP Peterborough (Owen, 2013: no pagination). In a similar vein, following the interim results Catch 22 publicly congratulated the pilot at HMP Doncaster on their website as 'the first step in the right direction towards reducing re-offending through a caseworker-led approach and a focus on improving outcomes'.[11] It is, however, notable that a very small proportion of penal voluntary organisations were directly involved in marketised reforms, but significant amounts of commentary surrounded this work.

Other organisations gave dissident responses, although these were ultimately not strong enough to counteract the MoJ's spokesperson power. Social Finance (who initially suggested and secured funding for the PbR pilot at HMP Peterborough) expressed dissidence towards the proposals in *Transforming Rehabilitation: A Strategy for Reform* (MoJ, 2013c). They publicly critiqued 'the suggestion that the progress of the Peterborough Social Impact Bond supports the case for the Transforming Rehabilitation initiative' (Howard League, 2013: no pagination) and explained that 'the success or otherwise of the Peterborough pilot is of limited relevance' to assessing the merits of the much wider changes envisaged by Transforming Rehabilitation (Howard League, 2013: no pagination), due to the unusual conditions of the pilot.

The Howard League and the Prison Reform Trust also expressed dissidence and resisted these reforms, producing briefing papers for MPs and the Lords attempting to prevent passage of the Offender Rehabilitation Bill. The Prison Reform Trust pointed out that the supervision requirement would add a 'further year to the ambit of the criminal justice system for all those sentenced to custody for any period of over one day and up to two years' (2013: 1). They explained its likely result of around 13,000 offenders being recalled to custody and cost of £16 million per year (Prison Reform Trust, 2013: 1). As such, the Trust advocated further consideration of whether these proposals were 'fair and proportionate and whether the proposed new arrangements should be voluntary or mandatory' across short-sentence prisoners (2013: 1). Similarly, the Howard League noted that the supervision requirement would 'result in a substantial increase in the number of short-term prison sentences' and that 'receptions to prison for breach or recall are already becoming one of the main drivers of the prison population' (Howard League, 2013: no pagination). They argued that the supervision requirement could see magistrates up-tariff and 'sentence offenders to a prison sentence when a community sentence would be more appropriate in order that they will qualify for the twelve months of statutory rehabilitation on leaving custody' and noted the increased costs should this occur (Howard League, 2013: no pagination). They also recommended that 'support for short-sentenced prisoners ought to be voluntary' (2013: no pagination). These dissident responses may have contributed to Lord Beecham's proposed amendment to the Bill when it was considered in the House of Lords, suggesting that changes to short-sentence offender supervision should be subject to an initial pilot, but this vote was lost with 188 for and 209 against.[12] The passage of the Bill and adoption of PbR throughout the delivery of penal services, despite dissidence from voluntary organisations, demonstrate how a powerful actor can mobilise other actors to achieve its own ends.

This account has focussed on the prison PbR pilots, roll out of PbR to pay penal service providers and new supervision requirement, but among multiple reforms *Transforming Rehabilitation* also part privatised probation. This process also had interesting consequences for charities. *Transforming Rehabilitation* established the public National Probation Service for high risk (ex-)offenders, and privatised probation supervision for medium and low risk (ex-)offenders by founding Community Rehabilitation Companies (MoJ, 2013c). These probation reforms also followed MoJ consultations on community sentences and probation (MoJ, 2012b; MoJ, 2012c), and voluntary organisations feature as junior partners in almost all of the partnerships now owning Community Rehabilitation Companies (which are partially remunerated via PbR and responsible for supervising those under the new supervision requirement) (NPC, 2015). Based on the

MoJ's consistent references to voluntary sector involvement and keenness to have a charitable prime contractor, some larger voluntary organisations decided to compete at Tier 1 in the commissioning process to own and run the new Community Rehabilitation Companies (NPC, 2015). However, none of the charities was successful at this level, although some were named as partners at Tier 2 and others are in conversation about potential future subcontracts at Tier 3 (NPC, 2015). This was seen as a disappointing outcome for the voluntary sector, which ultimately received nothing for its good faith and extensive efforts (NPC, 2015). It appears that they lost out on contracts as decisions were made on the basis of minimising financial risk and obtaining the best economies of scale, rather than the quality of services proposed (NPC, 2015). Although market policy reforms will only ever be a priority concern or even a possibility for a certain type of voluntary organisation (Unwin and Molyneux, 2005: 37), even the few organisations that were involved appeared ultimately to lose out in the *Transforming Rehabilitation* reforms to probation. This left the sense that the 'MoJ had behaved irresponsibly with charity resources and failed to grasp the moral implications' of wasting charitable resources 'in a fruitless (commissioning) process that might otherwise have been invested in frontline services to improve peoples' lives' (NPC, 2015: 7).

This analysis has illustrated how the externally proposed Social Impact Bond was translated into a PbR pilot with short-sentence prisoners at HMP Peterborough by the MoJ, which was subsequently used as a resource to support the proposals made in *Breaking the Cycle* (MoJ, 2010) and *Transforming Rehabilitation: A Strategy for Reform* (MoJ, 2013c). The PbR pilots undertaken with voluntary organisation involvement at HMPs Peterborough and Doncaster were translated into support for applying the PbR mechanism across penal service delivery and implementing the supervision requirement. The translation that followed *Breaking the Cycle* was underpinned by charities, which invented and implemented the Social Impact Bond that stimulated the PbR pilots and facilitated the roll-out of PbR throughout penal service contracting, thus creating cost savings to finance the supervision requirement. The MoJ's discursive 'voluntary sector' of biddable organisations and the small number of voluntary organisations practically involved in the translation facilitated the supervision requirement, which represents a significant expansion in community control (Cohen, 1985: 15) to include the new group of short-sentence prisoners. This idea is expanded and problematised in Chapter 7. Without actually providing evidence of their utility, the pilots supported PbR and the supervision requirement, and they were enabled and justified by the involvement of voluntary organisations. Although some voluntary organisations actively displayed dissident reactions to these proposals, e.g. through responses to policy consultations and briefing papers regarding the new supervision legislation (e.g. Howard League, 2013; Prison Reform Trust, 2013; Howard League, 2011), this dissidence was not powerful enough to counter the MoJ's multiple proposals, publications, pilots and position as spokesperson. Quite simply, the state's machinery was larger and stronger.

Notes

1 *Breaking the Cycle* was a point of departure for significant penal reform, but these reforms are not entirely discrete and align with the broader neoliberal project introduced by the Conservative Thatcher government in the 1980s (see Chapter 1).
2 As explained in Chapter 1, under PbR the contractor's payment is linked to results achieved, in order to encourage greater efficiency and effectiveness in service delivery.
3 Translation is the process through which multiple heterogeneous actors are integrated into a specific actor-network (Latour, 2005: 106–108). Chapter 3 provides a full description.
4 The supervision requirement has similarities to 'Custody Plus', a flagship of the Criminal Justice Act 2003. 'Custody Plus' involved a licence period of up to twenty-six weeks for short sentence prisoners with requirements aimed at reducing reoffending, but was never actually brought in due to concerns about inadequate resourcing and the potential for the system to become overwhelmed (Ashworth, 2010: 295).
5 Eligible prisoners must have been at least eighteen years of age when sentenced for a consecutive custodial period of fewer than 365 days (MoJ, 2011a: 34). They also had to be discharged from HMP Peterborough during the pilot to participate (MoJ, 2015c: 13).
6 While the intention was for the whole programme to operate under the Social Impact Bond, in practice this was only the case for the first two cohorts of 1,000 prisoners. The third cohort operated under a 'fee-for-service' arrangement rather than the original Social Impact Bond-unded PbR model (MoJ, 2015c: 1). Following the roll out of *Transforming Rehabilitation* reforms to probation, the third cohort operated under fee-for-service until the new Community Rehabilitation Company implemented its approach to rehabilitation (MoJ, 2015c: 1–2).
7 Social Finance set up a limited partnership called 'The Social Impact Partnership' to operate the pilot scheme. Here the nomenclature 'Social Finance' is used, to maintain clarity of expression (MoJ, 2011a: 13).
8 Drawing up these contracts required significant resource investment from the MoJ, Social Finance and its investors, and HM Treasury (due to new the payment mechanism for contractors and the unusual conditions of this pilot) (MoJ, 2011a: 15). Determining the outcome measurements and the payment model for the pilot was particularly time-consuming (MoJ, 2011a: 15). Social Finance's resource investment in developing this pilot scheme amounted to 2.5 person-years, specialist tax advice and over 300 hours of legal advice (secured on a *pro bono* basis) (MoJ, 2011a: 15).
9 For full details of this and other PbR models, see Independent Commission on Youth Crime and Antisocial Behaviour, 2011: 19.
10 Previous applications of translation illustrate that even non-human actors are usually seduced in some way (Callon, 1986). For example, Callon's scallops were attracted using towlines and collectors (see Chapter 3) and Sage *et al.*'s otters were interested using various means (2011: 283). The otters would be affected by the construction of a road bridge to Skye, Scotland. The devices of interessement used to enrol the otters included building new freshwater pools, which are essential to otter breeding, and constructing 1.5 miles of otter-resistant road walls and otter tunnels, which allowed the animals to pass under access roads on Skye and the mainland (Sage *et al.*, 2011: 283). The total cost of design changes to accommodate the otters was estimated at £3.8 million (Sage *et al.*, 2011: 283).
11 See   www.catch-22.org.uk/news/response-interim-results-pbr-pilot-hmp-doncaster/. Accessed: 10 December 2013.
12 See   www.parliament.uk/business/news/2013/may/lords-offender-rehabilitation-bill/. Accessed: 21 March 2014.

References

Afarikumah, E. and Kwankam, S. Y. (2013) 'Deploying Actor-Network Theory to Analyse Telemedicine Implementation in Ghana', *Science*, *1*(2): 77–84.

Ashworth, A. (2010) *Sentencing and Criminal Justice*. Cambridge: Cambridge University Press.

Callon, M. (1986) 'Some Elements of a Sociology of Translation: Domestication of the scallops and the fishermen of St Brieuc Bay', in Law, J. (ed.), *Power, Action and Belief: A new sociology of knowledge?* London: Routledge.

Callon, M. and Latour, B. (1981) 'Unscrewing the Big Leviathan: How actors macro-structure reality and how sociologists help them to do so', in Knorr-Cetina, K. and Cicourel, A. V. (eds), *Advances in Social Theory and Methodology: Toward an integration of micro and macro-sociologies*. Boston: Routledge and Kegan Paul.

Callon, M. and Law, J. (1982) 'On Interests and their Transformation: Enrolment and counter-enrolment', *Social Studies of Science*, *12*(4): 615–625.

Carrabine, E. (2000) 'Discourse, Governmentality and Translation: Toward a social theory of imprisonment', *Theoretical Criminology*, *4*(3): 309–331.

Cave, S., Williams, T., Jolliffe, D. and Hedderman, C. (2012) Peterborough Social Impact Bond: An independent assessment. Development of the PSM methodology. Available at: www.gov.uk/government/uploads/system/uploads/attachment_data/file/217392/peterborough-social-impact-bond-assessment.pdf. Accessed: 29 July 2015.

Clinks (2011) *Clinks Response to the Ministry of Justice's Green Paper 'Breaking the Cycle': Effective punishment, rehabilitation and sentencing of offenders'*. Available at: www.clinks.org/assets/files/PDFs/Clinks%20repsonse%20to%20Breaking%20the%20Cycle.pdf. Accessed: 4 January 2013.

Cohen, S. (1985) *Visions of Social Control: Crime, punishment and classification*. Cambridge: Polity Press.

Foucault, M. (1977) *Discipline and Punish: The birth of the prison*. London: Allen Lane.

Garland, D. (2001) *The Culture of Control: Crime and social order in a contemporary society*. Chicago: University of Chicago Press.

Gray, D., Graham, A., Dewhurst, Y., Kirkpatrick, G., MacDougall, L., Nicol, S. and Nixon, G. (2009) 'Scallops, Schools and Scholars: Reflections on the emergence of a research-oriented learning project', *Journal of Education for Teaching*, *35*(4): 425–440.

G4S (2011) *Breaking the Cycle. Effective Punishment, Rehabilitation and Sentencing of Offenders: Response by G4S Care and Justice Services (UK) to the Government's consultation*. Available at: www.g4s.uk.com/~/media/Files/United%20Kingdom/G4S%20Response%20to%20Government%20Green%20Paper%20-%20Executive%20Summary%20-%20March%202011.ashx. Accessed: 16 October 2013.

Hitchings, R. (2003) 'People, Plants and Performance: On actor network theory and the material pleasures of the private garden', *Social and Cultural Geography*, *4*(1): 99–114.

Howard League (2011) *Response to Breaking the Cycle*. Available at: http://d19ylpo4aovc7m.cloudfront.net/fileadmin/howard_league/user/pdf/Consultations/Response_to_Breaking_the_Cycle.pdf. Accessed: 16 October 2013.

Howard League (2013) *Offender Rehabilitation Bill. Report Stage and Third Reading*. Available at: https://d19ylpo4aovc7m.cloudfront.net/fileadmin/howard_league/user/pdf/Briefings/Briefing_for_ORB_Report_Stage_and_Third_Reading.pdf. Accessed: 10 April 2013.

Independent Commission on Youth Crime and Antisocial Behaviour (2011) *Payment by Results in Tackling Youth Crime.* Available at: www.police-foundation.org.uk/youth crimecommission/images/119_pbr%20seminar%20notes.pdf. Accessed: 17 October 2013.

Jessop, B. (1995) 'The Regulation Approach and Governance Theory: Alternative perspectives on economic and political change?' *Economy and Society, 24*(3): 307–333.

Jolliffe, D. and Hedderman, C. (2014) *Peterborough Social Impact Bond: Final report on Cohort 1 analysis.* Available at: www.gov.uk/government/uploads/system/uploads/attachment_data/file/341684/peterborough-social-impact-bond-report.pdf. Accessed: 29 July 2015.

Latour, B. (1999) 'On Recalling ANT', in Law, J. and Hassard, J. (eds) *Actor-Network Theory and After.* Oxford: Blackwell.

Latour, B. (2005) *Reassembling the Social: An introduction to Actor-Network Theory.* Oxford: Oxford University Press.

Law, J. (1992) 'Notes on the Theory of the Actor-Network: Ordering, strategy, and heterogeneity', *Systems Practice, 5*(4): 379–393.

Meek, R., Gojkovic, D. and Mills, A. (2010) 'The Role of the Third Sector in Work with Offenders: The perceptions of criminal justice and third sector stakeholders', *TSRC Working Paper 34.* Birmingham: Third Sector Research Centre.

Mission and Public Affairs Council of the Church of England (2011) *A Response to the Ministry of Justice Green Paper of December 2010 on Behalf of the Mission and Public Affairs Council of the Church of England.* Available at: www.churchofengland. org/media/1206139/breakingthecycleresp2011.pdf. Accessed: 16 December 2013.

MoJ (2010) *Breaking the Cycle: Effective punishment, rehabilitation and sentencing of offenders.* London: MoJ.

MoJ (2011a) *Lessons Learned from the Planning and Early Implementation of the Social Impact Bond at HMP Peterborough.* Available at: www.gov.uk/government/uploads/system/uploads/attachment_data/file/217375/social-impact-bond-hmp-peterborough. pdf. Accessed: 16 October 2013.

MoJ (2011b) *Breaking the Cycle: Government response.* Available at: www.gov.uk/government/uploads/system/uploads/attachment_data/file/186345/breaking-the-cycle-government-response.pdf. Accessed: 16 October 2013.

MoJ (2012a) *Findings and Lessons Learned from the Early Implementation of the HMP Doncaster Payment by Results Pilot.* Available at: www.catch-22.org.uk/Files/hmp-doncaster-payment-by-results-pilot.pdf?id=275e92a7-3ce6-4604-8760-a118010ebb54. Accessed: 18 October 2013.

MoJ (2012b) *Punishment and Reform: Effective community sentences.* Available at: https://consult.justice.gov.uk/digital-communications/effective-community-services-1/supporting_documents/effectivecommunitysentences.pdf. Accessed: 13 March 2015.

MoJ (2012c) *Punishment and Reform: Effective probation services.* Available at: https://consult.justice.gov.uk/digital-communications/effective-probation-services/supporting_documents/probationreviewconsultation.pdf. Accessed: 13 March 2015.

MoJ (2013a) *Statistical Notice: Interim re-conviction figures for the Peterborough and Doncaster Payment by Results pilots.* Available at: www.gov.uk/government/uploads/system/uploads/attachment_data/file/206686/re-conviction-results.pdf. Accessed: 17 October 2013.

MoJ (2013b) *Transforming Rehabilitation: A revolution in the way we manage offenders.* Available at: https://consult.justice.gov.uk/digital-communications/transforming-rehabilitation. Accessed: 17 October 2013.

MoJ (2013c) *Transforming Rehabilitation: A strategy for reform.* London: MoJ.

MoJ (2015a) *Interim Re-conviction Figures for Peterborough and Doncaster Payment by Results Pilots*. Available at: www.gov.uk/government/uploads/system/uploads/attachment_data/file/399312/annex-a-payment-by-results-jan15.pdf. Accessed: 15 March 2015.

MoJ (2015b) *HMP Doncaster Payment by Results pilot: Final process evaluation report*. Available at: www.gov.uk/government/uploads/system/uploads/attachment_data/file/449494/hmp-doncaster-pbr-final-evaluation.pdf. Accessed: 30 July 2015.

MoJ (2015c) *The Payment by Results Social Impact Bond pilot at HMP Peterborough: Final process evaluation report*. Available at: www.gov.uk/government/publications/social-impact-bond-pilot-at-hmp-peterborough-final-report. Accessed 1 February 2015.

Nacro (2011) *Breaking the Cycle: Effective punishment, rehabilitation and sentencing of offenders. Nacro's response*. Available at: www.nacro.org.uk/data/files/green-paper-2605-1-918.pdf. Accessed: 16 October 2013.

Nimmo, R. (2011) 'Actor-Network Theory and Methodology: Social research in a more-than-human world', *Methodological Innovations Online*, 6(3): 108–119.

NPC (2015) *Transforming Rehabilitation: The voluntary sector perspective*. Available at: www.thinknpc.org/publications/transforming-rehabilitation-the-voluntary-sector-perspective/. Accessed: 23 February 2016.

Owen, R. (2013) 'Probation Reform: Payment by results can reduce reoffending', *Guardian*. Available at: www.theguardian.com/society/2013/may/15/probation-reform-payment-results-reduce-reoffending. Accessed: 10 March 2014.

Porsander, L. (2005) 'My Name is Lifebuoy. An actor-network emerging from an action-net', in Czarniawska, B. and Hernes, T. (eds) *Actor-Network Theory and Organizing*. Malmo: Liber and Copenhagen Business School Press.

Prison Reform Trust (2011b) *Submission to the Ministry of Justice. Breaking the Cycle: Effective punishment, rehabilitation and sentencing of offenders*. Available at: www.prisonreformtrust.org.uk/Portals/0/Documents/Prison%20Reform%20Trust%20Response%20to%20Justice%20Green%20Paper.pdf. Accessed: 12 April 2015.

Prison Reform Trust (2013) *Briefing on the Offender Rehabilitation Bill*. Available at: www.prisonreformtrust.org.uk/Portals/0/Documents/Prison%20Reform%20Trust%20Briefing%20Offender%20Rehabilitation%20Bill%20HoC%202nd%20Reading%2011Nov13.pdf. Accessed: 10 March 2014.

Pudelek, J. (2013) 'HM Prison Peterborough Social Impact Bond has Led to a Fall in Reconvictions, Official Figures Show', *Third Sector Online*. Available at: www.thirdsector.co.uk/news/1186265/. Accessed: 10 March 2014.

Sage, D., Dainty, A. and Brookes, N. (2011) 'How Actor-Network Theories Can Help in Understanding Project Complexities', *International Journal of Managing Projects in Business*, 4(2): 274–293.

Sarker, S., Sarker, S., and Sidorova, A. (2006) 'Understanding Business Process Change Failure: An actor-network perspective', *Journal of Management Information Systems*, 23(1): 51–86.

Social Finance (2011) *Peterborough Social Impact Bond*. Available at: www.socialfinance.org.uk/sites/default/files/SF_Peterborough_SIB.pdf. Accessed: 3 January 2012.

St. Giles Trust (2011) *St Giles Trust: Our response to Breaking the Cycle, Green Paper consultation*. Available at: www.stgilestrust.org.uk/news/p102567-our%20response%20to%20the%20green%20paper%20breaking%20the%20cycle%20consultation%20.html. Accessed: 16 October 2013.

Tomczak, P. (forthcoming) 'The Voluntary Sector and the Mandatory Statutory Supervision Requirement: Expanding the carceral net', *British Journal of Criminology*.

Unwin, J. and Molyneux, P. (2005) 'Beyond Transfer to Transformation', in Paxton, W., Pearce, N., Unwin, J. and Molyneux, P. (eds) *The Voluntary Sector Delivering Public Services*. York: Joseph Rowntree Foundation.

7   The effects of charitable work

7.1 Introduction

Given the voluntary sector's significance in criminal justice policy, practice and scholarship, it is both surprising and problematic that we do not better understand either the effects of charitable work or its distinctiveness from the work of statutory and private agencies (Tomczak and Albertson, 2016; Armstrong, 2002). Many have acknowledged the benefits of charitable programmes for prisoners and probationers (e.g. Corcoran, 2012: 17; Maguire, 2012: 484; Mills *et al.*, 2012: 392; Meek *et al.*, 2010: 3–4; Neuberger, 2009: 7–17; Silvestri, 2009: 3; Lewis *et al.*, 2007; see also Chapter 2). Recent penal voluntary sector literature tends to follow the general 'presumption that ... there is something in the quality of being "non-profit" and "community-based" that meaningfully improves upon the model of "state" institutions' (Armstrong, 2002: 346). However, there is not an evidence base to support the alleged beneficial effects of charitable work, perhaps because the symbolic value of voluntary sector status 'seems to confer a kind of immunity which protects the nonprofit sector from scrutiny' (Armstrong, 2002: 362). Attempts to understand the effects of charitable work are further complicated by the net-widening literature, which suggests that voluntary organisations extend and reproduce exclusionary networks of state carceral control (e.g. Cox, 2013; Cohen, 1985; McWilliams, 1983; Ignatieff, 1978; Foucault, 1977; see Chapter 2). This gap in understanding is addressed in this chapter by examining the effects of charitable work, exploring how voluntary organisations can both extend control and positively mediate the experience of punishment.

In ANT terms, actors can be either intermediaries or mediators of an actor-network (Latour, 2005, 1996; see also Chapter 3). Intermediaries transport meaning or force without transformation and can be black-boxed in analysis, while mediators *transform, distort and modify* the meanings and elements that they are supposed to carry (Afarikumah and Kwankam, 2013; Latour, 2005). The net-widening literature (e.g. Ignatieff, 1978; Foucault, 1977) broadly implies an intermediary role for charities, which are considered to reproduce, transport and extend the force of the formal penal system without meaningfully transforming it (see Afarikumah and Kwankam, 2013; Latour, 2005). Literature which points to the potential enabling functions of charitable work (e.g. Lewis *et al.*,

2007; Liebling, 2004) broadly implies that charities *mediate punishment*, so transform, distort and modify the experience, meanings and elements thereof (see Afarikumah and Kwankam, 2013; Latour, 2005). Following ANT's aim of learning from actors without defining the effects of their actions a priori (Nimmo, 2011: 109; Latour, 1999: 20; Law, 2004: 157; see also Chapter 3), this chapter explores all of the potential effects of charitable work. This involves rejecting the Foucauldian position that all penal reforms are reducible to the will to power (Garland, 1990: 168–169), and avoiding the 'folly of the nihilistic net-widening literature, to reduce every change to no change at all', instead remaining open to exploring multiple consequences of work undertaken alongside penal institutions (Armstrong; 2002: 365).

Informed by original empirical data, I explore the effects of charitable work in this chapter. I consider how charities can reproduce, extend and transform punishment or, in other words, how charities can act as both intermediaries *and* mediators of punishment. The following section explores the potential control effects of charitable work, or examines charities as intermediaries of punishment. Then, the potential enabling functions of charitable work are considered, by exploring how charities can positively mediate or transform punishment. I conclude that both outcomes are possible. Charitable work can result in extended control at the micro and macro levels, sometimes through apparently inoccuous interactions in informal settings. Charitable work can also positively mediate punishment, most notably through distinctive relationships with prisoners and probationers which can enable desistance. Guided by ANT, I then revisit and problematise the concept of net-widening to propose a new avenue for politically enabling research and hybrid theorisation.

7.2 Expanding control, or charities as penal intermediaries

7.2.1 Introduction

Net-widening scholarship illustrates that intensified 'support' services and intervention can widen and deepen the carceral net, extending its exclusionary force (e.g. Cohen, 1985: 15, 268; see Chapter 2). For example, scholars have suggested that historical philanthropic work increased the scale of punishment and inserted the power to punish more deeply in the social body (e.g. Ignatieff, 1978: 213). Following this scholarship, charitable work can be considered an 'insidious means of netting more people into the formal criminal justice realm for more reasons' (Armstrong, 2002: 354). I now provide a reading of my data which suggests that charities may act as intermediaries which supplement, reproduce and expand statutory penal control without transforming it.

7.2.2 Small scale interactions

Drawing on the interview data, this section illustrates how small scale interactions between charitable staff, probationers and statutory staff can increase the scale of punishment and social control. It is also likely that charitable work in prisons can expand control. As this did not emerge from my data, I will not speculate, but future research could examine the potential net-widening functions of charitable work in prisons.

Jane explained how charitable work could increase the monitoring and surveillance of (ex-)offenders in the community. Jane described gaining privileged access to information about one of their service users, which the charity subsequently passed on to the probation service, resulting in the service user being recalled to prison. There is a clear argument to support the practice of monitoring known serious (ex-)offenders following their release into the community. Furthermore, charity staff may not always pass on the knowledge that they gain and create about (ex-)offenders (see Foucault, 1977: 125) to statutory criminal justice agencies, and sharing information must not always result in more punitive and controlling outcomes. But Jane's case illustrates how charitable work with probationers can expand the reach of the formal criminal justice system into the community:

JANE: I think there's a whole chunk of monitoring that goes on as well, I'm going to talk to someone after you on a video link who's been recalled to our local prison, but that was because we'd got some information and I think we stopped something happening to be honest. It was actually me who rang up the probation officer, because I had concerns, and then they got the police in, you know, but I view that as part of the job really.

(Regional project manager)

It is notable that charities may gain information about probationers during *apparently informal and non-punitive interactions*. Four interview participants explained how their charities invested in building supportive relationships and rapport with their service users. For Jane, this work occurred in apparently non-punitive, non-institutional community settings such as cafes. Similarly, Kylie explained how their charity's staff considered themselves to be 'separate' from the statutory criminal justice agencies, and emphasised this to their service users. Kylie also indicated that this information was well-received by their (ex-)offender service users:

JANE: I really am spending *a lot* of my time, I joke actually, I spend a lot of my time sitting in cafes with [serious] offenders having coffee, assessing them, getting relationships going, assessing who really could most use the volunteers (emphasis in recording).

(Regional project manager)

KYLIE: When we go and do our introductions to our service users, we try to tell them that we're not the system, you know, we're not the police, we're not probation, we're not prison, we're a charity that wants to help them.... We are independent, away from that sort of sector. And they do seem to respond to that quite well.

(Regional project manager)

Charity staff can also gain additional information about service users because they have more contact time with them than statutory staff. For example, Jacqui explained how her charity's staff had significantly longer and more frequent time periods to spend working with their (ex-)offender service users than probation officers or psychiatrists:

JACQUI: They (probation officers) have *the most ridiculous* caseloads. They have *really* high numbers of people.... We tend to see the women a lot. Erm, you know, if a woman ... sees her psychiatrist once every *six months*, and we see them every week (Emphases in recording).

(Regional project manager)

This emphasis upon building relationships and rapport, and having time to spend with service users may form valuable and enabling aspects of charitable work which are discussed later in this chapter. However, apparently non-punitive interactions between charity staff and (ex-)offenders in the community may also result in charities gaining privileged access to information about (ex-)offenders, with potentially insidious exclusionary effects. This privileged access to information may be lubricated by the relatively informal locations where contact occurs, the apparent separation between charitable staff and the statutory criminal justice agencies, and the capacity of charitable staff to interact with their clients more frequently than statutory staff are able to.

Charitable work may also enhance the physical monitoring of (ex-)offenders (see Garland, 1990: 148–149; Ignatieff, 1978: 77, 164; Foucault, 1977: 126). Morris worked for a charity which supported prisoners after release and provided housing. He explained that drug testing was a condition of entry into the accommodation. A positive result would deny access to the accommodation and be relayed to the Offender Manager:

MORRIS: We test on entry, if they are positive for Class A drugs we refuse entry, because that means they have taken drugs between prison and us, so they're not going to be ready. For cannabis, we're more flexible, 'cause that's in the system for longer. We say: 'we will take you in but if you're positive in twenty-eight days time, we will evict you'.... What we do is we'll say to the Offender Manager: 'this person turned up positive'.

(Charity director)

This section has illustrated how charitable work can lead to net-widening and extended control, through charities' privileged access to information about their service users and enhanced monitoring of them. The practices described in this section are all reasonable, but it is questionable whether (ex-)offenders who engage with charities *fully comprehend* that charitable staff may share information with statutory staff, which may have controlling and punitive implications. Kylie's charity informed (ex-)offenders that information may be shared with Offender Managers: 'We try to tell them that ... we will have to feed back if there's any issues, to the Offender Manager'. However, this potential implication of apparently non-punitive interactions with charitable staff may not always be made clear and understood. The next section considers how charitable work at the policy, or macro, level may expand control.

7.2.3 Macro level control

The MoJ sponsored translation of penal reforms that began with the problematisation set out in *Breaking the Cycle* (MoJ, 2010) was examined in Chapter 6. This analysis demonstrated how charities enabled and justified the significant expansion in community control (Cohen, 1985: 15) which resulted from the new supervision requirement for short-sentence prisoners (MoJ, 2013c: 6). The introduction of this 'unprecedented' supervision requirement for short-sentence prisoners (MoJ, 2013c: 6) presents particular parallels to the expansions of control illustrated in the historical literature, which are now explored.

As noted in Chapter 6, the new supervision requirement for short-sentence prisoners is predicted to significantly increase the *scale of punishment* by increasing recalls to custody and causing up-tariffing by magistrates (Howard League, 2013: no pagination; Prison Reform Trust, 2013: 1), being likely to result in around 13,000 recalls to custody at a cost of £16 million per year (Prison Reform Trust, 2013: 1). It spatially and temporally extends the carceral net by expanding community supervision to those with short prison sentences, who are unlikely to have committed serious or violent crimes. This mirrors historical increases in the scale of penality which were based on the desire to discipline less serious offenders. As explained in Chapter 2, the establishment of the penitentiary in the nineteenth century led to dramatic increases in the numbers imprisoned in England, through the apparent need to discipline petty offenders using the rules and regulations of the penitentiary to prevent them proceeding 'unimpeded to the commission of more dangerous offences' (Ignatieff, 1978: 28, 108). The establishment of probation in the late nineteenth and early twentieth century also increased the scale of punishment, e.g. through the Summary Jurisdiction Act 1879 which enabled supervision for cases only 'where the offences were thought so trifling as to make punishment unnecessary' (Jarvis, 1972: 10; see also Tomczak, forthcoming).

Furthermore, the supervision requirement inserts the power to punish more deeply into the social body (Ignatieff, 1978: xiii; Foucault, 1977: 82). The liberty that short-sentence prisoners were formerly automatically entitled to following their release from prison now has more restrictions and conditions attached to it. These prisoners' sentences therefore no longer end upon release from prison, and a 'further year' has been added 'to the ambit of the criminal justice system' (Prison Reform Trust, 2013: 1). Because short-sentence prisoners did not 'get support they need' to resettle in the community (MoJ, 2013c: 3), a mandatory and coercive supervision requirement was introduced. The liberty of short-sentence prisoners post-release has thus become conditional on their willingness and capacity to comply with the mandates of their supervision orders (see McWilliams, 1986: 256; Cohen, 1985: 286).

Furthermore, the reforms have further fragmented the legal power to punish and increased the 'army of technicians' involved in punishment (Foucault, 1977: 11; see also Garland, 1990: 136). The decentralising reforms draw on 'the expertise of everyone who can make a contribution' to improving offender rehabilitation and thus public safety (MoJ, 2010: 5). It is, however, questionable whether this represents progress towards more effective punishment and better public safety or further fragmentation of the legal power to punish (away from the state) and increases in the scale of punishment (see Garland, 1990; Foucault, 1977). That is, whether the effect of involving a broader set of 'providers from all sectors' (MoJ, 2010: 9) in competing for and delivering penal services is likely to be *more effective punishment, or merely more punishment* (see Cohen, 1985: 254). Voluntary sector staff participation in PbR pilots and supervision for short-sentence prisoners could therefore be equated to Foucault's subsidiary authorities of punishment and 'minor civil servants of moral orthopaedics', whose presence means that the penal system is 'constantly growing' (Foucault, 1977: 10). However, I problematise this idea later in this chapter and argue that their role went beyond reproducing penal control.

Voluntary sector involvement in penal policy can therefore result in and legitimise apparently inclusionary 'support' policies which mean that penal institutions remain, their remit is widened, intervention is intensified, control is extended and the net of carceral power is widened (see Cohen, 1985: 15, 286). The foundation of *Breaking the Cycle* was improving public safety, supporting prisoner resettlement and reducing the costs of punishment, but this translated into a mandatory and coercive supervision requirement estimated to cost £16 million annually. This expansion of penal power operated through voluntary sector involvement in the PbR pilots (see Carrabine, 2000: 319). This section has illustrated how charitable work at both the micro and macro level may transport the force of the criminal justice system and expand control. I now consider how charitable work can transform, distort and modify the meanings, elements and experience of punishment, and then problematise the ideas of net-widening and control.

7.3 Positive effects of charitable work, or charities as penal mediators

7.3.1 Introduction

Previous studies have indicated that charitable work may have valuable effects in terms of increasing the social capital of (ex-)offenders and enabling their desistance from crime (e.g. Brown and Ross, 2010; Mills and Codd, 2008; Lewis *et al.*, 2007; see Chapter 2). This section draws on the data to examine the positive effects which can result from charitable work. The value of charitable enrichment activities for prisoners is analysed first, making reference to the concepts of social and human capital (as defined in Chapter 2) to illustrate how charities may mediate, or transform the experience of imprisonment (see Afari-kumah and Kwankam, 2013; Latour, 2005). Charities are also likely to enhance the social and human capital of probationers, e.g. by providing education, support and training opportunities, but the data did not exemplify this so probationers are not referred to here. The role of *relationships* in mediating the experience of punishment and supporting desistance from crime is also examined. The data indicated that charitable staff can build distinctive relationships with prisoners and probationers as a result of their unique separation from the punitive and coercive aspects of punishment, and their positive conceptualisations of (ex-)offenders (see also Tomczak and Albertson, 2016).

7.3.2 Social and human capital

My data aligned with arguments that charities may widen the opportunities available to prisoners and thus enhance prisoner social and human capital (e.g. Meek *et al.*, 2010; Smith *et al.*, 1993). This section explores the range and value of these opportunities, which included learning in prison (e.g. to read or learning crafts) and the opportunity to volunteer in prison and community-based charitable programmes (e.g. as a peer mentor).

The work of the Shannon Trust demonstrates how charities may build social and human capital by widening the educational opportunities available to prisoners and addressing the very poor literacy amongst prisoners. Its peer-mentored reading plan has the vision: 'every prisoner a reader' (Shannon Trust, 2011: 3). The Trust aims 'to transform lives by inspiring prisoners who can read to teach prisoners with poor reading skills, thus providing learners with opportunities to develop *life skills* that better equip them for the challenges of living as contributing members of society' (Shannon Trust, 2011: 3, emphasis added). Learners can gain the life skill of reading competence and prisoner mentors may also develop new skills through the process, such as teaching and interpersonal skills. This mutual aid function (see Chapter 4) *creates capabilities* for both prisoner teachers and students, *enhancing their social and human capital* through both the teaching and network of mutual support and improvement operated by the Trust (see Faulkner, 2003: 291).

The Trust's website[1] provided convincing results from questionnaires in 2012 which suggest that its work is valued by prisoners and does create capabilities. Through participating in the reading plan, 95 per cent of learners and 85 per cent of mentors felt more confident about the future; 76 per cent of learners and 86 per cent of mentors felt that their communication skills had improved; 97 per cent of mentors felt that mentoring had given them new skills; and 98 per cent felt that they understood others better through the reading plan. There is no information available about the participant selection, data collection and interpretation procedures used to produce these results, so their validity cannot be considered. However, the website also included a 'Success Stories' section with a variety of case studies. This quotation from an ex-prisoner mentor indicates how the scheme could be beneficial:

An ex-prisoner reading mentor: 'Prison can be a place where your "real world" skills – especially as someone fortunate enough to have had a good education – are often ignored or devalued. Volunteering to ... (work) with other prisoners who genuinely want to *improve their reading skills* is a very practical way in which to rediscover *your own value and self-esteem.* Watching adults, who have often been excluded from school at an early age, suddenly realise that they can read letters from their loved ones without having to ask others for help (or even having to pay for assistance) is perhaps one of the *most rewarding experiences* anyone can have in an otherwise grim, custodial environment (emphases added).[2]

As indicated by the mentor, charitable work may provide *psychological benefits* for prisoners (see Digard *et al.*, 2007: 4; Lippke, 2003: 35; see Chapter 2) and opportunities for *self-development* (see Bilby *et al.*, 2013; Henley *et al.*, 2012; Tett *et al.*, 2012; Cohen, 2009), thus enhancing human capital. Prisoner Billy's story formed part of the 2010 Storybook Dads Annual Report and explained how engaging with this charity as a computer editor has affected him positively. Storybook Dads' work enabled imprisoned parents to record stories and messages for their children which were then edited and presented as a gift (Storybook Dads, 2010: 4, 5). In a related vein, Fine Cell Work 'trains prisoners in paid, skilled, creative needlework undertaken in the long hours spent in their cells ... to foster hope, discipline and self-esteem' (Fine Cell Work, 2010: 2). Prisoner Ross's story from their website indicated that this life-sentenced prisoner greatly valued the opportunity to sew whilst in his cell:

BILLY: Being part of Storybook Dads has made me believe that you can do anything if you put your mind to it. Not only have they given me computer skills but also a renewed vigour and confidence (which I admit was waning).

(Storybook Dads, 2010: 7)

ROSS: About nine o' clock I got it out and started sewing. Before I knew where I was they were unlocking us for breakfast, a whole night had come and gone with no thoughts of suicide and no tears of melancholy. I promptly joined the class as it offered me the escape I had been looking for.... The hope, the self-respect and pride. I am no longer dirty and smelly, I'm quite respectable, my self-worth has been restored.... How good it is to be alive, to feel that I am accomplishing something and that my life has real meaning.[3]

Psychological benefits for prisoners are illustrated by Ross, who explained how sewing helped him to find respite from melancholy and suicidal thoughts. Opportunities for self-development are illustrated by both quotations, which detailed how these prisoners gained a sense of increased confidence (Billy) and increased self-worth (Ross) through participating in these enrichment activities. Both quotations illustrate how charitable work created capabilities for the prisoners and enhanced their human capital, by developing their computer skills (Billy) and sewing skills (Ross). Charitable staff also described how charitable work could promote prisoner engagement with productive activities (Maguire, 2012; Mills *et al.*, 2012; Light, 1993; see also Bilby *et al.*, 2013; Tett *et al.*, 2012). For example, Holly explained the 'unusual' way that prisoners positively engaged with the charity's creative training opportunities, which would not be available in prisons if the charity did not offer them:

HOLLY: Prisons like it … it brings something else, that they can't, within their regime, offer. Or they don't have the resources or the manpower to actually offer…. The officers, yeah they do, they kind of have some value of what we do do and they see how the prisoners talk and how they engage and the positive way that they're willing to work, which to be honest is quite unusual.

(Central office project staff)

This section has explained some means through which charities can *mediate* punishment, such as providing additional opportunities for prisoners which may transform or modify the experience of imprisonment. The data illustrated that the social and human capital and engagement of prisoners could be enhanced through charitable enrichment activities. These activities had a stand-alone value in terms of improving the material experience of imprisonment (Liebling, 2004), but also supported engagement with productive activities and could thus enable desistance from crime (see McNeill *et al.*, 2012; Maruna, 2007; McNeill, 2006; see also Chapter 2). The next section examines how interpersonal relationships (see Liebling, 2004) between charitable staff and prisoners/probationers may also mediate the experience of punishment and support desistance, and explores the distinctiveness of these relationships. This suggests that the *providers of penal services can matter*.

7.3.3 Relationships

This section examines how interpersonal relationships with charitable staff and volunteers may mediate the experience of punishment and support the process of desisting from crime. Literature suggests that relationships between charitable staff and the prisoners and probationers with whom they work may be valuable and distinctive from those with statutory staff (Maguire, 2012; Mills *et al.*, 2012; Lewis *et al.*, 2007; Light, 1993). Although the evidence base to support these claims is limited, charitable staff might be able to pay attention to the needs of individual prisoners and probationers, and have the ability to provide personal and emotional support in a way that statutory staff do not (Lewis *et al.*, 2007: 47). This argument links to scholarship which has emphasised the importance of strengths-based interpersonal relationships in supporting desistance from crime (e.g. Phoenix and Kelly, 2013; Robinson and McNeill, 2008; McNeill, 2006).

Reflecting the data, this section principally refers to prisoner relationships with charitable staff. Data referring to probationers is labelled accordingly.

My analysis indicated that relationships between prisoners and charitable staff were valuable and could mediate the experience of imprisonment. New Bridge emphasised that the 'patience and support of our team' is instrumental in helping vulnerable prisoners 'eventually start to understand their potential and their worth' (New Bridge, 2010: 6). Fine Cell Work explained that their volunteers made a particularly special contribution and 'profoundly encouraged' the prisoners' motivation to engage with the charity (Fine Cell Work, 2010: 2). Billy's story from the 2010 Storybook Dads Annual Report noted that Billy valued his supportive relationships with the charity's staff and volunteers, stating 'the support that the team gives us is priceless' (Storybook Dads, 2010: 7).

Although the ability to create positive and enabling relationships with prisoners and probationers is by no means exclusive to charitable staff (see Phoenix and Kelly, 2013; Robinson and McNeill, 2008; McNeill, 2006), charitable staff may be able to create distinctively valuable relationships. Charitable staff seem to have some degree of *separation* from punishment, which can support their distinctive accepting and strengths-based conceptualisations of (ex-)offenders, and enable particularly positive and trusting relationships with (ex-)offenders which *distinctively mediate* their experience of punishment.

Charitable staff consciously adopted a non-judgemental and person-centred approach to their prisoner and probationer service users. The terminology used by charitable staff demonstrates accepting and strengths-based conceptualisations of service users, which are likely to be reflected in interactions. This terminology included: 'amazing women, who have faced *so much* and *still* keep going' (Jacqui, emphases in recording) and 'people with goodness inside them' (Solomon). Holly, Jacqui and Kylie detailed their non-judgemental, person-centred and strengths-based interactions with their prisoner and probationer service users. Holly explained that the judging of prisoners' offences was beyond their remit, being the concern of the judges who hand down sentences and the prison who administer them. Kylie also stated her charity's commitment to remaining non-judgemental of past offending by service users. Jacqui illustrated how the non-judgemental and person-centred approach of charitable staff was appreciated by probationers:

HOLLY: You know, it's not for us to make judgement about what they've done or what the prison (pause) you know, sentencing and all the rest of it.

(Central office project staff)

KYLIE (WORKED ALONGSIDE PROBATION): We have to take everybody on an individual basis and look at what they want to do. We take people as they come, I mean we've had a range of offences that come to us and obviously, through our training and induction and what we believe in, you know, you've got to remain non-judgemental and you know, you can't pass comment.

(Regional project manager)

JACQUI (WORKED ALONGSIDE PROBATION): What I am absolutely passionate about and I think, I know all my colleagues are, its about saying actually 'I know what you've done, *I'm not bothered what you've done* and *it's you now* that I'm interested in' and I think that's why we're so successful, because *women really feel that.*

(Regional project manager, (emphases added)

By distinguishing prisoner and probationer service users from their criminal offences and behaviours, charitable staff may have created some psychological separation from the 'offender' label, identity and behaviours. Such psychological distance could underpin strengths-based interactions and support willing prisoners and probationers to explore the new ways of being which underpin the cognitive transition from offender to resettled person (see Maruna, 2011, 2007; Burnett and Maruna, 2006; Giordano *et al.*, 2002). This process is illustrated by Billy's story, which formed part of the Storybook Dads 2010 Annual Report. Billy indicated that he had experienced some positive shifts in his identity (see Burnett and Maruna, 2006) through working with Storybook Dads, which may have positively affected his behaviour after release:

BILLY: It gives you a sense of responsibility and normality which helps in the planning for a life outside of prison, a life that doesn't involve ending up back inside.... If you ask me who I am, I no longer reply 'A criminal. One of life's screw-ups'.... I'll tell you now who I am; I am a father, an artist, an editor and producer, a teacher and a friend....]That's what I have found out about myself these last years with the help of the team at Storybook Dads. It's fair to say these last few years have changed my life because I've realised that people *do* care.

(Storybook Dads, 2010: 7, emphasis in original)

This is in line with the enabling, strengths-based interactions that have been cited to enable desistance (McNeill, 2006). However, charities are perhaps distinctively able to conceptualise their clients as being 'in need rather than a threat to public safety' and to focus primarily on socialisation and economic integration rather than risk management and security (Goddard, 2012: 357). This analysis does not imply that all prison and probation officers approach (ex-) offenders as one-dimensional characters or define them entirely by their offences. But charitable staff considered that their person-centred approach to prisoners and capacity for strengths-based interactions could never be replicated by statutory staff who can never have the same distance from coercive risk management and enforcement roles. It seems that involvement with these aspects of penal regimes can affect prisoner perceptions of staff and staff conceptualisations of prisoners, which are both in turn likely to affect relationships. The interview data suggested that *charitable staff have a unique relative separation from punishment* and may therefore *distinctively mediate the experience of punishment by offering distinctive interpersonal relationships to prisoners and probationers*, built on their accepting and strengths-based conceptualisations of (ex-)offenders. Because charitable practitioners often do not have direct involvement with the coercive aspects of punishment (although this may not be the case for some charities in certain marketised relationships providing core penal services for statutory criminal justice agencies), they may be better able to focus on the person behind the offence and remain non-judgemental.

For example, Adrian explained how their charity (and, in Adrian's opinion, all charities) saw themselves as providing interpersonal relationships that are different to interactions with statutory staff. For Adrian, charity staff were able to approach the prisoners they work with as women rather than offenders, because they did not have the same focus on prison security that officers must 'always' maintain. Jacqui also indicated that relationships between charity staff and their service users could be qualitatively different to those with statutory staff, who in her opinion too often lost sight of the people serving the sentences (see also Goddard, 2012: 357). Similarly, Aurora pointed out that charity staff could avoid interpreting all of their clients' behaviours 'through the lens of offending' and maintain focus on (ex-)offenders' strengths and 'potential'. Aurora also made the important point that this is not necessarily the case, as charities are always at risk of being 'captured' by the punitive concerns of the criminal justice system:

ADRIAN: If you're a prison officer, you key role is *always* security, it always has to be security, so when they're working with the women they're primarily defined by the fact that they're offenders, and then anything else will be secondary to that.... I think it is, all charities provide that, it is a different role, its seeing them *first as a woman* ... rather than as an offender.... We approach them as a woman ... that needs our support (emphases in recording).

(Charity director)

JACQUI (WORKED ALONGSIDE PROBATION): In criminal justice services it can be easy to lose sight of that *woman* in the prison sentence (emphasis in recording).

(Regional project manager)

AURORA: Instead of seeing people as offenders, which the criminal justice system too often does.... Instead of sort of seeing everything through the lens of offending, which is always through the lens of risk and, and the lens of need, so you define people as being risky and needy ... I think that is where the voluntary sector, if it doesn't get completely captured by the criminal justice system, if it doesn't *let itself* just be part of, ... a carceral experience, or an offender-based experience, that is where voluntary sector skills can come in. So viewing offenders as people with potential (emphasis in recording).

(Statutory staff)

A further quotation from Adrian explained how statutory staff's punitive and coercive roles may diminish their ability to maintain supportive and trusting relationships with prisoners. This demonstrates how the distinctive and valuable separation of charity staff from punishment may underpin trusting relationships and mediate the experience of punishment in a way that statutory staff never could, due to their control responsibilities:

ADRIAN: Lots of them [prison officers] are very good and provide lots of support to the women, but nonetheless (pause) in prison its just a thing, if you kick off on the landing, the same officer who may have been being really supportive earlier, their job is to take your privileges away and to lock you up and if necessary to drag you off somewhere if you're really kicking off and you won't go behind your doors. And I think the, the sort of care and control (pause), erm, aspect is very difficult to merge.

(Charity director)

This analysis does not suggest that charitable staff and volunteers are all non-judgemental and supportive to the prisoners and probationers that they work with, nor does it imply that all charitable staff have a degree of separation from punishment in the eyes of their prisoner and probationer service users. Chapters 4, 5 and 6 have detailed the important differences between charities and the context dependency of their programmes, which can affect the outcomes of their work with prisoners and probationers. But this section has demonstrated how charities and their staff can mediate the experience of criminal justice by providing distinctive relationship opportunities for prisoners and probationers. These distinctive relationships may improve the experience of punishment and could also support processes of desistance from crime. It seems that charitable staff have a unique position, being involved in punishment yet relatively separate from its more punitive and coercive aspects. This unique position may mean that charitable staff are viewed differently by prisoners and probationers, and possess a distinctive ability to psychologically separate them from their offending, which could support strengths-based interactions with service users and perhaps improve how prisoners see themselves. As such, although charities could be seen as subsidiary authorities of punishment (Foucault, 1977: 10), my data shows that they should not be reduced to intermediaries of punishment that merely expand the carceral net. This is not always the limit of their contribution. In light of this finding, I now revisit and rework my analysis of the PbR pilots (see Chapter 6) to provide a new avenue for research and integrated theory.

7.4 Problematising control

Whilst my analysis of the PbR pilots made a satisfying account of net-widening, positioning charities solely as intermediaries in this translation of penal power tells a partial story. Without denying that charitable work might not always differ from statutory penal programmes and recognising that it can often result in expanded control, the aim of ANT analysis is to multiply the 'mediating points between any two elements' rather than black-boxing actors as intermediaries (Latour, 1996: 378; see also Afarikumah and Kwankam, 2013). Indeed, a more nuanced reading of the data shows that charitable involvement in the PbR pilots did do more than merely reproduce existing criminal justice.

Available results from the PbR pilots did indicate falls in reconviction events across the board (MoJ, 2015a). I would much prefer that short-sentence prisoners were offered resettlement support on a voluntary rather than mandatory basis (and that broader social inequalities were addressed in non-punitive ways). It is, however, undeniable that short-sentence prisoners tend to have high reoffending rates and low levels of social and human capital, and are likely to experience difficulties (re-)integrating into the community post-release (MoJ, 2010). Furthermore, the PbR pilots did offer some *valuable avenues of practical and emotional support* to the prisoners with whom they worked. This practical support included providing access to a phone, arranging alcohol rehabilitation and mental health support, supporting housing and providing food vouchers. Whilst these forms of support may appear simplistic, they were apparently extremely valuable to some released prisoners and could play a role in enabling their desistance from crime, as the quotations below indicate:

> Staff on the Doncaster PbR pilot 'allowed offenders to use their work mobiles to make phone calls in order to resolve problems, such as with benefits, housing, drug support and debts. Staff stated that individuals typically had little income and could not afford the cost of lengthy phone calls to these agencies, which were often premium rate numbers'.
>
> (MoJ, 2015b: 27)

> Short-sentence prisoner released from HMP Peterborough: 'In prison itself, I spoke to the key worker a couple of times and explained that I needed, I used to go to [service] for alcohol, it's basically like rehabilitation. He got in contact with them for me and told them my release date.... He got in contact with a mental health service as well.... Yes, they helped me out a lot in prison'.
>
> (MoJ, 2015c: 42)

> Short-sentence prisoner released from HMP Peterborough: 'Personally, I think it's the housing because with me.... As soon as I'm out, I'm going to go back to ... what I know. If I've got my own roof, then I'm alright, basically. That's how I see it.... Obviously you need money to get your own deposit, so they're helping to do that for you.'
>
> (MoJ, 2015c: 44)

> Short-sentence prisoner released from HMP Peterborough: 'When I first got out of prison, for a good few months, the One Service were supplying [me] with food vouchers because my benefits were being messed up. Now if they

weren't there doing that for me, then I would have gone out and committed a crime to get the money, just to feed myself. So the fact that One Service[4] was there and helped me out with £25 a week in vouchers was brilliant. That prevented me from going out and committing a crime.'

(MoJ, 2015c: 48)

The emotional support included knowing that there was a service to turn to and being reassured by this, having help for the first time in one's life and having someone to talk to in times of need.

Short-sentence prisoner released from HMP Peterborough: 'I've been in jail five times and it's only this last time that I've been in jail that I've actually had any support or help offered. Before that, nothing.... Whereas this time round, having the One Service there, even though I haven't needed them much, knowing that they're there and if I need them they're there, it's been brilliant.'

(MoJ, 2015c: 47)

Short-sentence prisoner released from HMP Doncaster: 'Last time I had no clue as to where I was going or what I was doing! This time I knew I wouldn't just be thrown out on the street. I met [my case manager] on my release and [they] helped sort things. It was reassuring.'

(MoJ, 2015b: 30)

Short-sentence prisoner released from HMP Doncaster: 'Never had help like this before. First time in forty-five years. Already feel it's making a positive difference to my life.'

(MoJ, 2015b: 30)

Short-sentence prisoner released from HMP Peterborough: 'The thing with me, I lose my head sometimes and I've got mental health problems. They said they'd sit there and just listen to me if I've got problems and all that. I lost a few family members and all that just recently. Like I say, I knew they'd be there for me to talk to them. So that's the kind of stuff they do so supporting me in that kind of way.'

(MoJ, 2015c: 45)

It is important to note that the Peterborough and Doncaster PbR pilots offered support on a voluntary rather than mandatory basis, and that the new supervision requirement which emerged from them is very much the latter.[5] It is possible that the charitable work itself was not necessarily inherently controlling and exclusionary, but the supervision requirement resulted from the MoJ's translation of it. This translation illustrates that the powerful labels of charity and voluntarism (Armstrong, 2002; Crawford, 1999) can be adopted by the machinery of government and utilised to support certain purposes. In relation to

Canada, Hannah-Moffatt (2000: 528) has noted that 'the knowledges and resources of organizations like the Canadian Association of Elizabeth Fry Societies and Aboriginal groups are selectively used to legitimate penal strategies and to supplement deficiencies and gaps apparent in governmental programmes'. It is perhaps this selective adoption of aspects of charitable work by government and the powerful legitimating function of the charity label that are problematic, rather than (or combined with) the charitable work itself. When charitable work is reshaped by agencies such as the MoJ with negative consequences, charitable dissent to this has to counter the large and powerful machinery of the state.[6] As explained in Chapter 6, Social Finance, which proposed the Peterborough Social Impact Bond, later publicly critiqued 'the suggestion that the progress of the Peterborough Social Impact Bond supports the case' for the much wider changes envisaged by *Transforming Rehabilitation* (Howard League, 2013: no pagination). Nevertheless, and despite the vigorous dissent of charities such as the Prison Reform Trust and the Howard League, PbR was rolled out and the Offender Rehabilitation Act 2014 was enacted, thus instituting the supervision requirement and expanding carceral power in space and time.

Nevertheless, the data above indicate that the PbR pilots did do more than merely reproduce and extend existing criminal justice. In fact, their staff meaningfully improved the experience of punishment. The ultimate effects of the PbR pilots will depend upon how the new Community Rehabilitation Companies, which have responsibility for delivering the supervision requirement, see and implement their role, and how frequently breach proceedings which increase levels of incarceration are used. It is possible that there is space for innovation and person-, rather than compliance- and risk-, focussed work within the new Community Rehabilitation Companies (Robinson *et al.*, 2016: 172–173; see also Goddard and Myers, 2011), and perhaps the supervision requirement is, albeit in a problematic and coercive way, acknowledging the difficulties of short-sentence prisoners upon release. While I maintain that welfare is best delivered on a voluntary basis, and without detracting from the utility and validity of control and net-widening theories, focussing only on net-widening provides partial and limiting accounts which overlook variations in the *substance and qualities of the carceral net*, thus limiting possibilites for action: 'in order to begin imagining what a more just world might look like, it is crucial for criminologists to not only report the "bad news" about crime and punishment' (Goddard and Myers, 2011: 667; see also Zedner, 2002). Without denying the many problematic aspects of imprisonment and probation, a carceral net which supports, enables and encourages those caught within will be experienced differently and lead to different outcomes from one which is, for example, disabling, violent and depressing. I have no doubt that some charitable programmes 'clone' (Armstrong, 2002: 365; see also Garland, 1990; Cohen, 1985; Ignatieff, 1978; Foucault, 1977) and even amplify the controlling discourses and practices of criminal justice institutions, and my own analysis demonstrates how charitable work can lead to extended control. I therefore advocate that the control and net-widening implications of charitable work in criminal justice should be considered in *every* account of the penal voluntary sector, because charitable work is not an uncomplicated good. Apparently innocuous informal interactions may expand control and the label of charity has a very powerful legitimating function which can be attached to punitive and exclusionary policies.

However, the evidence also suggests that charities can valuably mediate punishment. Charities can widen the range of opportunities and material provisions available to prisoners (see Meek *et al.*, 2010; Smith *et al.*, 1993; see also Liebling, 2004), enabling prisoners to build social and human capital (see Brown and Ross, 2010; Lewis *et al.*, 2007) and promoting engagement with productive activities (see Maguire, 2012; Light, 1993). These 'extra' provisions are not necessarily distinctively valuable, although charities may offer distinctive interpersonal relationships to prisoners and probationers based on their person-centred, non-judgemental and strengths-based interactions with service users (Maguire, 2012; Mills *et al.*, 2012; Meek *et al.*, 2010) and unique separation from the punitive and coercive aspects of penal regimes (at least in some charitable programmes). The evidence presented in this chapter indicates that charitable work can transform the experience of imprisonment (see Liebling, 2004) and provide valuable support for probationers (see also Lewis *et al.*, 2007). All of these benefits may support willing service users to desist from crime (see McNeill *et al.*, 2012; Brown and Ross, 2010; Mills and Codd, 2008; Maruna, 2007; McNeill, 2006). By potentially interrupting the 'revolving door' of re-offending through interactions with prisoners and probationers, charities may enable the long process of liberation from the carceral net. However, the *context dependency* of charitable programmes also means that beneficial outcomes should not be assumed, and it is important to note that the ability of charities to mediate punishment is not unconstrained. Prisoners and probationers may benefit from engaging with charitable programmes, but this does not necessarily offset the pains of punishment and the broader social disadvantages that they are also likely to be facing (e.g. Corcoran, 2012: 22; Tett *et al.*, 2012: 172).

This analysis demonstrates that both the control and emancipatory literatures appear to be inadequate, suggesting that a more nuanced hybrid or integrated theorisation is required. The work of voluntary organisations can apparently result in both control and emancipation, or negative *and* positive effects. As charities' contributions to building social and human capital and expanding social control are not necessarily mutually exclusive, the task for scholars is to highlight how and under which conditions both of these overall outcomes can occur. I suggest that hybrid theory is required and offer the conceptual innovation of 'inclusionary control' to this end. Without denying the dangers of the expanding carceral net, it is reductionist and disabling not to simultaneously consider how its qualities can be changed, and the concept of net-widening does not facilitate such analysis. The idea of 'inclusionary control' is not to make excuses for exclusionary policies or problematic institutions, but to provide a means of examining how positive or improved outcomes can come from sites of control. A significantly expanded base of empirical evidence could underpin the development of theory accounting for such hybrid experiences, e.g. by examining the characteristics and qualities of the carceral net as it operates and is experienced by different people, in different places and at different times.

There are no unilateral effects to be assumed when considering the work of penal voluntary organisations, although the potential for increased control and exclusion must always be considered. The diversity of organisations within the sector and their varied relationships with the statutory agencies of punishment (e.g. lobbying, PbR, contractual and informal relationships at different scales, such as with the MoJ and with individual prisons) means that one analysis certainly does not fit all. Recent work from the USA notes that charities work with ex-prisoners 'in ways that vary across providers' religious and political orientations and corresponding funding sources' (Kaufman, 2015: 549), although notably *funding did not completely explain or determine* variations in charitable work. Although I would tend to agree with the assertion that smaller scale, possibly volunteer-led charities are 'more likely to bring the so-called 'added value' to their work with offenders, particularly the building of social cohesion through their connections to the local community' (Mills *et al.*, 2012: 401), the potential contributions of 'corporate-style' charities cannot be ignored. It seems that some prisoners greatly valued the contribution of the PbR pilot schemes. More evidence is required to assess the overlaps between empowerment and control, and to consider the relationship conditions which might influence these outcomes. For example, future work could assess if and how the effects of charitable work can vary with volunteer/paid staff ratios, mandatory programme participation, (non-)state (contract) funding and PbR funding. These avenues notwithstanding, commentators must always note that the powerful label of charity groups organisations which may have more points of difference than similarities (Armstrong, 2002: 356).

Notes

1 www.shannontrust.org.uk/our-work/our-achievements/. Accessed: 16 November 2013.
2 www.shannontrust.org.uk/our-work/success-stories/an-ex-reading-plan-mentor. Accessed: 9 February 2016.
3 www.finecellwork.co.uk/prison_stories/testimonials/279_ross_story. Accessed: 15 November 2013.
4 The One Service was the name for the PbR pilot which operated at HMP Peterborough between 2010 and 2015, providing 'through-the-gate' and post-release support to short-sentence adult male prisoners with the aim of reducing reoffending (MoJ, 2015c: 1). The consortium of service delivery organisations involved was described in Chapter 6.
5 As Christie notes, regarding the reshaping of Norwegian restorative justice boards into mechanisms for the control of deviant youth: 'boards with penal power will lose their civilising strength' (2015: 110).
6 Some charitable lobbying will be affected by new rules on the spending of government grant funding which came into effect in May 2016. The new rules mean that grant funds from central government must not be used to lobby government and Parliament, although privately raised funds can still be used for campaigning.

References

Afarikumah, E. and Kwankam, S. Y. (2013) 'Deploying Actor-Network Theory to Analyse Telemedicine Implementation in Ghana', *Science*, *1*(2): 77–84.

Armstrong, S. (2002) 'Punishing Not-For-Profit: Implications of nonprofit privatization in juvenile punishment', *Punishment and Society*, *4(*3): 345–368.

Bilby, C., Caulfield, L. S. and Ridley, L. (2013) *Re-Imagining Futures: Exploring arts interventions and the process of desistance.* London: Arts Alliance. Available at: www.artsalliance.org.uk/sites/default/files/Re-imagining_Futures_Research_Report_Final. pdf. Accessed: 3 November 2013.

Brown, M. and Ross, S. (2010) 'Mentoring, Social Capital and Desistance: A study of women released from prison', *Australian and New Zealand Journal of Criminology*, *43*(1): 31–50.

Burnett, R. and Maruna, S. (2006) 'The Kindness of Prisoners: Strengths-based resettlement in theory and action', *Criminology and Criminal Justice*, *6*(1): 83–106.

Carrabine, E. (2000) 'Discourse, Governmentality and Translation: Toward a social theory of imprisonment', *Theoretical Criminology*, *4*(3): 309–331.

Christie, N. (2015) 'Widening the Net', *Restorative Justice*, *3*(1): 109–113.

Cohen, M. L. (2009) 'Choral Singing and Prison Inmates: Influences of performing in a prison choir', *Journal of Correctional Education*, *60*(1): 52–65.

Cohen, S. (1985) *Visions of Social Control: Crime, punishment and classification.* Cambridge: Polity Press.

Corcoran, M. (2012) 'Be Careful What You Ask For: Findings from the seminar series on the Third Sector in criminal justice', *Prison Service Journal*, *204*: 17–22.

Cox, P. (2013) *Bad Girls in Britain, 1900–1950: Gender, justice, and welfare.* Basingstoke: Palgrave Macmillan.

Crawford, A. (1999) 'Questioning Appeals to Community within Crime Prevention and Control', *European Journal on Criminal Policy and Research*, *7*(4): 509–530.

Digard, L., Grafin von Sponeck, A. and Liebling, A. (2007) 'All Together Now: The therapeutic potential of a prison-based music programme', *Prison Service Journal*, *170*: 3–14.

Faulkner, D. (2003) 'Taking Citizenship Seriously: Social capital and criminal justice in a changing world', *Criminal Justice*, *3*(3): 287–315.

Fine Cell Work (2010) *Trustees' Report and Unaudited Accounts for the Year Ended 31 December 2010.*

Foucault, M. (1977) *Discipline and Punish: The birth of the prison.* London: Allen Lane.

Garland, D. (1990) *Punishment and Modern Society: A study in social theory.* Oxford: Clarendon Press.

Giordano, P. C., Cernkovich, S. A and Rudolph, J. L. (2002) 'Gender, Crime, and Desistance: Toward a theory of cognitive transformation', *American Journal of Sociology*, *107*(4): 990–1064.

Goddard, T. (2012) 'Post-Welfarist Risk Managers? Risk, crime prevention, and the turn to non-state community-based organizations', *Theoretical Criminology*, *16*(3): 347–363.

Goddard, T. and Myers, R. (2011) 'Democracy and Demonstration in the Grey Area of Neo-Liberalism: A case study of Free Los Angeles High School', *British Journal of Criminology*, *51*(4): 652–670.

Hannah-Moffat, K. (2000) 'Prisons That Empower', *British Journal of Criminology*, *40*(3): 510–531.

Henley, J., Caulfield, L. S., Wilson, D. and Wilkinson, D. J. (2012) 'Good Vibrations: Positive change through social music-making', *Music Education Research*, *14*(4): 499–520.

Howard League (2013) *Offender Rehabilitation Bill. Report stage and third reading.* Available at: https://d19ylpo4aovc7m.cloudfront.net/fileadmin/howard_league/user/pdf/Briefings/Briefing_for_ORB_Report_Stage_and_Third_Reading.pdf. Accessed: 10 April 2013.

Ignatieff, M. (1978) *A Just Measure of Pain.* London: Macmillan Press.

Jarvis, F. (1972) *Advise, Assist and Befriend: A history of the Probation and After-Care Service.* London: NAPO.

Kaufman, N. (2015) 'Prisoner Incorporation: The work of the state and non-governmental organizations', *Theoretical Criminology*, *19*(4): 534–553.

Latour, B. (1996) 'On Actor-Network Theory. A few clarifications plus more than a few complications', *Soziale Welt*, *47*(4): 369–381.

Latour, B. (1999) 'On Recalling ANT', in Law, J. and Hassard, J. (eds) *Actor-Network Theory and After.* Oxford: Blackwell.

Latour, B. (2005) *Reassembling the Social: An introduction to Actor-Network Theory.* Oxford: Oxford University Press.

Latour, B. (1996) 'On Actor-Network Theory. A few clarifications plus more than a few complications', *Soziale Welt*, *47*(4): 369–381.

Law, J. (2004) *After Method: Mess in social science research.* Abingdon: Routledge.

Lewis S., Maguire M., Raynor P., Vanstone M. and Vennard J. (2007) 'What Works in Resettlement? Findings from seven Pathfinders for short-term prisoners in England and Wales', *Criminology and Criminal Justice*, *7*(1): 33–53.

Liebling, A. with Arnold, H. (2004) *Prisons and Their Moral Performance: A study of values, quality, and prison life.* Oxford: Oxford University Press.

Light, R. (1993) 'Why Support Prisoners' Family-Tie Groups?' *The Howard Journal of Criminal Justice*, *32*(4): 322–329.

Lippke, R. L. (2003) 'Prisoner Access to Recreation, Entertainment and Diversion', *Punishment and Society*, *5*(1): 33–52.

Maguire, M. (2012) 'Response 1: Big Society, the voluntary sector and the marketisation of criminal justice', *Criminology and Criminal Justice*, *12*(5): 483–505.

Maruna, S. (2007) 'After Prison, What? The ex-prisoners' struggle to desist from crime', in Jewkes, Y. (ed.) *Handbook on Prisons.* Cullompton: Willan Publishing.

Maruna, S. (2011) 'Reentry As a Rite of Passage', *Punishment and Society*, *13*(1): 3–28.

McNeill, F. (2006) 'A Desistance Paradigm for Offender Management', *Criminology and Criminal Justice*, *6*(1): 39–62.

McNeill, F., Farrall, S., Lightowler, C. and Maruna, S. (2012) 'How and Why People Stop Offending: Discovering desistance', *IRISS Insights 15.* Available at www.iriss. org.uk/resources/how-and-why-people-stop-offending-discovering-desistance. Accessed: 19 February 2014.

McWilliams, W. (1983) 'The Mission to the English Police Courts 1876–1936', *The Howard Journal of Criminal Justice*, *22*(3): 129–147.

McWilliams, W. (1986) 'The English Probation System and The Diagnostic Ideal', *The Howard Journal of Criminal Justice*, *25*(4): 241–260.

Meek, R., Gojkovic, D. and Mills, A. (2010) 'The Role of the Third Sector in Work with Offenders: The perceptions of criminal justice and third sector stakeholders', *TSRC Working Paper 34.* Birmingham: Third Sector Research Centre.

Mills, A. and Codd, H. (2008) 'Prisoners' Families and Offender Management: Mobilizing social capital', *Probation Journal*, 55(1): 9–24.

Mills, A., Meek, R. and Gojkovic, D. (2012) 'Partners, Guests or Competitors: Relationships between criminal justice and third sector staff in prisons', *Probation Journal*, 59(4): 391–405.

MoJ (2010) *Breaking the Cycle: Effective punishment, rehabilitation and sentencing of offenders*. London: MoJ.

MoJ (2015a) *Interim Re-conviction Figures for Peterborough and Doncaster Payment by Results Pilots*. Available at: https://www.gov.uk/government/uploads/system/uploads/attachment_data/file/399312/annex-a-payment-by-results-jan15.pdf. Accessed: 15 March 2015.

MoJ (2015b) *HMP Doncaster Payment by Results Pilot: Final process evaluation report*. Available at: www.gov.uk/government/uploads/system/uploads/attachment_data/file/449494/hmp-doncaster-pbr-final-evaluation.pdf. Accessed: 30 July 2015.

MoJ (2015c) *The Payment by Results Social Impact Bond Pilot at HMP Peterborough: Final process evaluation report*. Available at: www.gov.uk/government/publications/social-impact-bond-pilot-at-hmp-peterborough-final-report. Accessed: 1 February 2015.

Neuberger, J. (2009) *Volunteering Across the Criminal Justice System*. London: The Cabinet Office.

New Bridge (2010) *Annual Report 2010*.

Nimmo, R. (2011) 'Actor-Network Theory and Methodology: Social research in a more-than-human world', *Methodological Innovations Online*, 6(3): 108–119.

Phoenix, J. and Kelly, L. (2013) '"You Have to Do It for Yourself" Responsiblization in youth justice and young people's situated knowledge of youth justice practice', *British Journal of Criminology*, 53(3): 419–437.

Prison Reform Trust (2013) *Briefing on the Offender Rehabilitation Bill*. Available at: www.prisonreformtrust.org.uk/Portals/0/Documents/Prison%20Reform%20Trust%20Briefing%20Offender%20Rehabilitation%20Bill%20HoC%202nd%20Reading%2011Nov13.pdf. Accessed: 10 March 2014.

Robinson, G. and McNeill, F. (2008) 'Exploring the Dynamics of Compliance with Community Penalties', *Theoretical Criminology*, 12(4): 431–449.

Robinson, G., Burke, L. and Millings, M. (2016) 'Criminal Justice Identities in Transition: The case of devolved probation services in England and Wales', *British Journal of Criminology*, 56(1): 161–178.

Shannon Trust (2011) *Financial Statements for the Year Ended 31 March 2011*.

Silvestri, A. (2009) *Partners or Prisoners? Voluntary sector independence in the world of commissioning and contestability*. London: Centre for Crime and Justice Studies.

Smith, D., Paylor, I. and Mitchell, P. (1993) 'Partnerships Between the Independent Sector and the Probation Service', *The Howard Journal of Criminal Justice*, 32(1): 25–39.

Storybook Dads (2010) *Annual Report 2010*.

Tett, L., Anderson, K., McNeill, F., Overy, K. and Sparks, R. (2012) 'Learning, Rehabilitation and the Arts in Prisons: A Scottish case study', *Studies in the Education of Adults*, 44(2): 171–185.

Tomczak, P. (forthcoming) 'The Voluntary Sector and the Mandatory Statutory Supervision Requirement: Expanding the carceral net', *British Journal of Criminology*.

Tomczak, P. and Albertson, K. (2016) 'Prisoner Relationships with Voluntary Sector Practitioners', *The Howard Journal of Criminal Justice*, 55(1–2): 57–72.

Zedner, L. (2002) 'Dangers of Dystopias in Penal Theory', *Oxford Journal of Legal Studies*, 22(2): 341–366.

8 Conclusions

Punishment and charity in a neoliberal age

8.1 Introduction

This text has addressed a significant gap in knowledge by *conceptualising the penal voluntary sector in England and Wales*, which was 'a descriptive rather than theoretically rigorous concept or empirically defined entity' (Corcoran, 2011: 33). Although the voluntary sector is broadly underresearched (Considine, 2003), there is a particular dearth of voluntary sector research in punishment (Corcoran, 2011: 33; Mills *et al.*, 2011: 195; Armstrong, 2002: 345). This is both surprising and problematic given that the sector is, and has a history of being, important in the operation of punishment (Martin, 2013; Mills *et al.*, 2012; Neuberger, 2009; Armstrong, 2002), and has been a significant feature of both recent penal policy reforms (e.g. MoJ, 2013c, 2010) and scholarship (e.g. Helminen, 2016; Hucklesby and Corcoran, 2016; Neilson, 2009).

In this text I have explored how the legacy of philanthropic work and neoliberal policy reforms over the last thirty years has created a complex three-tier penal voluntary sector of organisations, consisting of those which are largely state funded, those which are partly state funded and those not in receipt of state funding. I have three key findings: penal voluntary organisations are *diverse* and have a range of *interactions* with statutory criminal justice agencies, which extend beyond marketised service delivery relationships; the *marketisation* of penal services directly affects only a small number of large, corporate-style charities; and the *effects* of charitable work vary. This concluding chapter summarises the research findings, explains their implications for scholarship and reflects on areas for future research.

This conceptualisation has explored the critical what, how and so what questions in relation to the penal voluntary sector: namely, *what* voluntary organisations were doing with prisoners and probationers, *how* voluntary organisations managed to undertake this work, and the *effects* of charitable work on prisoners and probationers. In summary of the *what*, penal voluntary organisations were involved in both core (i.e. the essential work required by Prison Service Orders, Prison Service Instructions and Probation Instructions) and enrichment (i.e. optional or additional work, which may feed into core aims) work with prisoners and probationers. For example, Catch 22 worked to minimise reoffending through core offender management, sentence planning, case work and resettlement work in HMPs Doncaster and Thameside (Ainsworth, 2012), whilst Fine Cell Work trained and paid prisoners to do high quality, creative needlework in their cells and workshops in thirty prisons including HMPs Brixton, Gartree, Highdown, Leyhill, Northumberland and Wandsworth (Fine Cell Work, 2014; see also Chapter 4). In summary of the *how*, statutory criminal justice agencies and penal voluntary organisations established relationships through a variety of (in)formal and (non)contractual mechanisms. Catch 22 were paid for their core reoffending work by the private company Serco, which held the MoJ contract to operate HMPs Doncaster and Thameside which included elements of PbR (Ainsworth, 2012). Fine Cell Work sustained their operations through needlework product sales, donations and income from Trusts and Foundations such as the Philip King Trust, the Monument Trust and the Al Fayed Foundation (Fine Cell Work, 2014; see also Chapters 5 and 6). The *effects* of penal voluntary organisations' work included expanding control, e.g. through enabling and legitimising the new twelve-month mandatory statutory supervision requirement for short-sentence prisoners, and providing distinctive interpersonal relationships to prisoners and probationers, based on accepting and strengths-based conceptualisations of (ex-)offenders and a unique relative separation from punishment (see Chapter 7). This consideration of effects has illustrated a theoretical gap, to which end I offer the hybrid conceptual innovation of 'inclusionary control', which is fully explained below.

The unique contribution of this book has been to consider the heterogeneity of penal voluntary organisations, looking both within and beyond the penal service market and providing multi-level analyses of charities that are fully statutory funded, partly statutory funded and not statutory funded. This complex analysis has aimed to illustrate how and why charitable involvement in criminal justice is more complicated, concerning and full of potential than scholars have opined thus far. In terms of *complexity*, commentators considering the relationships between punishment and charity are speaking for an extremely heterogeneous range of penal voluntary organisations and a complex criminal justice system, which interact at a variety of levels through different mechanisms. In terms of *concern*, charitable activities can directly and indirectly result in the control and exclusion of those they purport to serve, and the label of charity has a powerful legitimating function which may be employed by state agencies and private companies for uncharitable and exclusionary ends. In terms of *potential*, charitable staff and volunteers seem, at least in some cases, to occupy a unique distance from punishment, which can transform the immediate experience of it and enable desistance from crime. In summary, there are no easy or definitive answers in this area.

ANT has provided an excellent means of exploring these diverse themes and rendered permission to undertake confusing and at times apparently contradictory analyses. It offered a structured theoretical framework which guided the research and underpinned my broader conceptualisation of the sector, which extends beyond the market policy reforms that form the focus of recent scholarship. The essence of ANT is to learn from the actors by tracing connections, without defining the effects of their actions a priori (Nimmo, 2011: 109; Latour, 1999: 20; Law, 2004: 157). This is particularly important for studies such as mine, where commentary tends to divide along partisan lines and be reliant on 'the imagery of what we think (voluntary organisations) are and do' (Armstrong, 2002: 362) rather than empirically derived understandings.

ANT's method of 'deploying uncertainties' guided an exploration of the sector's heterogeneities, and the principle of generalised symmetry was then applied to analyse the specific uncertainties of scale and agency. Small charities and charitable agency to resist and modify the expanding market for penal services were examined on the same terms as large corporate-style charities involved in macro scale policy reforms. The process of translation then provided a structured means of analysing the spectrum of interactions between various statutory criminal justice agencies and heterogeneous voluntary organisations. This body of analysis enabled an exploration of the effects of charitable work, using ANT's idea of mediating agents to problematise control and net-widening literature, and illustrated the potential enabling and inclusionary effects of charitable work for prisoners and probationers alongside exploring net-widening. This application of ANT has theoretical implications. ANT's ability to acknowledge the *agency of micro scale actors* using the principle of generalised symmetry (Herbert-Cheshire, 2003: 459; see also Nimmo, 2011: 109; Sage *et al.*, 2011: 275) and to map the transmission, extension, modification and subversion of penal power using translation forms an important counterpoint to the Foucauldian tradition of *reducing all penal reforms to the will to power* (Garland, 1990: 168–169). Translation provides a structured method of mapping exactly how control is expanded through disciplinary strategies *and* how penal power can be modified and resisted by heterogeneous actors.

Although values and power always exist in an integral relationship, Garland explains the need to adopt 'more pluralistic' accounts (1990: 157). Criminologists are well practised in explaining the forces that 'lock us into an institutionalised culture of control' (Garland, 2001: xii), but are perhaps less skilled at detailing resistances to, and means of escape from, controlling forces. ANT is not the only means of exploring these countervailing forces, but it provides useful conceptual tools for the task and can illuminate how texts affect practices by contributing to the formation of discourses (Carrabine, 2000). If it is possible for texts to further embed controlling practices, it follows that texts can contribute to alternative outcomes (Zedner, 2002). This argument is developed later in this chapter.

Future research could usefully examine the relative presence, activities and funding of voluntary organisations in public and private prisons in different jurisdictions, and consider the critical what, how and so what questions in their particular contexts. Such work could certainly draw on this case study of the penal voluntary sector in England and Wales, which I hope provides a useful framework of results for work to understand and perhaps compare practices elsewhere. However, results should be extrapolated between countries with *caution* and with an awareness of their specific penal and voluntary sector *contexts*. I also hope that the theoretical and methodological approach that I have adopted will be useful, for both future voluntary sector and broader criminal justice research. Although I do not claim to provide a programmatic or comprehensive 'ANT approach', I anticipate that the approach I have assembled and applied here will be useful for future research involving multiple partner organisations in the increasingly complex, hybrid and privatised landscape of penal service delivery (such as in restorative justice programmes), and for studying other parts of the voluntary sector at policy and practice level.

8.2 Summary of analysis

The aim of this research has been to appreciate the complexity of the penal voluntary sector rather than produce an absolute evaluation of it. Although this conceptualisation is broader than that provided by recent scholarship, it remains a partial conceptualisation of the sector. Conscious boundary choices were made due to the need to delimit an area for analysis (Pollack *et al.*, 2013: 1121; see also Chapter 3). The most significant exclusions were the interactions between charities and private companies which deliver penal services, although this was explored to some extent in the analysis of the PbR pilot scheme at HMP Doncaster (see Chapter 6). Private companies do mediate some translations involving charities and statutory criminal justice agencies, so it would be valuable if future work were to explore these interactions and consider how they can influence both charitable practices and the effects of charitable work.

Chapters 4, 5 and 6 illustrated the important diversities between charities, and the range of relationships through which charities interacted with statutory criminal justice agencies. ANT was used to examine this heterogeneity (see Chapter 3 for a full explanation). Chapter 4 explored diversities in the *scale* of charitable and statutory operations, along with the *agency* of charities to participate in, resist and negotiate neoliberal penal reforms (see also Chapters 5 and 6). The principle of generalised symmetry was applied by approaching apparently disparate bodies of voluntary and statutory sector actors from the same analytical perspective, and gathering empirical evidence by tracing connections between actors without defining the effects of their actions a priori (Nimmo, 2011: 109; Law, 2004: 157; Latour, 1999: 20). Marketisation is having a significant impact upon the operations of large, corporate-style charities or 'Big Players', who are most likely by far to participate in the penal service market and tend to be more dependent on statutory funding. However, such charities are atypical of the sector and comprise a minority of penal voluntary organisations (Corcoran, 2011: 41; Silvestri, 2009: 4; Corcoran, 2008: 37).

I neither discount the potential for the work of the 'Big Players' to positively mediate punishment nor assume the benefits of small charities' work, but it has been posited that the smaller (possibly volunteer-led) charities which form the majority of the sector are the most worthful, being 'more likely to bring the so-called 'added value' to their work with offenders, particularly the building of social cohesion through their connections to the local community' (Mills *et al.*, 2012: 401; see also Corcoran, 2011: 40). However, smaller voluntary organisations are almost entirely absent from recent penal voluntary sector literature, being notable only as a result of concerns about their 'future viability' (Mills *et al.*, 2011: 195). As such, we do not understand the 'vital array' of non-contractual prison and probation work which does not feature in recent policy discussions (Martin, 2013: no pagination), which seems to often be undertaken by the smaller voluntary organisations that we know very little about. Perhaps scholars have *neglected to analyse the most worthful organisations* in the sector. The broader analysis provided herein has addressed the lack of attention to smaller charities, emphasised charitable agency and problematised the argument that marketisation is seeing 'reformative' charitable agendas being appropriated by punitive concerns (Corcoran, 2012; Meek *et al.*, 2010; Neilson, 2009). At different scales of analysis and for different types of charity, marketisation is significantly less important.

Building on the analysis of charitable heterogeneity and awareness of scale and agency, the four-phase process of translation was applied to illustrate how charities *and* statutory criminal justice agencies (including the MoJ and smaller scale agencies) sponsor translations. Chapter 5 explained how charitable programmes became established *on a small scale and informal basis* in prison and probation settings, through relationships initiated by both charities and individual prisons and probation trusts (as they were at the time of the research). These informal relationships were 'below the radar' and largely absent from academic and political commentary, but may comprise the modus operandi for much of the penal voluntary sector (Martin, 2013; Joseph Rank Trust, 2012) and offer further services and opportunities for prisoners and probationers. As such, an array of prison and probation work is not understood. This informal model of relatively small scale interactions may also be where the sector undertakes some of its most valuable and innovative work (Martin, 2013; Mills *et al.*, 2012), with potential effects that include building social cohesion (Mills *et al.*, 2012), improving the experience of imprisonment (Liebling, 2004) and supporting desistance from crime (Burnett and McNeill, 2005).

Chapter 6 demonstrated how charities can be involved in and influenced by translations of penal policy. This chapter mapped the macro level translation which began with the publication of *Breaking the Cycle* Green Paper (MoJ, 2010) and ultimately expanded the spatial and temporal reach of carceral power and control through the introduction of a new twelve-month mandatory statutory supervision requirement for short-sentence prisoners. It demonstrated how charities acted as agents of social control, enabling and justifying this process of penal reform through involvement in the prison-based PbR pilots at HMPs Peterborough and Doncaster. These pilots initially emphasised voluntary participation, rehabilitation and resettlement, but led to significant expansions in carceral power and control. Mapping translations unpacks how governing is performed by networks of state and non-state actors whose activities are co-ordinated by shared objectives and understandings (Jessop, 1995: 317). But, illustrating how the power of the penal apparatus to regulate and/or transform the convicted *depends on and operates through* charitable work (see Carrabine, 2000: 319) at least to some extent, renders the act of governing far more precarious (Herbert-Cheshire, 2003: 460).

The final analysis chapter (Chapter 7) explored the complex and multiple effects of charitable work. Without applying ANT to 'deploy uncertainties' relating to the penal voluntary sector, this *range of effects* might have remained obscure (see Nimmo, 2011: 109; Law, 2004: 157) amid the debate about the macro level marketisation of penal services, and the dangers that state patronage apparently posed to organisations across the penal voluntary sector (Corcoran, 2011; Neilson, 2009). This consideration of effects has illustrated a gap requiring hybrid theory which can account for both exclusionary and inclusionary effects of charitable work, to which end I offer the conceptual innovation of 'inclusionary control', albeit with bated breath as I explain below. My key findings and their implications are now summarised in three sections, which are: the need to recognise diversities within the sector, questioning the effects of charitable work, and the political impacts of academic theorisation.

8.3   Recognising diversities within the sector

The symbolic value of the 'nonprofit' descriptor is very powerful; it encourages us to think of nonprofit status as the most important means of categorising extremely diverse organisations.

(Armstrong, 2002: 355–356)

Underpinned by the tenets of ANT, Chapters 4, 5 and 6 illustrated the diversities present amongst the 'bewildering variety' of penal voluntary organisations in England and Wales (Kendall and Knapp, 1995: 66). Key diversities included: charities' functions, the scale of charities' operations; the relative proportion of volunteers and paid staff within charities; charities' emphases on employing ex-service users; charities' focus on voluntary participation in their programmes; charities' income ranges and sources; and the varied interactions between charities and statutory criminal justice agencies. Indeed, the only constants amongst the diverse charities which comprise the penal voluntary sector were that they were registered as charities with the Charity Commission, and that their client group included (ex-)offenders and/or their families and victims.

Although all charities must demonstrate their pursuit of charitable objectives to comply with the requirements of the Charity Commission, these organisations have more points of difference than similarities. As such, it is almost impossible to make claims which hold across the penal voluntary sector. It is therefore crucial that scholars maintain awareness of the diversities within the sector, and note that arguments which are true for certain charities ought not to be extrapolated across the heterogeneous penal voluntary sector. Although there are some acknowledgements of this diversity within recent scholarship (see Chapter 2), it has not been sufficiently explored. The political impacts of this reductionism and the benefits of broader accounts are explored below.

The diversities illustrated in Chapters 4, 5 and 6 could indicate that the 'penal voluntary sector' nomenclature is inappropriate, suggesting that this should not be employed as a collective analytical concept. Perhaps conceptualising *the* 'penal voluntary sector' wrongly implies some unity of form or purpose which is not in reality present amongst this group of incredibly different organisations. Indeed, Armstrong (2002: 356) has queried whether 'a multi-million (or even billion) dollar nonprofit agency can and should be analysed in similar terms as a neighbourhood-based organisation with income in the tens of thousands, even if both provide services to the same population'. Conversely, there is a need to locate and identify this sector of organisations for analysis and theory-building, and these diverse organisations do all share the powerful and legitimating label of 'charity'. One way to proceed is by using the 'penal voluntary sector' terminology more cautiously and for scholarship to pay close attention to the heterogeneity of penal voluntary organisations (and the varying effects of their work). The sector can be explored as a three-tier entity, comprised of organisations which are largely state funded and which tend to be 'Big Players' or corporate-style charities (see Morgan, 2012: 478; Corcoran, 2012: 21; Benson and Hedge, 2009: 35; Corcoran, 2008: 37), those which are partly state funded and those not in receipt of state funding. Within these tiers organisations have varying proportions of paid and volunteer staff (with larger organisations appearing to draw on the volunteer workforce significantly less than smaller charities), and varying relationships with statutory criminal justice agencies (e.g. lobbying, informal, contractual and PbR). This tripartite classification is particularly useful for the debate about the effects of marketisation upon the sector, as these processes principally involve the small group of large charities or 'Big Players'. Although marketisation may 'trickle down' and affect smaller charities to some extent (see Chapter 6), it is very important that conclusions relating to the atypical 'Big Players' (see Corcoran, 2011: 41; Silvestri, 2009: 4) are not extrapolated across the sector.

Adopting this tripartite classification is one means of moving towards a broader approach to studying this sector. Maintaining awareness of these three classifications of charities could stimulate a more complete debate about marketisation by addressing commentators' tendency to over-estimate its importance across the sector (see Chapters 2 and 4) and encouraging an examination of how marketisation is affecting all three 'types' of charity. This tripartite classification also has implications for considering the effects of charitable work and the political impacts of voluntary sector scholarship, which are explored below. However, the suggested classification has not been drawn from a representative sample of charities, so could be tested in future work.

8.4 The effects of charitable work

Chapter 7 explored the effects that charitable work may have upon prisoners and probationers, illustrating how it can extend power and control, and can contribute to the widening of the carceral net (Garland, 1990; Cohen, 1985;

Foucault, 1977; see also Chapter 2). For example, charities may increase the monitoring and surveillance of service users, and share knowledge so created with the statutory criminal justice agencies. At the micro level, these control effects were particularly prominent in analyses of charitable work with probationers, where knowledge sharing could directly result in probationers being recalled to custody. It was particularly concerning that knowledge was often gathered through apparently informal and non-punitive interactions, which could lead to insidious exclusionary effects. At the macro level, a notable example of net-widening was the introduction of the mandatory statutory supervision requirement for short-sentence prisoners following the PbR schemes run with charitable involvement at HMPs Peterborough and Doncaster.

My findings therefore align with Armstrong's recommendation (2002: 365) that the net-widening and control implications of charitable work require further acknowledgement and analysis. I advocate that the exclusionary control and net-widening implications of charitable work should be included in *every* account of the penal voluntary sector. However, although charities may extend control, this argument should not be unduly extrapolated across the sector or considered in isolation. Following ANT's aim of multiplying the mediating points in translations (see Chapter 3), analysis also explored how charities can valuably mediate punishment. Charities can widen the range of opportunities and material provisions available to prisoners (see Meek *et al.*, 2010; Smith *et al.*, 1993; see also Liebling, 2004), enabling prisoners to build social and human capital (see Brown and Ross, 2010; Lewis *et al.*, 2007) and promoting engagement with productive activities (see Maguire, 2012; Light, 1993). These 'extra' provisions are not necessarily distinctively valuable, although charities can offer distinctive interpersonal relationships to prisoners and probationers based on their person-centred, non-judgemental and strengths-based interactions with service users (Maguire, 2012; Mills *et al.*, 2012; Meek *et al.*, 2010) and unique separation from the punitive and coercive aspects of penal regimes (at least in some charitable programmes). But if the reach of market reforms extends beyond larger corporate-style charities in future, or comes to affect micro level charitable action more significantly (see Chapter 6), this contribution could be at risk as a result of charities becoming more involved with the punitive and coercive aspects of criminal justice work (Corcoran and Hucklesby, 2013).

However, my findings also demonstrated a theoretical gap, suggesting that both the control and emancipatory literatures appear to be inadequate, and more nuanced hybrid or integrated theorisation is required. The work of voluntary organisations can apparently result in both exclusion and inclusion, control and emancipation, or negative *and* positive effects. As charities' contributions to building social and human capital and expanding social control are not necessarily mutually exclusive, the task for scholars is to highlight, using evidence, how and under which conditions both of these overall outcomes can occur. I suggest that hybrid theory is required and offer the conceptual innovation of 'inclusionary control' to this end. It is hard to see how the work of penal voluntary organisations could always avoid extending or amplifying control, as it is undertaken alongside the most controlling institutions that we have. However, and without denying the dangers of the expanding carceral net, control is not all that occurs. It is reductionist and disabling not to simultaneously consider how the qualities of the carceral net can be changed, and the concept of net-widening does not facilitate such analysis. The idea of 'inclusionary control' is not to make excuses for exclusionary policies or problematic institutions, but to provide a means of examining if and how positive or improved outcomes can come from sites of control. A significantly expanded base of empirical evidence could underpin the development of theory accounting for such hybrid experiences, e.g. by examining the characteristics and qualities of the carceral net as it operates and is experienced by different people, in different places and at different times.

Simultaneously, charities may expand 'exclusionary control' and may make little contribution to the prisoners and probationers that they work with. Future research could therefore consider how the heterogeneity of charities influences the effects of their work upon prisoners and probationers. It seems clear that enabling and controlling outcomes can result from charitable work, so which aspects of charitable heterogeneity may contribute towards these outcomes? Mapping the interactions between charities and statutory criminal justice agencies using ANT's four-phase process of translation provides a specific means of analysing how these outcomes occur, and could better illustrate which aspects of the interactions affected these outcomes (as explained in Chapter 3 and applied in Chapters 6 and 7).

Recent work from the USA notes that charities work with ex-prisoners 'in ways that vary across providers' religious and political orientations and corresponding funding sources' (Kaufman, 2015: 549), although notably *funding did not completely explain or determine* variations in charitable work. Although I would tend to agree with the assertion that smaller scale, possibly volunteer-led charities are 'more likely to bring the so-called "added value" to their work with offenders, particularly the building of social cohesion through their connections to the local community' (Mills *et al.*, 2012: 401), the potential contributions of 'corporate-style' charities cannot be ignored. It seems that some prisoners greatly valued the contribution of the PbR pilot schemes, which offered some valuable avenues of practical and emotional support. Even at the 'sharp end' of charitable work, e.g. Catch 22's core offender management work in Serco-run HMPs Doncaster and Thameside, effects may not be limited to control. Catch 22 claim to have implemented their principle of 'one assessment, one case worker, one relationship' into the way Serco delivers these services (Ainsworth, 2012). More evidence is required to assess the overlaps between inclusionary control and empowerment, and exclusionary control, and to consider the relationship conditions which might influence these outcomes. For example, future work could consider whether the *type of charity* and the *form of its interactions* with statutory criminal justice agencies (e.g. contractual, PbR, informal) affect its *effects* upon prisoners and probationers. How do the effects of charitable work vary with volunteer/paid staff ratios, mandatory programme participation, (non)statutory (contract) funding and PbR funding. What effects do corporate-style charities have upon prisoners and probationers? Are charity staff working under contract relationships with the MoJ valued less than volunteer staff by prisoners and probationers? If so, why? Conversely, are volunteer staff working under informal relationships with the statutory criminal justice agencies valued more? If so, why? Does working under contract with the MoJ necessarily negate all positive or enabling effects of charitable work? Can charities with existing social-welfarist orientations (Goddard, 2012; see Chapter 2) preserve these in contractual relationships? Can any positive outcomes result when prisoners/probationers are forced to engage with charitable programmes? Are charities which focus on employing ex-service users particularly valuable because they offer employment opportunities to (ex-)offenders?

This book has provided an exploratory analysis of the effects of charitable work, finding that enabling and controlling outcomes are possible. Hybrid theory which can account for both of these outcomes is required and I have offered the conceptual innovation of 'inclusionary control' to this end. Assessing if and how the *heterogeneity* of charities and their diverse interactions with the statutory criminal justice agencies can *influence the exclusionary and inclusionary effects of charitable work* would provide valuable conclusions. In addition, the effects of charitable work and the effects of statutory translations of charitable work could be untangled through a focus on direct exclusionary effects and indirect exclusionary effects, as it was perhaps the latter that occurred in the policy translation analysed in Chapter 6. These conclusions could be applied to practice and would contribute to the marketisation debate by discerning the value of the 'Big Players' who are involved in these reforms. Translation provides a specific means of mapping these circumstances and conditions. However, my strongest recommendation for future research is that it should directly seek the experiences of prisoners and probationers. There is hardly any independent information or research considering whether prisoners and probationers engage with charitable programmes voluntarily, whether they consider such programmes beneficial, and what their experiences of interacting with charities are (see Bosworth *et al.*, 2005). Data from charity and statutory publications and interviews with charity and statutory staff were essential to understand the heterogeneity of charitable relationships with statutory criminal justice agencies in this research. Chapter 7 does contain a small number of quotations from prisoners, but from secondary sources. The experiences of the prisoners and probationers who are most affected by the operations of charities and statutory criminal justice agencies are *crucial* to the debate about the effects of charitable work (see Bosworth *et al.*, 2005) and theory should be built on their evidence.

8.5 A politically enabling conceptualisation of the sector

Recent penal voluntary sector scholarship has focussed heavily on the potential neutralisation of distinctive charitable qualities through marketisation and associated closer involvement with the punitive and coercive aspects of criminal justice work (Corcoran and Hucklesby, 2013; see also Chapter 2). These reforms are certainly important for some charities and charitable involvement in the market for penal services must be discussed. But it is also important to remember that the theorisation of processes has political impacts (Goddard and Myers, 2011: 667; Hart, 2002: 813; Zedner, 2002). Following ANT, sociological texts do not merely represent reality, but also order and organise reality to some extent (Hitchings, 2003: 100; see Chapter 3). Accepting market reforms, and the associated potential for penal expansionism, as monolithic and inexorable forces is reductionist and likely to create a self-fulfilling prophecy (Tomczak, 2014). This approach also diverts attention from insufficient scholarly understandings of *why* charities are valuable, e.g. they may extend control, improve the experience of punishment and support desistance from crime.

Corcoran (2011: 48) claims that the 'business' case for marketising penal services in policy rhetoric works to commodify voluntary sector expertise and 'does the voluntary sector a disservice at many levels'. However, by mirroring the statutory conceptualisation of the sector, commentators have also done it a disservice. Recent penal voluntary sector scholarship has provided a significant contribution to the body of knowledge, by defining the terrain of this topic and constructing the foundations for further analysis (see Chapter 2). However, the focus on the market for penal services has thus far come at the expense of analysing the diversity, agency, innovation and resistance amongst voluntary organisations. The existence of these qualities must not be overstated, but ignoring them provides an impoverished account of the sector, works to denigrate those qualities and prevents analysis of *how* charitable work can usefully mediate the experience of punishment.

This book has provided a broader and *more theoretically complete* conceptualisation of the penal voluntary sector in England and Wales by applying ANT to move beyond the macro scale, marketised account of the sector. This has been achieved by examining the heterogeneity of penal voluntary organisations, and scoping a wider set of interactions between charities and statutory criminal justice agencies, following the process of deploying uncertainties, the principle of generalised symmetry and the process of translation. In addition to exploring contractual relationships driven by macro level policy reforms (see Chapter 6), Chapters 4 and 5 analysed smaller scale and informal relationships between charities and statutory criminal justice agencies. Chapter 6 also considered how charities can exercise resistance to policy reforms, drawing on the publications of the Prison Reform Trust and the Howard League.

This conceptualisation has multiplied the mediating points (Latour, 1996: 378; see Chapter 3) in translations involving the penal voluntary sector, by focussing on interactions between actors rather than relying on agent and subject dichotomies to characterise the MoJ and penal voluntary sector respectively. It has illustrated that there are limits to the influence of marketised penal policy reforms, and that these reforms are neither monolithic nor cohesive forces in shaping the sector (see Hart, 2002: 813). Assessing the heterogeneity of penal voluntary organisations and mapping their diverse relationships with statutory criminal justice agencies are valuable because they have laid the foundations for a more complete and politically enabling understanding of the penal voluntary sector and the array of 'under the radar' work it does alongside prisons and probation. As explained in Chapter 5, the extent of informal work alongside prisons and probation appears not to be appreciated by charities themselves, policy makers or academics. This analysis has illuminated possibilities for collective charitable resistance to problematic penal policies, although many service delivery organisations appear to be self-censoring in order to maintain their access to prisons (see Chapter 5).

The scholarly tendency to present neoliberal penal reforms as inexorable forces, and to produce 'grimly pessimistic' accounts of the 'criminal justice state' is problematic, and risks reinforcing the very situation that commentators seek to expose (Zedner, 2002: 342; see also Goddard and Myers, 2011; Hart, 2002). Determinedly pessimistic commentary creates its own set of problems, because the emphasis upon dystopic visions of crime control leads scholars to overlook trends that point in a different direction (Zedner, 2002: 342, 355) and prevents analysis of how punishment could be improved. Identifying the 'dangers and harms implicit in the contemporary scheme of things' is a crucial task for commentators (Garland, 2001: 3). But, producing partial scholarship that is essentially a justification of political beliefs does not advance our craft.

In earlier work, Garland emphasised the need to avoid reducing all changes to the will to power (1990: 168–169). This tendency is the 'folly of the nihilistic net-widening literature' (Armstrong, 2002: 365). There is, therefore, an equally important need to consider the representativeness of conceptualisations of the penal voluntary sector and their political impact. Regarding the potential risks posed to charities by the further marketisation of penal services, Maguire pointed out that 'there is no certainty that the fears of pessimists will materialise. Whether they do or not depends to a considerable extent on the attitudes, actions and decisions of individuals across the system' (2012: 491). But this is one of very few such acknowledgements in recent commentary.

Armstrong (2002: 365) counsels that 'by remaining open-minded about the meaning of reform we can better understand the implications of its consequences'. It is therefore important that theory can describe and envision alternative possibilities and countermovements to neoliberal penal reforms, penal expansionism and the extension of control. As such, I suggest that we gather empirical evidence and base theoretical advancements upon it. I hesitated to propose the concept of 'inclusionary control', because the predictable 'critical' responses almost drowned it out in my mind. But being 'critical' should not over-ride what our data tell us. Mine indicated that there is the potential for charitable work alongside coercive carceral institutions to make people's lives better (see also Tomczak and Albertson, 2016). Even marketised charities might make valuable contributions, or offer additional services alongside contractual work which could make a valuable impact (e.g. New Bridge's befriending service transformed the experience of imprisonment for at least some of its service users). Legitimising or 'shoring-up' problematic institutions does not delete these contributions. My academic training has illuminated that the institutions of criminal justice are 'bad' institutions, which allocate personal responsibility for structural problems, and within which terrible things happen. Nevertheless, it is a problem if our theoretical tools do not enable accurate description of those phenomena which we observe.

Although pluralistic accounts may be messier and lack the satisfaction provided by reductionist 'critical' conclusions, they are more practically and politically enabling. By mapping the diverse forms of charitable work, this book has provided a greater awareness of its enabling and controlling effects upon prisoners and probationers (e.g. social capital and net-widening), and a greater awareness of the factors which may influence these eventual outcomes (e.g. employing ex-service users, and maintaining non-judgemental and strengths-based interactions with service users through separation from the coercive aspects of criminal justice work). This provides a springboard from which future work can seek to identify exactly *how* charities can make a positive and distinctive contribution to prisoners and probationers, *how* their inclusionary and exclusionary effects balance, *how* charities can resist net-widening and the extension of control, and the factors which may mean that they do *not* achieve these outcomes.

References

Ainsworth, D. (2012) Interview: Chris Wright. *Third Sector.* Available at: Available at: www.thirdsector.co.uk/interview-chris-wright/management/article/1150049. Accessed: 5 April 2016.

Armstrong, S. (2002) 'Punishing Not-For-Profit: Implications of nonprofit privatization in juvenile punishment', *Punishment and Society, 4(3)*: 345–368.

Benson, A. and Hedge, J. (2009) 'Criminal Justice and the Voluntary Sector: A policy that does not compute', *Criminal Justice Matters, 77(1)*: 34–36.

Bosworth, M., Campbell, D., Demby, B., Ferranti, S. M. and Santos, M. (2005) 'Doing Prison Research: Views from inside', *Qualitative Inquiry, 11(2)*: 249–264.

Brown, M. and Ross, S. (2010) 'Mentoring, Social Capital and Desistance: A study of women released from prison', *Australian and New Zealand Journal of Criminology, 43(1)*: 31–50.

Burnett, R. and McNeill, F. (2005) 'The Place of the Officer–Offender Relationship in Assisting Offenders to Desist from Crime', *Probation Journal, 52(3)*: 247–268.

Carrabine, E. (2000) 'Discourse, Governmentality and Translation: Toward a social theory of imprisonment', *Theoretical Criminology, 4(3)*: 309–331.

Cohen, S. (1985) *Visions of Social Control: Crime, punishment and classification.* Cambridge: Polity Press.

Considine, M. (2003) 'Governance and Competition: The role of non-profit organisations in the delivery of public services', *Australian Journal of Political Science, 38(1)*: 63–77.

Corcoran, M. (2008) 'What Does Government Want from the Penal Voluntary Sector?' *Criminal Justice Matters, 71(1)*: 36–38.

Corcoran, M. (2011) 'Dilemmas of Institutionalization in the Penal Voluntary Sector', *Critical Social Policy, 31(1)*: 30–52.

Corcoran, M. (2012) 'Be Careful What You Ask For: Findings from the seminar series on the Third Sector in criminal justice', *Prison Service Journal, 204:* 17–22.

Corcoran, M. and Hucklesby, A. (2013) 'Briefing paper: The Third Sector in Criminal Justice'. Available at: www.law.leeds.ac.uk/assets/files/research/ccjs/130703-thirdsec-crimjust-briefing-2013.pdf. Accessed: 12 August 2013.

Fine Cell Work (2014) *Trustees' Report and Unaudited Accounts for the Year Ended 31 December 2014.*

Foucault, M. (1977) *Discipline and Punish: The birth of the prison.* London: Allen Lane.

Garland, D. (1990) *Punishment and Modern Society: A study in social theory.* Oxford: Clarendon Press.

Garland, D. (2001) *The Culture of Control: Crime and social order in a contemporary society.* Chicago: University of Chicago Press.

Goddard, T. (2012) 'Post-Welfarist Risk Managers? Risk, crime prevention, and the turn to non-state community-based organizations', *Theoretical Criminology*, *16*(3): 347–363.

Goddard, T. and Myers, R. (2011) 'Democracy and Demonstration in the Grey Area of Neo-Liberalism: A case study of Free Los Angeles High School', *British Journal of Criminology*, *51*(4): 652–670.

Hart, G. (2002) 'Geography and Development: Development/s beyond neoliberalism? Power, culture, political economy', *Progress in Human Geography*, *26*(2): 812–822.

Helminen, M. (2016) 'Nordic and Scottish Civil Society Organisations Working with Offenders and the Effects of Service Delivery: Is pursuing mission impossible whilst bidding for contracts?', *The Howard Journal of Criminal Justice*, 55 (1–2): 73–93.

Herbert-Cheshire, L. (2003) 'Translating Policy: Power and action in Australia's country towns', *Sociologia Ruralis*, *43*(4): 454–473.

Hitchings, R. (2003) 'People, Plants and Performance: On actor-network theory and the material pleasures of the private garden', *Social and Cultural Geography*, *4*(1): 99–114.

Hucklesby, A. and Corcoran, M. (2016) (eds) *The Voluntary Sector and Criminal Justice.* Basingstoke: Palgrave.

Jessop, B. (1995) 'The Regulation Approach and Governance Theory: Alternative per-spectives on economic and political change?' *Economy and Society*, *24*(3): 307–333.

Joseph Rank Trust (2012) *Collaboration or Competition? Cooperation or Contestability?* Available at: http: //theosthinktank.co.uk/research/theos-reports. Accessed: 7 June 2012.

Kaufman, N. (2015) 'Prisoner Incorporation: The work of the state and non-governmental organizations', *Theoretical Criminology*, *19*(4): 534–553.

Kendall, J. and Knapp, M. R. J. (1995) 'Boundaries, Definitions and Typologies: A loose and baggy monster', in Davis Smith, J., Rochester, C. and Hedley, D. (eds) *An Intro-duction to the Voluntary Sector.* London: Routledge.

Latour, B. (1996) 'On Actor-Network Theory. A few clarifications plus more than a few complications', *Soziale Welt*, *47*(4): 369–381.

Latour, B. (1999) 'On Recalling ANT', in Law, J. and Hassard, J. (eds) *Actor-Network Theory and After.* Oxford: Blackwell.

Law, J. (2004) *After Method: Mess in social science research.* Abingdon: Routledge.

Lewis S., Maguire M., Raynor P., Vanstone M. and Vennard J. *(2007)* 'What works in Resettlement? Findings from seven Pathfinders for short-term prisoners in England and Wales', *Criminology and Criminal Justice*, *7*(1): 33–53.

Liebling, A., with Arnold, H. (2004). *Prisons and Their Moral Performance: A study of values, quality, and prison life.* Oxford: Oxford University Press.

Light, R. (1993) 'Why Support Prisoners' Family-Tie Groups?' *The Howard Journal of Criminal Justice*, *32*(4): 322–329.

Maguire, M. (2012) 'Response 1: Big Society, the voluntary sector and the marketisation of criminal justice', *Criminology and Criminal Justice*, *12*(5): 483–505.

Martin, C. (2013) *Dazzled by the Fireworks: Realising detail in the overwhelming scale of reform*. Clinks Blog Post. Available at: www.clinks.org/community/blog-posts/dazzled-fireworks-realising-detail-overwhelming-scale-reform. Accessed: 25 May 2013.

Meek, R., Gojkovic, D. and Mills, A. (2010) 'The Role of the Third Sector in Work with Offenders: The perceptions of criminal justice and third sector stakeholders', *TSRC Working Paper 34*. Birmingham: Third Sector Research Centre.

Mills, A., Meek, R. and Gojkovic, D. (2011) 'Exploring the Relationship Between the Voluntary Sector and the State in Criminal Justice', *Voluntary Sector Review*, *2*(2): 193–211.

Mills, A., Meek, R. and Gojkovic, D. (2012) 'Partners, Guests or Competitors: Relationships between criminal justice and third sector staff in prisons', *Probation Journal*, *59*(4): 391–405.

MoJ (2010) *Breaking the Cycle: Effective punishment, rehabilitation and sentencing of offenders*. London: MoJ.

MoJ (2013c) *Transforming Rehabilitation: A strategy for reform*. London: MoJ.

Morgan, R. (2012) 'Crime and Justice in the "Big Society"', *Criminology and Criminal Justice*, *12*(5): 463–481.

Neilson, A. (2009) 'A Crisis of Identity: NACRO's bid to run a prison and what it means for the voluntary sector', *The Howard Journal of Criminal Justice*, *48*(4): 401–410.

Neuberger, J. (2009) *Volunteering Across the Criminal Justice System*. London: The Cabinet Office.

Nimmo, R. (2011) 'Actor-Network Theory and Methodology: Social research in a more-than-human world', *Methodological Innovations Online*, *6*(3): 108–119.

Pollack, J., Costello, K. and Sankaran, S. (2013) 'Applying Actor-Network Theory as a Sensemaking Framework for Complex Organisational Change Programs', *International Journal of Project Management*, *31*(8): 1118–1128.

Sage, D., Dainty, A. and Brookes, N. (2011) 'How Actor-Network Theories Can Help in Understanding Project Complexities', *International Journal of Managing Projects in Business*, *4*(2): 274–293.

Silvestri, A. (2009) *Partners or Prisoners? Voluntary sector independence in the world of commissioning and contestability*. London: Centre for Crime and Justice Studies.

Smith, D., Paylor, I. and Mitchell, P. (1993) 'Partnerships Between the Independent Sector and the Probation Service', *The Howard Journal of Criminal Justice*, *32*(1): 25–39.

Tomczak, P. (2014) 'The Penal Voluntary Sector in England and Wales: Beyond neo-liberalism?' *Criminology and Criminal Justice*, *14*(4): 470–486.

Tomczak, P. and Albertson, K. (2016) 'Prisoner Relationships with Voluntary Sector Practitioners', *The Howard Journal of Criminal Justice*, *55*(1–2): 57–72.

Zedner, L. (2002) 'Dangers of Dystopias in Penal Theory', *Oxford Journal of Legal Studies*, *22*(2): 341–366.

Index

Page numbers in *italics* denote tables. End of chapter notes are denoted by a letter n between page number and note number.